Isis Mary Sophia

ISIS MARY SOPHIA

Her Mission and Ours

Selected lectures and writings by
Rudolf Steiner

Edited and introduced by Christopher Bamford

STEINERBOOKS

The original German of the lectures and writings contained in this book are contained in the Rudolf Steiner Gesamtausgabe (The Collected Works of Rudolf Steiner). Translations are from the following volume numbers: 1, 4, 13, 26, 38, 55, 57, 94, 100, 103, 144, 148, 149, 180, 202, 211, 243. Rudolf Steiner Verlag, Dornach, Switzerland, publishes the Rudolf Steiner Gesamtausgabe. Chapter 6 is translated from *Schickzalszeichen auf dem Entwicklungswege der Anthroposophischen Gesellschaft*, also published by Rudolf Steiner Verlag, Dornach, Switzerland, in 1943. Translations by permission of the publishers.

Publication of this volume was made possible by generous gifts from Janet Clement, Julie Neander, Mary H. Miller, and Mary E. Jennings. The publisher is especially grateful to Mary E. Jennings for her commitment and understanding.

Book Design by Will Marsh

Library of Congress Cataloging-in-Publication Data

Steiner, Rudolf, 1861-1925.
  [Selections. English. 2003]
  Isis Mary Sophia : her mission and ours : selected lectures and writings / Rudolf Steiner ; selected, edited, and introduced by Christopher Bamford.
    p. cm.
  ISBN 0-88010-494-5
  1. Anthroposophy. 2. Wisdom—Religious aspects. I. Bamford, Christopher, 1943- II. Title.
BP595.S894 I8513 2003
299'.935—dc22
                                        2003015104

10   9   8   7   6   5   4   3   2

Printed in the United States of America

Contents

Introduction

by Christopher Bamford

Let it be known: today, the Divine Feminine
Is descending to Earth in an incorruptible body.
In the unfading light of the new Goddess,
Heaven has become one with the depths.
—Vladimir Solovyov, "Three Meetings"

Omnia Conjungo. I unite all.
—Sophia's motto, cited by Pavel Florensky

Over the past centuries, the being of Sophia, or feminine Divine
Wisdom, has been emerging from the mists of ancient history, like
Venus from the waters, to become a sign and mystery of our times.
Though it is difficult to say who she is, wherever we turn, we see
traces of her coming—as if tracking the fringes of her mantle as it
brushed aside the tangled, sclerotic cobwebs of centuries of cerebra-
tion. As she draws near, much that was forgotten is reentering consciousness, not only as memory but also from the future, *as possibility.*
It demands that we rethink who we are, whence we have come, and
whither we are going. We see her in the crumbling of the old social
order and in the dawn light breaking through the night of patriarchal dominance in ways of knowing. Feminist philosophers of science have shown us that a magical, holistic, and participatory
"Hermetic" alternative to reductive, mechanistic science—post-
modern before the fact—contested the rise of modern science from
the start. At the same time, scientists are turning from a manipula-
tive, control-oriented science to a more loving, phenomenological
approach to nature. No less pioneering, historians and medievalists
have uncovered whole lineages of women philosophers, mystics, and

theologians whose work is forcing us to rethink the whole meaning of Christianity and Western civilization. Mention could be made too of the efflorescence of feminine spiritualities and of the recovery of the women of the Gospel who sustained Jesus with their own substance. Then there are the Marian apparitions which, since the 1840s, have accompanied the end of modernism.

But there is still more. A new mood is abroad, a kind of heart's yearning for what Sophia has traditionally always provided—a seamless vessel of harmony and meaning, uniting Heaven and Earth, within which we may live, move, and have our being. Those who experience their lives as empty or meaningless are beginning to recognize that simply to oppose spirit to matter and locate all problems in "materialism" does not work. A "spiritual" path in a void leaves the world untouched. Context is necessary. Humanity and the world—the cosmos—are indivisibly one. To walk a path in isolation from the world, to fragment ourselves, leaves us unchanged. "Secularism"—the lack of the spiritual in everyday life, in nature—is thus a more useful description of our state than "materialism." Epitomized by the split between faith and reason, theology and philosophy, science and spirituality, secularism, which means the separation of the spiritual from the rest of life, gives us fundamentalism—abstraction and literalism—and consequently, ironically, terrorism. Marxist-Leninist materialism was simple by contrast. What we need now is something that places spirit once again at the heart of our existence. Sophia gives us this ethical directive, calling upon us to sacralize—consecrate, make spiritual—the whole world and all our lives, not just on Sundays. "Everything that lives is holy," said Blake.

An Evolving Reality: The Mystery of Christ and Sophia

Sophia is a still-evolving mystery. She is a great secret, an open secret perhaps, but one at once so profound that it reaches to the very substance of the world and so close to our essential humanity, who we are, that we cannot see her. Beginning in God before creation, she unfolded through creation and now participates in creation's redemption. Coming from the Father, she is present and active not only in the birth, death, and resurrection of the Son of God, but also in the descent and dissemination of the Holy Spirit. Thus, she holds within her being every aspect of human, cosmic, and—may we say it?—even divine evolution. She is, to mention a few of her titles, the Mother of God, the Mother of Humanity, the Soul of the World, the Holy Spirit, and the Goddess Natura. She is also the human soul. No wonder it is hard to grasp her.

We have been made aware, by theological and mystical traditions as well as contemporary teachers like Rudolf Steiner, of some of Christ's meaning for humanity, divinity, and the cosmos. But full revelation of the mystery of Sophia, according to Steiner, will occur only in the future, in the next (sixth or so-called Slavic) cultural epoch.

Today, Sophia is a sign of the times; we sense her coming under many different forms and intuitions. But to say with any precision *who* she is—in her fullness, breadth, height, and depth—eludes us. She is a truly *spiritual* being, who must be understood and encountered spiritually. "True understanding of and insight into the Sophia mystery," according to Sergei Prokofieff, "is even more foreign to our materialistic age than the Christ mystery."

A First Glance at Who She Is

Following Blake, we may begin with "life" and "holiness." Sophia is *life*—the life of the spirit. She is the common "Life" of the Trinity, as she is the "common" life of creation. Thus, Sophia is twofold: divine and creaturely. As twofold, she ensures *the presence of holiness*—that where there is life there is spirit. At the same time, she ensures the *unity* of creation and the uncreated—for there is but one life. Present in both divinity and creation, she is the indissoluble *bond and mediator* between them. She is the means or way by which divinity bodies forth in creation. As the container or receptacle—as well as the unity—of the divine ideas, she is divine *wisdom*. As its manifestation,

she is divine *glory*. Put another way, she is the principle of *theophany*—
the revealing of God. As such, she is intimately related to *humanity*,
for it is through human beings that the presence of God—or
theophany—is cognitively realized in the universe. Sophia is also
inseparable from the *Holy Spirit*, the Spirit of Wisdom, who, according to the Nicene Creed, is "the Lord, the Giver of Life," the breath
of life "from the mouth of God." Jesus names this spirit "the Spirit
of truth" or "the Comforter," who will guide us into all truth. For
this reason, according to a secret tradition as old as Christianity
itself and only now coming into the open, the Holy Spirit is feminine—and closely linked with Sophia in the form of Mary. An
ancient Coptic life of the Virgin confirms this. After quoting Jesus'
familiar saying, "After not many days, I will send the Spirit, the
Comforter, unto you in my place," it adds something new. It
announces that with Pentecost, "Behold, she who was My dwelling
place, and I was her Son in the flesh and in the Godhead, even she
who in the flesh looked like me, behold, *she is with you now.*" It is this
Holy Spirit that overshadowed Mary and came down—even
incarnated—through her who gives birth to the Son of God. She is
the spirit who transforms wisdom into reality, into love, into creation, into a world existing with *the actual life of God.* This life, as Sergei Bulgakov puts it, "in its own full transparency is *beauty*, which is
the self-revelation of the deity, the garment of God as it were." At
the same time, this living spirit—who is wisdom, beauty, and truth—
is also the *uniting* spirit, the spirit of true community. This is the
spirit that makes it possible that, when "two or three are gathered"
in Christ's name, he is there.

Put another way, Sophia is a divine feminine spiritual being who
knows, feels, and acts from the very highest spheres of divinity to
the lowliest, humblest clefts and corners of the Earth—passing
through all the many levels of the starry heavens. She is, we may say,
the very "soul" of God, of the world, and of humanity. Threefold,
like the Godhead, she leads us toward the wisdom of the heart that
she is. In the words of Hildegard of Bingen:

O energy of Wisdom,
you circled circling
encompassing all
in the one path of life
with three wings:
one flies on high,
one distills from the earth,
and the third flies everywhere.
Praise to you, as is fitting,
O Wisdom.

Steiner and Sophia

Rudolf Steiner (1861–1925) was one of the most extraordinary figures of the last two centuries. A great spiritual philosopher, visionary thinker, and teacher, he was also eminently practical and farsighted in what he saw as humanity's needs. Around the world today we see the always growing fruits of his inspiration and research in movements as varied as, for instance, Waldorf education, biodynamic agriculture, the Camphill movement for the care of the handicapped, and anthroposophically extended medicine. This collection presents many of Rudolf Steiner's statements about Sophia. One would think that assembling these would have been an easy matter— that there would have been an embarrassment of riches on this topic. Steiner, after all, is the creator of "Anthroposophy," which is made of two Greek words—*Anthropos* (human being) and *Sophia* (wisdom). Both of these may be understood in either a "low" or a "high" sense. In the low or obvious sense, Anthroposophy is "human wisdom," the wisdom that is humanity or human nature. The high sense specifies the esoteric ground of this nature.

Uniting (uppercase) Anthropos and Sophia, in fact, invokes the mystery of a divine, original, "cosmic humanity" almost as alluded to by some early Gnostics. The Valentinians, for instance, maintained that, after the Incarnation of Christ, God's previously hidden, unspoken name could finally be revealed. It was *Anthropos!* This was why, they said, "the Savior styled himself the 'Son of Anthropos.'" Confirming this view of humanity's high origin, another fragment preserved by Clement of Alexandria tells the story of the creation of Adam by the angels. It describes how "fear fell on the angels in the presence of the creature they had created when it emitted greater sounds than its creation justified. For Adam, being fashioned in the name of *Anthropos* inspired fear of the pre-existent *Anthropos*, because he was in him."

Sophia likewise has both high and low connotations. At one level, she invokes the human soul as feminine, divine, but fallen. To rescue this Sophia—destined to be the bride of Christ—the Word descended from Heaven to Earth and incarnated in a human body, and through his death, resurrection, and ascension made possible the return of Sophia to her divine condition. In other accounts, Sophia is God's feminine aspect. From this point of view, Sophia is linked either with the Holy Spirit or the Divine Being or Ground (*Ousia, Substance*) as the common element, the "abyss" around which the Persons of the Trinity—Father, Son, and Holy Spirit—dance their "round dance (*perichoresis*)." As such, She is the Holy of Holies, "the silence and mystery of the Godhead," the innermost ground of all that is.

Anthroposophy, which invokes all these meanings, is also called spiritual science, which, as a "science of the spirit" is, it may be said, even a science of the Holy Spirit. Thereby, Anthroposophy announces a new Age of the Spirit in accord with the prophetic vision of Joachim of Fiore, the twelfth-century Calabrian mystic. Joachim prophesied that the pre-Christian Age of the Father, which was followed after the coming of Christ by the Age of the Son, would in turn be followed by an Age of the Spirit:

The first age was the age of knowledge, the second of understanding, and the third age will be the period of complete intelligence.

The first was servile obedience, the second filial servitude, and the third will be freedom. The first was affliction, the second action, and the third will be contemplation. The first was fear, the second faith, and the third will be love. The first was the age of slaves, the second the age of sons, and the third will be the age of friends.

Spiritual intelligence, freedom, contemplation, love, friendship—these "Sophianic" realities implicitly occupy the very center of Anthroposophy, or spiritual science. As for the basis of these, if we study Steiner's directions for spiritual practice, we find that *Sophia pervades Anthroposophy from the ground up.* For the foundations of Anthroposophy—in a sense, its beginning and end—are reverence or devotion, service, and selflessness. Steiner frequently refers to these three practices (which are also principles and virtues). For confirmation of this, readers may like to reread the first and last chapters of *How to Know Higher Worlds.* However, he never calls them "Sophianic" or relates them to Sophia (nor to Isis or Mary), though they certainly are.

In other words, *Sophia lies at the esoteric heart of Steiner's mission.* Perhaps that is precisely why Steiner is notably reticent, even modest, when speaking of Sophia, circling suggestively around her, now at one level, now at another, without ever fully defining her or coming right out and saying exactly what he means. Between the lines, however, he tells a profound story—or rather, a number of profound stories that must be read and meditated slowly. Steiner's vision, like any truly spiritual vision, is not a system or an ideology. We should not try to force it into a rationalized or mechanical structure. A spiritual teaching is more like a living organism that must be intuited whole than a mechanism that can be analyzed. To understand it requires what the poet John Keats called "negative capability"—that is, one must be "capable of being in uncertainties, mysteries, doubts, without any irritable reaching after fact and reason."

Wisdom and Love

According to Steiner's account of our present evolutionary state, which he calls the "Earth stage of evolution," and our particular epoch within it, the "consciousness soul," humanity's task is the transformation of wisdom into love. The substance of the Earth is Wisdom, the work of the gods, inscribed in the substance of the galaxies and the movements of the stars, as well is in the rocks, plants, and animals that surround us. This Wisdom must become Love. In earlier epochs, the knowledge that we now acquire by deliberate exercise of our intelligence was received simultaneously and directly with sense perception. Such knowing was itself a remnant of a still more ancient, universal supersensible consciousness. After Christ's Incarnation, however, fewer and fewer human beings possessed this capacity. In its place, people began to develop conscious cognitive powers (Imagination, Inspiration, and Intuition). Steiner writes: "The task of these new initiates was to recognize, through their own faculties, what had once been comprehended through ancient Mystery wisdom and to add to this knowledge of the essential nature of the Christ event." By this means, a certain "hidden knowledge"—which Steiner calls "Grail knowledge"—began to flow into humanity. As a result of this influx, we will gradually develop a new, conscious clairvoyance which, in practice, implies the transformation of "wisdom" into "love." As the fruit of evolution, we are everywhere—in nature, the cosmos, our own bodies—surrounded by wisdom. We live in a world made by the gods. The power of love allows our "I" to harmonize and transform this wisdom into what can grow into the future. Love, as Georg Kühlewind says, is always creative of what "is not yet." Through love, outer wisdom becomes inner wisdom: the world is turned inside out. Steiner writes: "Beginning with the Earth phase of evolution, *the wisdom of the outer cosmos becomes inner wisdom in the human being.* Internalized in this way, it becomes the seed of love. Wisdom is the prerequisite for love; love is the result of wisdom that has been reborn in the I."

Sophia, Philosophia, Anthroposophia

In his inaugural lecture to the First General Meeting of the Anthroposophical Society in 1913, Rudolf Steiner spoke of the being of Anthroposophy—"Anthropo-Sophia." He began by citing the poet Dante's great love for Lady Philosophy. Dante's love was no mere allegory. According to Steiner, it was "a concrete experience of a passionate relationship, immediate and of the soul, with Lady Philosophy." Turning then to the ancient Greeks, Steiner pointed out that they did not know "Philosophia," but only "Sophia." For the Greeks, this Sophia was a living being, just as Lady Philosophia was for Dante. But she was distant. She began to draw closer around the fifth century after Christ—we meet her as Philosophia in Boethius's *Consolation of Philosophy.* By the Middle Ages, she inspired the most ardent feelings as she approached from the clouds. But she was becoming distant again. Indeed, by Dante's time, her appearance in the form Lady Philosophy represented a last vestige of an immediate personal connection with the spiritual worlds. Today, this vestige seems to have disappeared. How then, do we encounter Sophia today? Steiner says that, in the contemporary age of the consciousness soul, Sophia must become "the being who directly enlightens human beings." Having entered us, Sophia "will take our being with her and present it to us outwardly—as Anthroposophia." "In this form," he says, "she will confront enlightened human beings as the objective being Sophia who once stood before the Greeks."

Speaking of Dante's feelings for the Lady, Steiner suggests a link between Wisdom and Mary the mother of Jesus: "Anyone who can feel such things will find a direct connection between Raphael's Sistine Madonna floating on the clouds and the exalted Lady Philosophia." We may then ask if this connection illuminates what Steiner alluded to as a kind of "incarnation" of Sophia when he spoke of Sophia's passage through humanity to become Anthropo-Sophia or—may we say?—Mary-Sophia. Did Isis-Sophia enter the earthly stream of world evolution through Mary?

Mary

Mary is the great mystery of the Christian tradition. Nothing would have happened without her assent to God's desire that she conceive and bring forth a son—to be called Jesus, who would bear the Christ. Without her astonishing "Behold the handmaid of the Lord, be it unto me according to thy word," there would have been no Incarnation, no "Word made flesh," no death and resurrection, no ascension. Yet the Gospels mention her rarely. It is as if she lived in effacement. Some have suggested the very reticence of the Scriptures speaks to her greatness and spiritual depth—that she is "a secret revelation." Certainly, whenever she appears her presence is fraught with consequence. She is intimately linked to Jesus as mother, friend, and disciple. She participated in his ministry and his miracles. She stood at the foot of the cross, where Christ gave her to be the mother of us all when he said to John, the Beloved Disciple, "Behold, your mother," and to Mary, "Behold your son." She was indispensable to the descent of the Holy Spirit at Pentecost. It is difficult not to conclude that she is close to the inner core of Christ's mission, as well as his teaching and ministry.

History bears this out. Whether by oral tradition or by the Holy Spirit, Mary's stature grew and grows still. Very early, she became at once the figure of the striving Christian soul—the prototype of true faith and real works—and of Christ's "mystical body," an expression encompassing multiple realities from the community of believers through the universal Church of all humanity to the Universe itself. She was recognized from the beginning to be the new Eve (as Christ was the new Adam). Irenaeus, Bishop of Lyons and disciple of the Beloved Disciple, writes in the second century: "As Eve was seduced by the word of an angel to flee from God . . . so Mary by the word of an angel received the glad tidings that she would bear God by obeying His Word. The former was seduced to disobey God, but the latter was persuaded to obey God, so that the Virgin Mary might become the advocate of the virgin Eve. As the human race was subjected to death through a virgin, so it was saved by a Virgin." Thus the ninth-century *Ave Stella Maris* (Hail, Star of the Sea) proclaimed (as Steiner also mentions), "Gabriel's Ave spoken long ago reversed Eve's [Eva's] name." No wonder the Third Ecumenical Council of Ephesus (431 C.E.) declared her *Theotokos*, Mother of God. Deeply meaningful mystical titles proliferated—Morning Star, Gate of Heaven, Beauty of the World, Queen of Life, Mother of All Living, Mirror of Justice, Seat of Wisdom, Mystical Rose, Ark of the Covenant, Refuge of Sinners, Comforter of the Afflicted, Queen of Angels, Lamp-Stand of Seven Branches, and so on. As her presence grew, her appearances become more frequent. After all, she was a being. By the Middle Ages, that being began to overlight Western culture, initiating an inner transformation centered on the "knowing heart." More recently, we have seen the movement to declare her "Co-Redemptrix" (Co-Redeemer) gaining ground.

Steiner's view, based on his own research, is different, but consonant with the historical evolution of consciousness regarding Mary. To understand it, we need a little background.

As readers of the Gospels well know, St. Matthew and St. Luke give quite different genealogies for Joseph, Mary, and Jesus. Biblical scholars as well as theologians have mostly ignored these differences or merely drawn what symbolic meaning they could from them. Spiritual research, however, revealed to Rudolf Steiner that the reason for the separate genealogies was quite simply that that there were two holy families—two Josephs, two Marys, two Jesuses!

Of the Mary of Luke's Gospel, about whom we know very little from tradition, Emil Bock—drawing on Steiner's indications—writes in *The Childhood of Jesus* in glowing, meditative words filled with wisdom and truth:

She was the focus of rays that penetrated only once from the highest heavenly spheres to Earth in this particular way. In complete pristine purity and perfection, a divine archetype that surrounds humanity in the spiritual world was mirrored in her being and countenance. Even as the archetype of the child and childlikeness . . . was reflected in the child she was to bear, so too the Mary of Luke seemed like the archetype of all virginal womanhood come down to Earth, the incarnation of eternal femininity, the woman of women.

People of antiquity looked up to the virginal world-mother in many forms and perceived in her the actively working existence of a being who, as the soul of the universe, is the macrocosmic correspondence of the soul mystery of the individual human being. For the same reason that the soul of the universe was viewed as a goddess, not a god, the human female is a clearer image of the human soul than the human male. In paradisal primordial stages, the nature of the feminine human being, as yet not having drawn into solid earthly corporeality, was a more direct, unsullied, and complete replica of the virginal-maternal world soul. In Eve, before the Fall, the biblical story of creation gives an inkling of this replica, which is identical with the prototype. After the Fall into solid dark matter, the earthly female nature could never be anything but a deformed and distorted reflection of the eternal female element. Still, in the young Mary of Luke's Gospel, freed from all distortion, the primal being of virgin and mother appeared to have taken on form once again. Even as the paradisal being of Adam before the Fall, which had been preserved in the spirit realm, as to incarnate in the [Luke] Jesus child, so, in his mother, the conserved paradisal Eve seemed to become physically visible. Here in all outward unpretentiousness, a human soul was through and through surrounded and imbued with the world soul and, through it, by the pure light of the cosmos, the same which in the ancient world was called Isis-Sophia and, in Christianity, the "Holy Spirit."

As Eternal Femininity, Madonna of Purity, and Virgin Mother Goddess with Child, this Mary of Luke's Gospel was the fulfillment of ancient prophecies and the embodiment of humanity's deepest destiny. A "young soul," she lived a "hidden" life. The "other" Mary—of St. Matthew's Gospel—led a more open life. Various Apocryphal texts—the Protoevangelium of James, the so-called Arabic Infancy Gospel, and the Gospel of Pseudo Matthew—refer to this Mary, the daughter of Joachim and Anna. Like her heavenly sister, she too "was surrounded with the radiance of a miracle." Drawn from her earliest years into the presence of the Temple, she was an "old soul," deeply pious, holy, and devout. A "Temple Maiden," she lived in great intimacy with the spiritual world and recapitulated in her development the religious development of humanity.

Leaving aside details incidental to our theme of Sophia, the first fusion of the two holy families occurred after that moment spoken of in the Gospels when Jesus was lost in the temple at the age of twelve. He was found again, full of knowledge and wisdom. He taught as one who had authority, revealing that the "I" of the Matthew Jesus (which was ancient and wise) had passed over into the Luke Jesus. Soon thereafter, according to Steiner's researches, the Luke Mary died, as did the Matthew Mary's son. The Matthew Mary (whose aged husband had likewise died) then married the newly widowed Joseph. Thus, the Matthew Mary became the stepmother of the Luke Jesus, so that there was now but one holy family.

The next great event occurred when Jesus and his stepmother have a "farewell" conversation just before Jesus goes up to the Jordan to be baptized by John. This Mary has grown very close to her stepson, sharing as friend and confidante in all his experiences—above all, the fruits of his huge compassion and his pain at humanity's distance from God and the spiritual world. As Emil Bock writes, this last conversation before—in Steiner's Christology—the descent of the Christ at the Baptism simply continued the intimate conversation that Jesus had enjoyed with Mary over the years. But there was something different. The intensity of the moment opened both their souls to the breaking point of new birth. Their conversation became an event. As Jesus told of the pain that he experienced at gazing into humanity's future, his whole being began to loosen in anticipation of the entry of the Christ into his soul. Mary, listening with absolute compassion, suddenly understood the destiny of the one she loved now as her own. In Bock's words, "A mighty presentiment of perception told her that a wise providence had been at work in all her painful blows of destiny, a providence that was intent on turning her into *one who would share in carrying an incomprehensible event of Salvation.*" However, he continues, "The transformation of soul that took place in Mary consisted not only in a new insight and understanding which overwhelmed her. The lightning flash of recognition that struck her at the same time opened her soul to an actual heavenly force by which henceforth she remained overshadowed and imbued." At this moment, the paradisal, virginal soul of Luke's Mary, irradiated by the divine Isis-Sophia entity, descended upon the Matthew Mary's soul. As a result, she was permeated by a kind of "cosmic virginity" Henceforth, Mary was "ensouled and inspired by heavenly divine being and consciousness" and became, as she now is, the Blessed Virgin. As Emil Bock points out, "In archetypal form, the tremendous change that was evoked in Mary by the farewell conversation represents a transformation that every human soul must struggle to attain." He quotes Angelus Silesius:

> You must be Mary and give birth to God in you
> If God is to grant you eternal bliss too.

Bock also points out, following Steiner, Mary's capital role in the first of Jesus' miracles or signs, the "Sun-miracle" of the wedding at Cana, where the water was turned into wine, foreshadowing the Eucharist. According to Steiner, this miracle "grows out of a mystery that operated between the soul of Jesus and his mother. At the wedding, they ran out of wine. Mary turns to Jesus for help, but Jesus apparently rebukes his mother, saying, "Woman, what have I to do with thee." These words are mistranslated. No rebuke is intended. They are a formula from the Mysteries and in fact should be translated, "What is it that works and weaves between us?" It is the first time they have met since the conversation that transformed them both. Mary now bears the "virgin Mother-soul of the world." At the wedding, she sees Jesus—now the Christ-bearer—again. As Bock says, "Two exalted beings find each other again on Earth. In this hour of meeting there operated between these two transformed beings something that might be described as the divine octave of the human Mother-Son relationship. By the radiant light of the being that ensouled her, Mary recognized intuitively in her completely changed Son the power of the Sun-being, Christ. This it is that brought about the miracle of Cana."

At Pentecost, all of the disciples—along with Mary and the other women—were gathered in one place. Tradition has them surrounding Mary, in a circle. She was at their center when a mighty sound as of a rushing wind was heard. A fiery ray descended upon her, spreading out to light in tongues of flame upon all those present. They were filled with the Holy Spirit and began to speak in tongues which each understood as if it was his or her own language. It is not surprising, therefore, that in the Middle Ages we find representations of the Trinity in which the Third Person—the Holy Spirit—is depicted as a woman.

Mary lived long after that—with the Beloved Disciple in his house at Ephesus. They had a community, whose teaching (it is said) we may find in John's great letter of love (I John). When Mary died, it was said she went to sleep and was assumed bodily into Heaven. Above all, Mary pondered (and ponders still) in her heart. Her assent and receptivity, humility and poverty, her radical presence—all add up to the supreme virtue of the dedication of the heart to truth.

The New Isis-Mary-Sophia

To put it as succinctly as possible, for Rudolf Steiner Sophia is wisdom in all its manifestations—divine, heavenly, cosmic, earthly. From this perspective, wisdom is everywhere. She is an evolutionary reality surrounding and permeating us. To truly acknowledge reality, we must say that we live and move and have our being in her. Traditionally, the study of this reality—the path and way of knowing the wisdom that we are and that surrounds us—is called *science*. Science, before the modern age of duality, abstraction, objectification, manipulation, and control, was always devoted to the great project of self-knowledge, which is the transformation of wisdom into love. Steiner therefore also calls Anthroposophy "spiritual science," and he tried throughout his life to explain the nature and methods of that science. His whole work, in fact, is dedicated to this project. But his readers and listeners—because they were so thoroughly conditioned, as we are still today, by the materialist-mechanist assumptions of the modern world—had great trouble understanding him. Sometimes, he spoke more esoterically to try to convey the inner meaning of what spiritual science involved and told quasi-humorously of the need for a "new Isis myth." This myth, he emphasized, was not an abstraction but *a reality*. He said that behind the wooden sculpture of Christ—the Representative of Humanity carved (between Lucifer and Ahriman, the two beings of "evil") in the Goetheanum, the headquarters of Anthroposophy in Switzerland— there was a fourth, invisible, figure, a being, Isis. Mostly she was invisible, but sometimes especially intuitive visitors glimpsed her. They saw that, in fact, she was asleep and that beneath her was the inscription "I am humanity. I am the past, present, and future. Every mortal should lift my veil."

Without going into details (the text may be found on page 193), we may say that a new Typhon, the very personification of calculating intellect, dupes her and creates a mechanical pseudo-offspring. Poor Isis! For the illusion of a child all she has is a simulacrum of wisdom. Then she notices—clairvoyantly—that she still has cow horns, just as she had in ancient Egypt. Her clairvoyance grows. Through it she commands Typhon—or, some say, Hermes—to place a crown upon her head. Sadly, it is only a paper crown, covered with scientific writing. But her clairvoyance continues to grow and with its help she begins to understand the meaning of the *Word*, or *Logos*, taught by St. John in the Prologue to his Gospel. And, as she begins to understand the meaning of the Logos, her paper crown turns to gold. Scientific abstraction becomes living reality. Sophia becomes *alive*.

As Steiner says in "The Search for the New Isis":

> Isis-Sophia
> Wisdom of God
> Lucifer has slain her,
> And on wings of cosmic forces
> Carried her away into the depths of space.
> Christ-Will
> Working in us
> Shall tear her from Lucifer
> And on grounds of spiritual knowledge
> Call to new life in human souls
> Isis-Sophia
> Wisdom of God.

A Single Femininity

Leaving aside the vexed question of the historical existence of a universal "Great Mother" culture predating the advent of the newer "patriarchal" religions, the feminine divine is clearly present everywhere in the founding civilizations of our present moment. She is called by many names—Inanna in Sumeria; Astarte among the Hittites; Ishtar in Babylon; in Egypt (among many others), Isis, Maat, Hathor, Nut, and Neith; in Greece, Demeter, Persephone, Artemis, Athena, Hecate. The list is endless—Sophia and Mary are only two more. The more one seeks, the more Goddesses one finds. This apparently riotous confusion should *not* be taken as evidence of polytheism—far from it. These figurations—all of whom may be said to be aspects of Sophia—represent different states of one and the same primal principle, acting according to successive phases of becoming. "There is only a single femininity, but it acts differently in different environments," as Schwaller de Lubicz says.

Wisdom Literature

In the Judeo-Christian tradition, Sophia appears first in the guise of *Hokhmah* in the postexilic so-called Wisdom Books. We find her in Job, Proverbs, Jesus Sirach, and the Wisdom of Solomon. The literature is extraordinarily rich, every phrase and line deserving of meditation. In the earliest account, Job 28, we find:

> But where can Wisdom be found?
> Where is the place of understanding?
>
> No one can set a value on it;
> It cannot be found in the land of the living.
> The deep says, "It is not in me."
> The sea says, "I do not have it."
> It cannot be bartered for gold;
> Silver cannot be paid out as its price. . . .
>
> Whence does Wisdom come?
> Where is the source of understanding?
>
> It is hidden from the eyes of all living,
> Concealed from the fowl of heaven. . . .
> God understands the way to it;
> He knows its place;
> For he sees to the ends of the earth,
> Observes all that is beneath the heavens.
> When He fixed the weight of the winds,
> Set the measure for the waters;
> When He made a rule for the rain

And a course for thunderstorms,
When He saw it and gauged it;
He set it up and searched it out.

He said to man,
"See! Fear of the lord is Wisdom;
To shun evil is understanding."

For Job, Wisdom is of God. Embedded in creation, she is its language—"the 'meaning' implanted by God in creation." Humans, however, do not yet have a way to understand her. She is not yet a person, a being. Wisdom is here feminine only because *Hokhmah* is feminine.

Proverbs 8 presents a different view. Wisdom now stands on Earth, and addresses human beings. She wants them to find her and to follow her. In return, she promises shrewdness, justice, truth, counsel, resourcefulness, understanding, courage, and righteousness. "Wisdom is better than rubies; / No goods can equal her." Then she gives her pedigree.

The Lord created me at the beginning of his course
As the first of his works of old.
In the distant past I was fashioned
At the beginning, at the origin of the earth.
There was still no deep when I was brought forth,
No springs rich in water.
Before the mountains were sunk, before the hills, I was born.
He had no yet made earth and fields,
Or the world's first clumps of clay.
I was there when he set the heavens into space;
When he fixed the horizon upon the deep;
When he made the heavens above form,
And the fountains of the deep gushed forth;
When he assigned the sea its limits,

So that its waters never transgress his command;
When he fixed the foundations of the earth,
I was with him as a confidant,
A source of delight every day,
Playing in front of him all the time,
Playing in his inhabited world,
Finding delight with humankind.

This Wisdom was created before Heaven and Earth. She was in
fact the very beginning of God's creation: the first created being, the
closest to him. Present at creation, she is the daughter of God, his
joy and delight. She is his presence, his messenger in the world. She
plays not only before him, but also among us, human beings in the
world. She finds delight with us too. Unlike Job's portrayal, Wisdom in Proverbs wishes to be recognized. She seeks us out. She is
God's revelation on Earth, speaking through creation. To find her is
life, because she is life.

Happy is he, who listens to me,
Coming early to my gates each day,
Waiting outside my doors.
For he who finds me finds life
And obtains favor from the Lord.
But he who misses me destroys himself;
All who hate me love death.

Jesus Sirach, composed in Hebrew around 190 B.C.E. and translated into Greek about 132 B.C.E., amplifies the vision in Proverbs.
Again, Wisdom speaks in the first person, explaining how she runs
through all creation. She tells how she came forth from the mouth
of the Most High, covering the Earth like a mist, yet dwelling in the
heavens and taking her course through the abyss—all the while holding sway over the Earth and her peoples. The text implies that,
though beginning in Heaven and present everywhere, *Wisdom seeks a*

home on Earth. God, in fact, commands her to find an earthly dwelling. She settles in Israel, first in the Tabernacle, then in the Temple. In this process, she becomes identified with and embodied in the Torah, God's law expressing the covenant between God and humanity.

In the Wisdom of Solomon, Wisdom has come to Earth. Solomon himself speaks for Wisdom. "What Wisdom [*Sophia*] is, and how she came into being, I shall tell you." It is God who reveals this to Solomon. God and his *Sophia* are two sides of a single coin. What joins them is Spirit (*pneuma*)—"the Spirit of Wisdom." Wisdom is a spirit—"a kindly spirit"—and it has a spirit. "In Wisdom there is a spirit intelligent and holy, unique in its kind and yet made up of many parts, subtle, free-moving, lucid." Twenty-one (3 x 7) qualities are named. This spirit is almost equated with God—"for the Spirit of the Lord fills the whole earth, and that which holds all things together knows very well everything that is said." At this point (7:25–28), the clearest description of Wisdom's origin in and relationship with God is given:

> Like a fine mist she rises from the power of God,
> A clear effluence from the glory of the Almighty;
> So nothing defiled can enter into her by stealth.
> She is the radiance that streams from everlasting light,
> The flawless mirror of the active power of God
> And the image of his goodness.
> She is but one, yet can do all things,
> Herself unchanging, she makes all things new;
> Age after age she enters into holy souls,
> And makes them friends of God and prophets,
> For nothing is acceptable to God
> But the person who makes his home with Wisdom.

It is also said that she "sits beside God's throne" and "adds luster to her noble birth because it is given her to live with God." Further, she is God's "coadjutor," his beloved, even his spouse. Solomon too takes her for his wife: "Wisdom I loved; I sought her out when I was young and longed to win her for my bride; I was in love with her beauty. . . . So I determined to take her home to live with me."

Greece

In Greece, the mood is at once similar, different, and as always, ambiguous. Wisdom is divine concord and harmony. To the extent that human beings acquire wisdom, they share in the divine fullness. To do so is the foundation of all piety and the true desire of the philosopher, who loves wisdom. Courage, self-control, temperance— such virtues are fine, as far as they go. But "the one currency for which all should be exchanged is wisdom." Wisdom makes virtue possible. From this point of view, "wisdom itself is a kind of *purification*," which, for the Greeks, was a purification of the body—from the body. As such, in an absolute sense, wisdom is not to be found in this world, which is why the philosopher must practice dying, as Socrates teaches.

> Surely there are many who have chosen of their own free will to follow dead lovers and wives and sons to the next world, in the hope of seeing and meeting there the persons whom they loved. If this is so, will a true lover of wisdom who has firmly grasped this same conviction—that he will never attain to wisdom worthy of the name anywhere than in the next world—will he be grieved at dying? Will he not be glad to make the journey? We must suppose so—that is, if he is a real philosopher, because he then will be of the firm belief that he will never find wisdom in all its purity in any other place. (*Phaedo*)

Elsewhere, Plato attributes Wisdom—in the sense of that "single science that were it removed from humanity, or had never appeared, human beings would become the most foolish of creatures"—to Uranus, the heavens, the source of all numbers.

> If we but reach a right contemplation of him, we may call him by the name of Cosmos, Olympus, or Uranus, as we please. Let us only follow him in his course as he bespangles himself and wheels his stars through their courses in the act of providing us with seasons and daily food. And with the gift of the whole number series, he gives us likewise the rest of understanding, and all other good things. But it is the greatest gift of all, if we accept the gift of number, and let our minds expatiate over the whole heavenly circuit. (*Epinomis*)

Sophia as the starry sky is, in fact, a constant—from the Egyptian Nut to Steiner's lectures on the "New Isis." Plato makes this Wisdom male—but such gender slippage should not disturb us. A certain misogyny runs through our tradition.

Before philosophy (and after it, too, for the gods did not "die" until much later), there were the Goddesses—Demeter, Persephone, Hera, Athena, Metis, Aphrodite, Artemis, Gaia, Rhea, Semele, and so on. Of these, only Metis ("wise counsel") and the owl-eyed virgin Pallas Athena are explicitly associated with wisdom. All, however, as Jung recognized, are soul qualities. Of Demeter, the Earth Mother, and Persephone, Steiner says, "With these two names we touch on what are really two souls in modern human beings—two souls whose union is achieved only through the severest ordeals." Persephone, taken down to Hades, is our ancient heritage of clairvoyance, raped by modern knowledge. Demeter is "the ruler of the greatest wonders of nature, an archetypal form that points to the time when the life of the human brain was not yet cut off from the general bodily life." She is "the archetypal mother of the human soul and the fruitful sources of nature," out of whom what is born elementally becomes Persephone in the human being.

Philo

Uniting Greek philosophy and biblical wisdom, Philo of Alexandria wrote philosophical commentaries on the Bible. These are full of references to Sophia. For example, here is Sophia as bride of God and mother of the world: "We should rightly say and without further question that the Architect who made this universe was at the same time father of what was thus born, while its mother was the knowledge possessed by its maker. With this knowledge God had union, though not as human beings have it, and begot created being. And knowledge, having received the divine seed and when the travail was consummated, bore the only beloved son who is apprehended by the senses, the world that we see."

Wisdom for Philo is above all the mediator, the way God reaches from Heaven to Earth, channeling gifts of goodness, virtue, and knowledge. He speaks of "the solid and indestructible Wisdom of God, which feeds and nurses and rears to sturdiness all who yearn after imperishable sustenance." She is "the mother of all that are in the world, affording her offspring, as soon as they are born, the nourishment which they require from her own breasts." Elsewhere, Philo plays with Sophia's gender. Though she is female in relation to God, through her activity in the world she is more masculine. "Let us pay no heed to the discrepancy in the gender of words," he concludes, "and say that the daughter of God, even Wisdom, is not only masculine, but father, sowing and begetting in souls aptness to learn, discipline, knowledge, sound sense." In other words, though feminine, Sophia is by no means passive!

Christianity and Gnosis

At the heart of Christianity are two beings: the being of Christ, who entered our world and turned creation inside out, and the being of Mary—for Christ could enter this world only through the being of Jesus-and-Mary. The presence of Christ, who entered our world through Jesus-and-Mary, means—for Christians—that human nature and divine nature, God and cosmos, are no longer two but one. By uniting with human nature, God entered the earthly, evolutionary world. The Word became flesh, but not only the Word. As the early Christian Fathers recognized, the Persons of the Trinity—the Father, the Son, and the Holy Spirit—though distinct, are indivisible. They cannot be separated. Through the Incarnation of the Son, the entire Godhead entered the stream of world evolution. As a result, there is no longer any transcendent outside. The transcendent is in *this* world. One need no longer seek causes or explanations outside experience. There is no beyond. Each thing in our experience can open to infinite depth and height. The universe has been turned inside out. This is why Rudolf Steiner repeatedly calls the "Mystery of Golgotha" a cosmic, universal event.

When the events of the Incarnation occurred, few people noticed them beyond the small circles of the disciples and the women and friends around Christ. Fewer still understood. The first people to try to understand the significance of what had happened out of their own spiritual experience were early Gnostics like Valentinus. In doing so, it was they who encountered and named Sophia for the first time, for they saw creation and redemption as the drama of Christ and Sophia.

The first couple, incomprehensible Depth and ineffable Silence, created the first seed, from which arose the first pair, Conscience and Truth. From these gushed forth the other Aeons—Reason and Life, Anthropos and Community, and so forth down—always in pairs. The last to arrive, unpaired, was Sophia, the youngest of the Aeons. Like the other Aeons, Sophia enjoyed the fullness of all life. But she felt far removed from the Source. Impetuous and impatient, her passion got the better of her. Refusing to wait to know the ineffable One from whom she sprang, she rushed forward. Much then happened to her, many adventures, and perhaps she would have reached her goal, but she met *Horos* (limitation), who separated her from her passion—dividing her—and exiled that passion (now called

"Achamoth," or Lower Sophia) from the spiritual world. Expelled from the spiritual world, Sophia brought forth Jesus as a remembrance of it. But he would not stay with her. He returned to the spiritual world. This was before creation or the Fall, as we know it.

Left alone, cast out, Achamoth-Sophia suffered agonies of fear, despair, passion, and ignorance. Her suffering was not ineffective. It produced a false, alien, aborted world whose very matter, soul, and spirit mimicked that of the Truth. As Valentinus says, "Ignorance of the Father brought about anguish and terror. And the anguish and terror grew thick like a fog, so that no one was able to see. For this reason error became powerful; it fashioned its own matter. . . . It set about making a creature, with all its might preparing in beauty as substitute for the truth."

Meanwhile, above, the heavenly Sophia, together with Jesus and all the Aeons, looked down with pity, sadness, and compassion as the Sophia below, born of passion, labored in ignorance, suffering, and anguish. Finally, at the last moment, they decided to rescue her. They sent the celestial bridegroom Christ, "a being of perfect beauty, the very star of the spiritual world, its perfect fruit," into the world she had made.

From the Gnostics, we learn that Sophia is threefold. First, she is present with God before the creation. In a sense, she is uncreated creation itself in God. Second, she aids the creation and—this is the Gnostic insight—partially falls with it, so that the suffering of the world, as it falls out of Paradise and hurtles further and further away from direct participation in divine wisdom, is the suffering of Sophia herself. Finally, there is renewed, redeemed Sophia. Rooted in, and reunited with, the divine as the source of the divine-human relation, Sophia now works at the new creation in time. She is the New Jerusalem, a new Heaven and a new Earth—at once the preexistent and eternal and built in time. These three, who are one, are made one through the collaboration of Christ and Sophia.

These different images of Sophia show us how important it is not to literalize her. We must begin to understand Sophia-Wisdom as an activity that we can embody and participate in. The guiding image for this among Christians has always been Mary. But we must understand this Mary not only as the Virgin Mother of Jesus Christ, transparent to the Holy Spirit, but as coextensive both with Jesus' human bodily nature and with the body of Christ. Christ's body is that invisible body built up by its members through their love—that is, by all those who walk the way of love of Sophia-Mary-Jesus. It is the interpenetrated, interconnected solidarity of love, which is not any political institution but is coextensive with the universe itself.

The Middle Ages and After

The Middle Ages was a turning point in Sophia's evolution. It was the moment of "the discovery of the individual," marking the opening of a new kind of human interiority—from Abelard's discovery of the inner voice of moral responsibility to Aquinas's majestic unfolding of the personality in pure thinking. It was also the time of the great Grail cycles, as well as the *Tale of Flor and Blanchflor* and the *Roman de la Rose*—all "Sophianic" in their essence. Above all, and uniting these, was the explicit dawning of the divine feminine— marked by the birth of a new devotion to Mary and to the humanity of Jesus. Echoing this, at the School of Chartres hermetic Platonists sought to reopen the Book of Nature and create a new sacred science of the Goddess *Natura*. It was the time, too, of the first translations of alchemical texts from Arabic into Latin—alchemy being the "Sophianic science" *par excellence*—and of the creation of the book Bahir and Moses de Leon's compilation of the Zohar, revolutionary works of Jewish Kabbalah, written in southern France. These introduced the figure of the *Shekinah*, the feminine presence of God.

The book Bahir which takes its name from Job 37.21—"But now one does not see the light [any more], it shines [*bahir hu'*] in the heavens"—presents a dynamic, evolving God, unfolding into creation in a series of potencies or emanations called "*Sefirot.*" There are ten of these, of which the tenth is the Shekinah. She is the vessel into which all the others flow and at the same time the "heart" of God, with direct access to the thirty-two hidden paths of wisdom by which the world was created. A precious stone that God loves more than his "kings," she may well remind us of the stone from Lucifer's crown that became the stone of the Grail in Wolfram von Eschenbach's *Parzival.* While low or "immanent," the Shekinah is also connected to the highest and most transcendent source. Like Sophia, "There is a Shekinah below, just as there is a Shekinah above." She hands over the divine powers to this world, while also directing them from above. Thus she is described as "united yet separated." Above all, like Mary, she is the mediatrix between Heaven and Earth. As such, she is God's own embodiment in the world. Seeking an origin for the Shekinah, who is not fully predictable by prior Jewish thinking on the subject, the scholar Peter Shäfer points to the growing Marian theology of the period. Mary likewise was from above and below. Identified with Wisdom, the "firstborn of all creation," she was born on Earth to give birth to Jesus, but assumed into Heaven. She was both human and deified. She is simultaneously the daughter, the mother, and the bride of God. Like the Shekinah, Mary is the great mediatrix and co-redemptrix—in Hildegard, she is even *salvatrix,* the feminine savior.

> O *Salvatrix,*
> You who bore the new light
> For humankind:
> Gather the members of your Son
> Into celestial harmony.

Mary is the new Eve; Heaven and all the angels and Earth and all its creatures revolve around her, just as the Sefirot revolve around the Shekinah.

At the same time as these more theological events were unfolding, women mystics among the Beguines and in the new Cistercian "schools of love" were initiating a new, nondualistic spiritual path that likewise united Heaven and Earth. Meanwhile, to the south, in Languedoc and Provence, the Troubadours and Cathars were drawing together Christian, Ismaili, Manichaean, and Sufi teachings to create a new, vernacular feminine culture of love for transforming the world in the human soul. Underlying all of these was a new understanding of the centrality of the *heart*, the *purified soul*, and the *feminine* (three aspects of a single reality)—and also of the unity of the individual soul and the world soul, the *Anima Mundi*. The task was to become one with the heart of the world, the divine-human heart of Jesus Christ opened up *in* the world by the spear of Longinus to become a fountain of living water for the sake of the world's transformation. From this opened heart, slain from the foundation of the world, water and blood poured over and into the Earth, permeating it, filling it with the spirit of creative love, ennobling it as the growing heart of creation. As invoked by the mystics, this "heart" is not simply located. It is not a thing to be located anywhere, inside or outside the body. Rather, it is the activity that is the center of all things: the potential center of every perception, the magical fulcrum of every marvel. It is the realization of Christ in all things: Mary makes this possible.

Hildegard of Bingen (b. 1098) gives us another clue. For Hildegard, Sophia, whom she calls either *Sapientia* (Wisdom) or *Caritas* (Love) is the reality—the cosmic glue—harmonizing and connecting many things we usually keep separate. She is the living bond between creator and creation, God and cosmos. By her perpetual mediation the divine manifests and can be known. This Sophia lives in the encounter of God and creation. She is where God stoops to humanity and humanity aspires to God. As the cosmogonic, playful companion of the creator, Sophia makes possible not only creation itself, but the incarnation of that creation in time. This is the redemption or new creation in and through Christ, which for Hildegard is the center and cause of all, the event for which the world has been made. A woman, Mary, accomplished the new creation that is the threefold union of divinity, humanity, and the Earth. Woman, the feminine, is the means of God's becoming all in all. And this means that the feminine—Sophia: Wisdom and Love—is not limited just to Mary. It extends, first, to Jesus, the Humanity of Christ— "Jesus, our mother"—and then, by extension, to the "Church," humanity, the Earth—which we are and which is, in turn, one with the cosmos itself. Jesus, the crucified Christ-bearer, humanity, matter, the Earth, the cosmos, is Sophia, the place where the heart of Christ must come to dwell. The hearts of Jesus and Mary are one heart—Sophia's heart. They are the heart or center of the cosmos itself, as well as the center of the person. The dawning realization among twelfth- and thirteenth-century adepts was that one could create such a heart by radically purifying and transforming the soul. Thereby—having made ready the dwelling—one could receive the divine guests, the indwelling of Christ and the gift of the Holy Spirit. At its highest level, it was understood that this inner work was a grace made possible by Mary-Sophia, the Second Eve, who renewed humanity's fitness to assume its proper cosmogonic or "Adamic" function. Once the soul was purified and united with Sophia—was Sophia or Wisdom and Love—the soul was perfected in the three realms that are, traditionally, the perfection of the human state—spirit, body, and soul or Heaven, Earth, and the sublunary sphere between.

By the Renaissance, this movement of the heart inward intensified. For Jacob Boehme, for instance, God—what he calls the *Ungrund*, the fundamental reality—is dark. It eludes cognition. His view is anthropological. All we cognize in this darkness is—and is in—the light of Sophia. Sophia is the pure, chaste, integral "whole person." Through the Fall, we lost our purity and virginity. Sophia flew off to the heavens, while on Earth Eve arose. Thereafter, all human life longs for the lost Sophia—she who is within us still as our ground and likewise still also shines in the heavens. "The Wisdom of God is an eternal Virgin, not a female, but chasteness and purity without blemish, and represents an image of God, like an image in the form of the Trinity." And again, "The Virgin of the Wisdom of God, which God the Father spoke through the Word, is the spirit of the pure element, and is therefore called a Virgin, because it is so chaste, and generates nothing. As the flaming spirit in our body generates nothing but opens all secrets . . . so also here the Wisdom (or Virgin) of God opens all the wonders in the holy element, for there are the essences wherein the fruits of Paradise spring up." The pure element is *barmherzigkeit*, warmheartedness. This element allows God to know himself through us.

Boehme initiated a new path of Christian inwardness. Following him, a scattered but persistent and widespread school of Sophianic mystics arose, forming small communities of seekers who sought to realize the cognitive soul path of Sophia. In this school, which could broadly be said to have culminated in Romanticism, Steiner, too, studied. Steiner was likewise aware of the Russian school of Sophiology stemming primarily from Vladimir Solovyov, whose philosophy Steiner once described as Anthroposophy without the name. Solovyov speaks of a twofold unity in the integrity of the divine being: "the acting, or producing, unity of the creativity of the Word and the produced, or actualized unity." He likens these to soul and body. The first he calls Christ; to the second, the produced unity, he gives the mystical name Sophia, who, he says, is the principle of humanity. Thus "Sophia is ideal or perfect humanity, eternally contained in the integral divine being, or Christ." He continues,

This second, produced unity—in contrast to the primordial unity of the divine Logos—is, as we know, the world soul, or ideal humanity (Sophia), which contains within itself and unites with itself all particular living entities, or souls. As the realization of the divine principle, its image and likeness, archetypal humankind, or the world soul, is both one and all. The world soul occupies a mediating position between the multiplicity of living entities, which constitute the real content of its life, and the absolute unity of Divinity, which is the ideal principle and norm of its life. As the living focus, or soul, of all creatures and the real form of Divinity, the existent subject of creaturely being and the existent object of divine action, partaking of the unity of God and at the same time embracing the whole multiplicity of living souls, the all-one humankind, or the world soul, is a dual being. Containing within itself both the divine principle and creaturely being, the world soul is not determined exclusively by either one or the other, and it therefore remains free. The divine principle, which is present in the world soul, liberates it from its creaturely nature, while this nature in turn liberates it with respect to Divinity. Embracing all living entities (souls) and, in them, all ideas, the world soul is not exclusively bound to any one among them, is free from all of them. However, since it is the immediate center and real unity of all these entities, the world soul receives in their individuality independence from the divine principle and the possibility of acting upon the latter as a free subject. Insofar as it receives the divine Logos into itself and is determined by the divine Logos, the world soul is humanity, the divine humanity of Christ, the body of Christ, Sophia. Receiving the one divine principle and uniting with this unity the whole multiplicity of entities, the world soul thereby gives the divine principle complete actual realization in the all. Through the world soul, God is manifested as the living active, force in all creation, as the Holy Spirit. In other words, in being determined or formed by the divine Logos, the world soul enables the Holy Spirit to actualize itself in the all, for that which in the light of the Logos is disclosed in ideal forms is actualized by the Holy Spirit in a real action.

No better philosophical description of Anthroposophy exists.

Other Streams

Mention must also be made of Theosophy, which was the immediate context of Steiner's beginning to teach. As in Anthroposophy, Sophia lies at the unacknowledged center of Theosophy. Madame

Blavatsky's first—Rosicrucian—work was, after all, entitled *Isis Unveiled*. For HPB, Isis (who is Sophia) stands for "Divine Intelligence." She is also known as the Archaeal Soul," the "primeval architecturess," or the Holy Spirit. In *The Secret Doctrine*, we read that the "higher gods of antiquity"—the *logoi*—were all originally "sons of the Mother." The original deity was feminine! Blavatsky writes, "The gnostic Sophia, 'Wisdom' who is the 'Mother' of the Ogdoad [the other gods] . . . is the Holy Ghost and creator of all, as in all the ancient systems. The 'father' is a much later invention. The earliest manifested logos was female everywhere—the mother of the seven planetary powers." As for Sophia-Achamoth, she is the source of "the spiritual principle" in human beings.

Anna Bonus Kingsford, Blavatsky's rival and an esoteric Christian seer, relates a similar view in *The Perfect Way:*

> As Living Substance, God is One. As Life and Substance, God is twain. He is the Life, and She is the Substance. . . . As original Substance, the substance of all other substances, She underlies that whereof all things are made; and, like life and mind, is interior, mystical, spiritual, and discernible only when in operation. In the unmanifest, She is the great Deep, or Ocean, of Infinitude, the Principium or Arche, the heavenly Sophia or Wisdom who encircles and embraces all things; of whom are dimension and form and appearance; Whose veil is the astral fluid, and Who is herself the substance of all souls.
>
> On the plane of manifestation, as the Soul macrocosmic and microcosmic, she appears as the Daughter, Mother, and Spouse of God. Exhibiting in a perfect Humanity the fullness of life she has received from God, she is mystically styled the Blessed Virgin Mary. . . . As Venus . . . she corresponds to the spirit of counsel. . . . She is portrayed as Aphrodite. . . . She appears as Sodium of salt. . . . As Pallas or Minerva she is "Our Lady of Victories." . . . As Isis or Artemis, she is preeminently the initiator, and the Virgin clothed in white, standing on the Moon and ruling the

waters. . . . In the Macrocosm, She is that Beginning or Wisdom wherein God makes the heavens and the earth.

In *The Mahatma Letters to A. P. Sinnett*, even the Mahatmas M. and K.H. weigh in with a similar consideration:

Well may the Geometer of the R.S. [Royal Society] not know that the apparent absurdity of attempting to square the circle covers a mystery ineffable. . . . To many such metaphysical minds it would be worse than useless to divulge the fact that the Unmanifested Circle—the *Father* or *Absolute* Life—is non-existent outside the Triangle and Perfect Square, and is only manifested in the Son; and that it is when reversing the action and returning to its absolute state of Unity, and the square expands once more into the circle, that "the Son returns to the bosom of the Father." There it remains until called back by his Mother, the "Great Deep," to remanifest as a *triad*—the *Son* partaking at once of the Essence of the Father and of that of the Mother—the active Substance, *Prakriti*, in its differentiated condition. "My Mother—(Sophia, the manifested Wisdom)—took me," say Jesus in a Gnostic treatise; and he asks his disciples to tarry *till he comes*

It is no coincidence that this was occurring at the time of the women's movement and all that it entailed, and also of the appearances of the Virgin Mary. These appearances, which began with Catherine Labouré in the rue du Bac in Paris in 1830, have by now become frequent, worldwide, and apocalyptic. Announcing a new epoch—whose realization depends upon humanity's returning to the universal spiritual law of prayer, love, and sacrifice—Mary comes as the mother of all humanity and the being closest to Christ, and speaks to her earthly children as a suffering mother. Her heart weeps for our human souls and our predicament. Healing mediator, nurturing comforter, queen, exemplar, and teacher, she calls for a new birth of Christ in humanity and the Earth. First, prayer; then, love and an open heart. Above all, she calls for peace and the unity of all through mutual reconciliation and forgiveness. The messages are staggering in their simplicity and repetitiveness: pray, pray, pray; love, love, love; open your hearts; pray with your hearts; clean your hearts; fast and pray with your hearts; open your hearts to the Spirit. More specifically: "Each child of God must seek reconciliation with every other person immediately for the love of God." And again: "I invite you to prayer of the heart. If you pray from your heart, dear children, the ice-cold hearts of your brothers will be melted and every barrier will disappear." And again, still more specifically: "I call you to love your neighbors, to love those people from whom evil is coming to you."

The Primacy of Cognition

For Steiner, cognition is primary. Sophia is a being. *A being is consciousness,* a mode of cognition. Sophia, then, is "Sophia consciousness." What we have lost and must find again is Sophia consciousness. Filled with Christ, reverence of Christ, we must go in search of his mother, Isis-Sophia. Strangely, it is not that we do not know where she is—she is there in the stars, she shines in the cosmos, she surrounds the Earth in an aura of beauty. But we do not know *how to see her.* She must be seen and known from within. And for this we need the Isis-power—the Sophia-power—of Christ. As Steiner says, "It is not the Christ we lack, but the knowledge and wisdom of Isis, the Sophia of the Christ." At the same time, strangely again: *"What we have lost is the cognition, the intuition of Jesus Christ. This is what we must find again, with the help of the force of Jesus Christ in us."* Jesus Christ and his mother Isis-Mary-Sophia are interdependent. They go together; you can't encounter one without the other. For Steiner, much depends on bringing them together —more perhaps than we can imagine. Without Sophia we cannot know the Risen "etheric" Christ. Steiner says: "Christ will appear in spiritual form during the twentieth century not simply because something happens externally, but to the extent that we find the power represented by holy Sophia."

Wisdom Lives in the Light

Here are four meditations given by Rudolf Steiner:

I

Wisdom in the Spirit
Love in the Soul
Power in the Will:
They guide me
They hold me.
I trust them.
I offer myself to them.

2

Working—in love
Coming to life—out of power
Striving—in Wisdom
I fulfil my I
(Christ)

3

On the Cross of the World Body,
The World Soul reveals Herself:

Living in five radiant streams
Through Wisdom,
Love,
Power of Will,

All-sense
And I-sense,

She finds
In herself
The World Spirit.

4

Finally, Steiner gave a series of meditations around "I am," "It thinks," "She feels," "He wills." During the first, roughly speaking one concentrates the attention in the area of the "third eye." During the second, one concentrates on a point behind the larynx. During the third, the concentraaton is focused on the two arms and hands. During the fourth, one concentrates on the whole bodily self. *It* is "universal cosmic thinking." *She* is "the Cosmic Soul. *He* is God "within whose will we instate our whole being."

Bibliography and Further Reading

Allen, Paul M. *Vladimir Soloviev: Russian Mystic*. Blauvelt, NY: Steinerbooks, 1978.

Bock, Emil. *The Childhood of Jesus*. Edinburgh: Floris Books, 1997.

———. *The Three Years*. Edinburgh: Floris Books, 1987.

Bulgakov, Sergei. *Sophia, The Wisdom of God*. Hudson, NY: Lindisfarne Press, 1993.

Florensky, Pavel. *The Pillar and Foundation of the Truth*. Princeton: Princeton University Press, 1997.

Godwin, Joscelyn. *The Theosophical Enlightenment*. Albany: SUNY Press, 1994.

Matthews, Caitlin. *Sophia, Goddess of Wisdom*. London: Mandala/HarperCollins, 1991.

MacDermott, Violet. *The Fall of Sophia: A Gnostic Text on the Redemption of Universal Consciousness*. Great Barrington, MA: Lindisfarne Books, 2001.

Newman, Barbara. *Sister of Wisdom: St. Hildegard's Theology of the Feminine*. Berkeley: University of California Press, 1987.

———, trans. *Saint Hildegard of Bingen: Symposia*. Ithaca: Cornell Univ. Press, 1988.

Prokofieff, Sergei O. *Eternal Individuality: Towards a Karmic Biography of* Novalis. London: Temple Lodge, 1992.

——. *The Twelve Holy Nights and the Spiritual Hierarchies.* London: Temple Lodge, 1990.

——. *The Spiritual Streams of Eastern Europe and the Future Mysteries of the Holy Grail.* London: Temple Lodge, 1993.

Schipflinger, Thomas. *Sophia-Maria: A Holistic Vision of Creation.* York Beach, ME: Samuel Weiser, 1998.

Schäfer, Peter. *Mirror of His Beauty: Feminine Images of God from the Bible to the Early Kabbalah.* Princeton: Princeton University Press, 2002.

Schwaller de Lubicz, R.A. *The Temple of Man: Apet of the South at Luxor.* Rochester, VT: Inner Traditions International, 1998.

Solovyov, Vladimir. *Lectures on Divine Humanity.* Hudson, NY: Lindisfarne Press, 1995.

Versluis, Arthur. *Theosophia: Hidden Dimensions of Christianity.* Hudson, NY: Lindisfarne Press, 1994.

——. *Wisdom's Children: A Christian Esoteric Tradition.* Albany: SUNY Press, 1999.

——. *Wisdom's Book: The Sophia Anthology.* St. Paul. MN: Paragon House, 2000.

Prologue
LIVING THINKING

We find in the Spirit
The path to soul illumination
And in that light
The Word of God
That serves as our support in joy and sorrow.

I. Thinking Is an Organ of Perception
FROM NATURE'S OPEN SECRET

EMPIRICAL SCIENCE FORGETS that thousands upon thousands of people may have observed a sense-perceptible fact and passed by it without noticing anything remarkable. Then along comes someone who sees it and perceives within it the working of an important law. How do we explain this? The discoverer must have been able to look in a way different from those who came before. He or she perceived the fact with different eyes—had a certain thought about *how* to relate that fact to others, about what was significant in it and what was not. In this way, those who make scientific discoveries comprehend and order their experience through *thinking* and, consequently, see more than others do. *They see with the eyes of the spirit.* All scientific discoveries stem from the circumstance that the observer is able to observe in a way guided by the right thought. It is natural that *thinking* should guide observation. But it cannot do so when the researcher has lost confidence in it and does not understand its scope and significance. Empirical science helplessly roams the world of phenomena; the world becomes for it a confusing multiplicity of particulars because it lacks the energy of thought to penetrate its experience.

People speak of limits to knowledge today because they fail to understand the task of thinking. . . .

Whoever attributes to thinking a perceptive capacity going beyond that of the senses must also acknowledge that this capacity directs itself toward objects lying beyond sense-perceptible reality. The objects of thinking are ideas. When our thinking comprehends an idea, it unites with the foundations of universal existence. What is actively at work in the outer world enters the human spirit. The human being unites with objective reality in its highest potency. *Beholding the idea in outer reality is the true communion of humanity.*

Thinking relates to ideas as the eye relates to light and the ear to sound; *it is an organ of perception.*

II. *Thinking Unites Us with the Cosmos*
FROM INTUITIVE THINKING AS A SPIRITUAL PATH

Without a doubt: *in thinking we hold a corner of the world process* where we must be present if anything is to occur.

[Steiner comments on this sentence in *Mystery Knowledge and Mystery Centers.*] That may be a simple way of putting it. But what it means is that it is impossible, in a true experience of thinking, to go on feeling the world mystery to be inaccessible: one is inside it. One no longer feels oneself outside the divine, but within it. *To lay hold on thinking in oneself is to lay hold on the divine.*

[And again, in a lecture (GA 205):] Our modern world is still far from being in a position to study our interwovenness with the cosmos, our at-oneness with it. I made a special point of calling attention to this in my *Philosophy of Freedom*. There you will find key passages intended to show that beneath our ordinary level of consciousness we are related to the whole cosmos. These passages show that we are an integral part of the cosmos, and that our individual humanness, making its appearance clothed in ordinary consciousness, blossoms forth from the commonality of the cosmos.

★

We must first consider thinking completely neutrally, without reference to a thinking subject or a thought object. For in subject and object we already have concepts that are formed by thinking.

★

Unprejudiced observation shows that nothing can be attributed to the essence of thinking that is not found within thinking itself. One cannot arrive at anything that causes thinking if one leaves the realm of thinking behind.

★

It is through the thinker that thinking is linked to observation. Human consciousness is the stage where concept and observation meet and are connected to one another. This is, in fact, what characterizes human consciousness. It is the mediator between thinking and observation. To the extent that human beings observe them, things appear as given; to the extent that human beings think, they experience themselves as active. They regard things as *objects*, and themselves as thinking *subjects*. Because they direct their thinking to what they observe, they are conscious of objects; because they direct their thinking to themselves, they are conscious of themselves, they have *self-consciousness*. Human consciousness must necessarily be at the same time *self*-consciousness, because it is a *thinking* consciousness.

For when thinking directs its gaze toward its own activity, it has before it as its object its own very being, that is, its subject.

But we must not overlook that it is only with the help of thinking that we can define ourselves as subjects, and contrast ourselves to objects. Therefore thinking must never be regarded as merely subjective activity. Thinking is *beyond* subject and object. It forms both these concepts, just as it does all others. Thus, when we as thinking subjects relate a concept to an object, we must not regard this relationship as something merely subjective. It is not the subject who introduces the relationship, but thinking. The subject does not think because it is a subject; rather it appears to itself as a subject because it can think. The activity that human beings exercise as *thinking* beings is therefore not merely subjective, but is a kind of activity that is neither subjective nor objective; it goes beyond both of these concepts. *I should never say that my individual subject thinks; rather, it lives by the grace of thinking.* Thus thinking is an element that leads me beyond myself and unites me with objects. But it separates me from them at the same time, by setting me over against them as subject.

*

In thinking we are given the element that unites our particular individuality with the whole of the cosmos. When we sense, feel (and also perceive), we are separate; when we think, we are the all-one being that penetrates all. This is the deeper basis of our dual nature. Within us we see an absolute force come into existence, a force that is universal. Yet we do not know it as it streams forth from the center of the world, but only at a point on the periphery. If we knew it as it streamed forth from the center of the world, then we would know the whole riddle of the world at the instant we came to consciousness. Since we stand at a point on the periphery, and find our existence enclosed within certain limits, we must find out about the realm situated outside our own being with the help of thinking that extends into us from universal existence.

✿

III. *The Holy Spirit and the Christ in Us*

FROM A LETTER OF AUGUST 19, 1902

It is certainly true that the "*Christ in us*" is essentially none other than what dogmatic theology calls the "Holy Spirit." But it seems to me that from another point of view these two concepts should be distinguished. The history of Catholic dogma here seems to have fallen into great confusion. Yes, the "Holy Spirit" and the "Christ in us" are one and the same—*but at different stages or levels of development.* One could also say that the "Holy Spirit" is the (feminine) "Mother" principle of the (male) "Son" principle, Christ. We owe the development of the "Christ in us" to the "Holy Spirit" (the female creator of Christ). Originally, the "Holy Spirit" was nothing other than the Divine Mother (Isis, etc.). Christianity rejected this feminine (Isis) principle and retained only the Son (Christ). In the "Holy Spirit," however, Christianity still retains the rudiments of the earlier feminine principle. Therefore, in Christian dogma, the "Holy Spirit" melds quite naturally with the "Son." They become one and the same, while on the one hand the rejected Isis principle becomes incomprehensible as the "Holy Spirit," and on the other hand the Virgin Mary is taken up exoterically. First, Isis is volatilized as the Holy Spirit and then she is reestablished as "Mary" without any consciousness of the connection.

I

SOPHIA, THE HOLY SPIRIT, MARY, AND MARY MAGDALENE

❄

I. The Virgin Sophia and the Holy Spirit

MUNICH NOVEMBER 5, 1906

. . . WHAT DOES A STUDENT RECEIVE after being brought through initiation to the summit of the mountain? He or she receives something very real. Remember our description of the human being. At the time of Jesus Christ, most human beings had developed a part of the astral body and a part of the etheric body. It was different with those who were initiates. What was asked of them? Candidates for initiation were required to have fully worked through their entire astral body. There could not be anything in their astral body that they had not brought under control—that they did not rule. Generally, our passions rule us; we do not usually rule our passions. If we wish to become students, however, we must become the masters of our desires and passions. We must work on our etheric bodies. We must transform the qualities of our temperament—to the extent that we can, for instance, consciously alter our movements, our gait, and our handwriting. It is not enough to become a more ethical person. We must become *a different person*.

When the entire astral body has been worked through, it becomes *Manas*, Spirit Self. The transformed etheric body is called

Buddhi. It has become Life Spirit. And if we manage to transform the physical body, we become able to work on the planets, to become centers of cosmic force. At this point we develop *Atman,* the Father, the Spiritual Human Being in us.

Initially, the work done by human beings on their etheric and astral bodies is quite unconscious. It occurs simply in the general evolutionary development of humankind. The *chela,* or disciple, starts taking this work consciously in hand. Persistent practice brings one to the point where the whole astral body is transformed. Then all that lives in the astral body can penetrate the etheric body. If this were to happen any earlier, it would have harmful effects, because what is achieved in this way accompanies the causal body through all incarnations. To eternalize and enliven all that the astral body contains is an immensely important process, for this can no longer be discarded in any purgatorial *kamaloka.* It is a part of the human being forever, which is why the earlier purification was so important.

In the old initiations, the imprinting of the etheric body with the contents of the astral body was done in the following way. The student was brought to an underground crypt and laid in a kind of coffin. Sometimes he or she would be tied to a kind of cross and put into a lethargic state which raised the etheric and astral bodies out of the physical body. Something similar happens when one of your limbs goes to sleep; you can witness a part of the etheric body "hanging," as it were, out of the body. Such an initiation required someone who was already quite highly initiated. Many other things were done according to prescribed rules.

The sleep induced during initiation was no ordinary sleep. Only the physical body remained in the coffin—the etheric and astral bodies left. Therefore the sleep was a kind of death. This was necessary to free the etheric body so that the astral body could imprint itself on it. This condition lasted three days. When the initiator returned the novice to the physical body, a last formula was impressed upon him or her. With this, the novice awoke. The formula was "Eli, Eli, lama sabachthani!"

At that point, the novice was shown a particular star. In Egypt, the star was Sirius. Now the candidate was a new person. For quite specific reasons, the fully spiritualized astral body was now also given a special name. This astral body was called "Virgin," or "the Virgin Sophia." The etheric body that received what the Virgin Sophia was carrying was called the "Holy Spirit." And the fruit of their meeting was called "the Son of Man." These mysteries are at the root of the annunciation and birth of Jesus of Nazareth.

This inner experience was also represented in the image of the Holy Spirit hovering in the form of a dove above a chalice. This is the moment described in the Gospel of John (1:32): "And John bore witness and spoke: 'I saw the Spirit descending like a dove from the Heavens, and it rested above Him.'" This is an actual occurrence, provided you think of it as happening on the astral plane. The person who was allowed to experience such things outside of initiation, on the physical plane, was allowed to initiate others. In John 11:1–45, the resurrection of Lazarus is nothing but an initiation of this kind performed on Lazarus.

It is impossible ever to go too deeply into the Gospel of John. Naming is particularly important here. The assigning of names in the Bible is conducted on the basis of the person's inner being. This is so in the case of the names of the twelve apostles. Their names point to the relationship between the twelve and their master, the Christ, who is the head, and whose sign is the Ram, or Lamb. The name John designates the one who announces the *Buddhi*. We can distinguish twelve beings in the human being. The twelve-part human being as we know it today is the result of a gradual evolution. Every time the Sun entered a new zodiacal sign, a new organ developed in the human being. For instance when the Sun was in Leo, the heart evolved. As human beings rise, they get involved in a group soul. You will find the twelve parts of the human being reproduced and concealed in the names of the apostles. The twelve apostles are to the collective Body of Christ as the twelve parts are to the ordinary body. The part representing the "I" dominated by egotism, which eventually causes the death of the Christ, is Judas Iscariot.

The importance of naming may also be seen in the fact that the one who, on the larger cosmic scale, was the spiritual representative of human development was named the "Son of Man." His father is the "Holy Spirit," his mother the "Virgin Sophia" This appears in John's Gospel 19:25–27, at the foot of the cross: "Woman, this is your son!" and "Son, this is your Mother!"

❁

II. Mary and Mary Magdalene

BASEL, NOVEMBER 20, 1907

"The law was given by Moses, devotion—grace—and truth by Jesus Christ" (John 1:17). If we can fully understand this passage, we can also understand the deeply meaningful rupture that Christ's appearance occasioned in human history. In previous lectures, I have described humanity's development in broad strokes. I showed how "I-consciousness" evolved. In the most distant past, whole groups and generations thought of themselves as "I." The great longevity attributed to the patriarchs can be understood in this way. Gradually, this feeling of being "I" increasingly narrowed down to individual personalities. I also showed how in the course of this evolution two distinct streams appeared. One was the stream of blood kinship that aimed at uniting people on the basis of natural bonds. The other was the Luciferic stream that placed people on their own and prepared them for the coming purely spiritual union.

Throughout the period covered by the Old Testament, law meant something coming from the outside that brought order into human society. After blood relationships lost their binding power, human beings needed to be connected through an external, intellectual order. The law was perceived as coming from the outside. This externally imposed law is valid until the sacrifice—grace—and truth that came to us through Christ have created an understanding of true knowledge in us. Devotion and truth can evolve only gradually. Christianity, which is meant to put devotion where the law was, is still in its very beginning. The more the Earth evolves, the stronger the influence of Christianity will become on humanity. Humanity needs to rise to a level of being able to love together where every human being, acting from an inner impulse, will enter into a brother-sister relationship with his or her neighbor. Humanity would not have been able to rise to this high level of evolution on its own strength. It is the task of Christianity to help in this process. Human beings will no longer need outer laws when they are inwardly impelled to conduct their lives so that devotion and truth are used to guide all their actions.

This should not be understood to mean that humanity no longer needs a law; but that this is an ideal toward which we should strive. Bit by bit, humanity will come to a point where free human activity will create world harmony. To achieve this goal requires the intervention of the power that the Gospels call Christ. What the esoteric schools describe as "carrying the Christ in oneself" means, for individuals, to be capable of establishing such a relationship with one's fellow human beings that one can freely, without any compulsion, enter into the harmony.

To understand what follows it is necessary once again to recall the composition of the human being:

"I"

astral body	Spirit Self
etheric body	Life Spirit
physical body	Spirit Human

The "I" working on the astral body transforms it into Spirit Self. This happens in stages, as first the "sentient soul" is formed, then the "intellectual soul," and finally the "consciousness soul." The Spirit Self flows into the matured purified consciousness soul.

The "I" also works on the etheric body. The impulses that have the greatest effectiveness here are those that work through art, religion, and esoteric schooling.

Esoteric schooling—Mystery Schools—existed already in pre-Christian times and was able to develop students to the point where they could see the higher worlds. But this seeing was accessible only to serious students in the most hidden of the initiation schools, and then only in the course of the actual initiation rituals, when their etheric body was separated from their physical body. Initiation in this pre-Christian context means an actual "raising" of the human being to allow one to see the higher worlds. In all pre-Christian initiations, the novice had to be put into a kind of sleep. The initiatory sleep is different from ordinary sleep in that in ordinary sleep the etheric body remains connected with the physical body, whereas in initiatory sleep the etheric body was briefly separated from the physical body. During this time the hierophant had to keep the body alive. The removal of the etheric body made it possible to conduct novices with the rest of their bodies into the higher worlds, and to allow them experiences that could later be registered by the physical brain. Such were the only initiation methods during pre-Christian times.

With the advent of Jesus Christ, something entirely new appeared in relation to the process of initiation. Imagine that you have transformed your entire astral body into Spirit Self. Your Spirit Self would then imprint itself into your etheric body like a seal into sealing wax, and give it its form. In this way your etheric body is transformed into Life Spirit. When this is done, the Life Spirit penetrates the physical body and transforms it into the Spirit Human (the Risen Body). Only with the appearance of Christ did it become possible for the Life Spirit to *directly* influence the life body.

This means that the experiences attained in the higher worlds could now be incarnated in the human brain without the need for a preliminary separation of the etheric body. The first being whose etheric body was completely penetrated by the Spirit Self and whose physical body was completely penetrated by the Life Spirit was Jesus Christ. When Jesus Christ came to the Earth, it became possible for those connected with him to undergo the same initiation, without needing to separate the etheric body from the physical body.

All initiates in pre-Christian times, however, had experienced out-of-body initiation and had then returned to the physical body, able to give an account that was actually their own direct experience of the spiritual worlds.

This was the kind of initiation undergone by Buddha, Moses, and others. But in Jesus, a being came to Earth who could see the higher worlds while remaining in a physical body. The teachings of Buddha, Moses, and so on are completely independent of the Master's personality. A person is a Buddhist or a "Mosaist" by following the teachings of Buddha or Moses. It doesn't matter whether a person acknowledges Buddha or Moses (as individuals), for these founders were only transmitters for their experiences in the higher worlds.

Christ's teachings on the other hand become "Christianity" only through incarnation in an individual human being, and to be a Christian it is not enough to follow Christian teachings. Only those who feel connected with the historical Christ are truly Christian. Individual tenets of the Christian beliefs have existed before, but this is not the issue. It is rather that the Christian believes in Jesus Christ, that the Christian believes Jesus to represent the perfect human being transformed in the flesh.

In the old days, people used to talk of initiates as "divine humans." This was because the initiate had risen during the initiation ceremony to the spiritual worlds and "lived" with spiritual or divine beings. The initiate was therefore a "divine human." Before Jesus Christ, however, it was impossible in fact to see a divine human in the physical body. We must therefore take literally the passage in John 1:18: "No one has ever seen God; the only begotten Son, who is in the bosom of the Father, he has proclaimed him." Earlier, only those who had themselves ascended could have the experience of God. In Christ however, for the first time, the Godhead became visible on Earth. This was stated in John 1:14 ("And the Word was made flesh, and dwelt among us") and was also taught in the schools of Dionysius the Areopagite. Christ existed to show human beings the way; human beings must become his followers, must prepare themselves to imprint what is in the etheric body into the physical body—that is, allow the Christ Principle to develop in them.

The Gospel of John is a book of life. No one who researches it merely intellectually will understand it. To know it, one must live it. Anyone who meditates the first fourteen verses daily for a certain length of time will discover why the words are there. They are the stuff of meditation, and awaken in the human soul a capacity to see *as one's own experiences* in great astral tableau such individual episodes of the Gospel as, for instance, the wedding at Cana or the conversation with Nicodemus. We can become clairvoyant through exercises, and then we can experience the truth of what is written in John's Gospel. Hundreds of people have done that. The writer of the Gospel was himself a high clairvoyant, initiated by Christ himself.

The disciple John is nowhere named in the Gospel. The only reference to him is as "the disciple whom Jesus loved" (John 19:26). This is a technical expression designating a person initiated by the Master himself. When John describes the raising of Lazarus (John 11), he describes his own initiation. Only because the writer was himself initiated by the Lord do the most secret relationships between Christ and world evolution become visible in this Gospel. I have mentioned before that the old initiations used to last three and a half days. This explains Lazarus's rising on the fourth day. It is also said of Lazarus that "Jesus loved him" (John, 11:3, 35, 36). Here again we have the technical expression for a favorite student. While Lazarus's body lay in the grave, apparently dead, his etheric body was taken out to undergo initiation and receive the very same power that resides in Christ. Thus he became a "Risen One," the person whom the Lord loved and who wrote the Gospel. If we read through the Gospel, we notice that not a single line contradicts this, although the process of initiation itself is described "under a veil."

Let us consider another view of the Gospel of John. John 19:25 says, "And now there stood by the cross of Jesus his mother, and his mother's sister, Mary the wife of Cleophas, and Mary Magdalene."

To understand the Gospel, we need to know who these women were. Today you would not find three sisters in a family all bearing the same name. This was unusual in those days too. The passage indicates that, for the writer of the Gospel, Jesus' mother was not called Mary. Nowhere in the Gospel is Jesus' mother called Mary. At the wedding in Cana (John 2), the text says, "the mother of Jesus was there." This points to an important fact that we can understand only if we know how the writer of the Gospel uses his words.

What does "the mother of Jesus" mean?

As we have seen, the human being consists of physical body, etheric body, and astral body. The transition from astral body to Spirit Self should not be understood so simply. As we have said, the "I" slowly and gradually transforms the astral body into sentient soul, intellectual soul, and consciousness soul. The "I" always continues to work, and only when it has transformed the astral body completely into the consciousness soul is it in a position to purify the latter (the transformed astral body) so that the Spirit Self may arise within it. The human being is composed of

Father	7. Spirit Human	Transformed physical body
Son	6. Life Spirit	Transformed etheric body
Holy Spirit	5. Spirit Self (purified consciousness soul)	Virgin Sophia,
	4. intellectual (mind soul, astral soul)	Mary, wife of Cleophas
	3. sentient soul, sentient body	Mary Magdalene
	2. Etheric body	
	I. Physical body	

The Spirit Human will evolve only in the distant future. The Life Spirit now exists only in embryonic form in most humans. The evolution of the Spirit Self, however, has presently begun. It is inseparably connected with the consciousness soul, like a sword with its sheath. The sentient soul in turn is sheathed by the sentient or astral body. In our human organization, we therefore have nine members or parts. Spirit Self and consciousness soul are, like the sentient soul and the astral body, inseparable. For this reason theosophical literature usually speaks of only seven bodies. Spirit Self is identified with the Holy Spirit, which in the Christian sense is the guiding being on the astral plane. The Life Spirit is called "Word" or "Son." The "Spirit Human" is the "Father Spirit" or the "Father."

Those who have given birth in themselves to the Spirit Self are called the "Children of God." Through them, "The Light shines in the darkness." They have "received the Light." Outwardly, they are human beings of flesh and blood, but they bear in themselves a higher human being. In their inner being, the consciousness soul gives birth to the Spirit Self.

The "mother" of such a spiritualized individual is not the physical mother. The mother dwells within. She is the purified and spiritualized consciousness soul. She is the principle from which higher human beings are born. John's Gospel describes this spiritual birth, which is a birth in the highest sense of the word. The Spirit Self or Holy Spirit flows into the purified consciousness soul. As it says in the Gospel, " I saw the Spirit descending from heaven like a dove from the sky and it abode upon him" (John 1:32).

Since the consciousness soul is the principle in which the Spirit Self has evolved, we call it the "mother of Christ" or, in the esoteric schools, the "Virgin Sophia." Through fecundation of the Virgin Sophia, the Christ could be born in Jesus of Nazareth. In the esoteric schools of Dionysius, the intellectual and sentient souls were called, respectively, Mary and Mary Magdalene. . . .

❋

III. Sophia Is the Gospel Itself

BASEL, NOVEMBER 25, 1907

. . . Those who live with John's Gospel will awaken in themselves the power of seeing. The Gospel of John is a visionary book, written to train us in clairvoyance. Those who experience it sentence by sentence will witness the powerful effect of spiritually coming face-to-face with Christ.

Before we know that Christ is a reality, it is difficult to convince us that we have to work on ourselves. John's Gospel is the way to Christ. The writer gives the reader every opportunity to understand. Those who purify their astral bodies and develop Spirit Self in themselves will approach in spirit the wisdom in themselves that allows them to understand what Christ is. Christ himself indicated this way. He hangs on the cross. Below him stand his mother and the initiated disciple whom he loves. The disciple is expected to bring to humanity wisdom, knowledge of the meaning of Christ. Then, Mother Sophia is evoked in these words: "Here is your mother, whom you must love."

The spiritualized mother of Jesus is the Gospel itself. She is wisdom, leading humanity to the highest insights. The disciple gave us Mother Sophia, meaning he wrote a Gospel for us that allows anyone who looks into it to learn to know Christ, who is the source and goal of this great movement (spiritual science).

2

WISDOM AND HEALTH

Berlin, February 14, 1907

SPIRITUAL SCIENCE AIMS TO BE AN INFLUENCE in practical life, a source of strength and confidence. It is for people who wish to be effective in life, not for the merely curious. Knowledge of the spirit has always existed. It has been fostered in circles where it was recognized that human beings are capable of developing spiritual forces of greater capacity than the ordinary intellect. In these circles there was awareness of the fact that healing was connected with holiness; it was felt that the Holy Spirit was the wholly healthy spirit that united itself with the souls of human beings to bring healing to the world.

This is the least understood aspect. Spiritual knowledge guides the human soul away from narrow attitudes and egoistic aims; it points to universal issues that unite the individual with the cosmos. Nevertheless, the higher forces it bestows often are used as an incentive for egoistic striving. It is often made to serve egoism despite the fact that its very nature is to lead human beings away from the personal; people demand that egoistic wishes should be fulfilled from one day to the next through spiritual science.

There once existed in Africa a brotherhood, the Therapeutae, that fostered spiritual knowledge. The same sect was known as the Essenes in the region where Christianity arose. The name indicates that the brotherhood was concerned with healing, which they practiced by combining their spiritual insight with knowledge of matter. When spiritual knowledge is absorbed, healing forces are also absorbed. Spiritual science is an elixir of life; though it cannot be proved by argument, the proof will be seen when it is assimilated, then applied to life, and health follows.

However, people might as well know nothing about spiritual science if all they can do is talk glibly about reincarnation and karma. One's whole inner being must be steeped in spiritual science if its effect is to be experienced; one must live it every hour of the day, and be able to wait calmly. In this connection Goethe's saying is apt: "Consider the what, but even more consider the how." Spiritual science is rightly understood if it is assimilated like a spiritual food, and allowed to grow and mature within. It is rightly understood if in moments of sorrow or happiness, of devotion and exaltation, or when life threatens to fall apart, one experiences the hope, strength, and incentive to action it brings.

Spiritual science must become a personal quest. The striving human being, looking at the stars, will recognize the eternal laws that guide them through cosmic space. When clouds sail across the vault of heaven or when the Sun rises in splendor, or the Moon in silent majesty, a person will see all these phenomena as the expression of soul-spiritual universal life. Just as we recognize the look on a face or the movement of a hand as the expression of the soul and spirit in human beings, when we look at the past we look at the same time up to the spirit whose imprint in the physical is everywhere evident.

Absorb the spirit, and you absorb health-giving forces! Not, however, in lazy comfort; there are people who entertain the most trivial notions while declaring that all one needs is to be in tune with the infinite. That has nothing to do with knowledge of the spirit. Spiritual knowledge must penetrate an individual's innermost being. It is not through some magical formula that we discover the spiritual world. What is required is that we enter with patience and love into every being, every event. The spiritual world is there; it should not be sought as if it has no connection with the physical. Wherever we find ourselves placed in life, there we must seek it; then spiritual knowledge becomes a personal quest.

There are people who have no sense for music or paintings; likewise there are people with no sense for what is spiritual. The following incident illustrates a common notion of what is spiritual: One evening in a small town, a strange light was noticed to pass across the church wall. Soon it was a topic of conversation all over the town. As no natural explanation was found, it was determined that it was a spiritual phenomenon. Actually, the fact that it was seen by many already made this highly unlikely. For a person to be able to perceive a genuine spiritual event, certain spiritual organs and capabilities must first be developed. In our time this is a rare event; so the fact that the strange light was seen by many people is a sure proof that it was not a spiritual manifestation. And indeed an explanation was soon forthcoming: An elderly lady with a lantern was in the habit of walking her dog in the evening. On one particular night the light happened to be noticed. Investigation of such meaningless suppositions is pointless. The most significant spiritual manifestations are to be found in the objects and events around us every day.

Wisdom is science, but also more than science. It is science that is united with, not apart from, reality. At any moment it can become decision and action. Someone who is knowledgeable about scientific laws is a scientist; someone who immediately knows how to apply knowledge so that it becomes reality is wise. Wisdom is science becoming creative. We must so contemplate, so merge with the laws of nature that they become an inner force. Through his contemplation and exact observation of individual plants, Goethe arrived at his inner perception of the archetypal plant. The idea of the archetypal plant is a product of spiritual intuition; it is a plant image that can come to life within us; from it numberless plants can be derived which do not as yet exist, but could exist. In someone who has become a sage, laws are not bound to the particular; they are eternal living entities. This is the realm of Imagination, of ideas that are not abstract but creative images. Abstract concepts and ideas may lead to science, but not to wisdom. Had Goethe remained at the conceptual stage, he would never have discovered the archetypal plant. It must be seen so vividly and so exactly that one can draw it, including root, stem, leaves, and fruit, without it resembling any particular plant. Such an image is not a product of fantasy. Fantasy is related to imagination as shadow is to reality; however, it can be transformed and raised to become Imagination.

We may not yet have access to the world of Imagination, but it is a world that is attainable. We must develop soul forces that are objective, comparable to the forces active in our eyes. We would be surrounded by perpetual darkness if the eyes did not transform the light falling upon them into colored images and mental pictures. Anyone who believes we must just wait for some nebulous manifestation of the spirit to appear has no comprehension of the inner work required of human beings. The soul must become active, as the eyes are active transforming light. Unless the soul creates pictures and images within itself, the spiritual world cannot stream in. The pictures thus created will maintain objectivity provided they are not prompted by egoistic wishes; when their content is spiritual, then healing forces stream into a person's soul. When the ability to transform the concepts of spiritual science into vivid pictures full of color, sound, and life is attained, when the whole world becomes such a picture, then this wisdom becomes in all spheres of life a healing force, not only for ourselves, but for others, for the whole world. Even if the pictures we create in the soul are not accurate, it will not matter; they are corrected by what guides us. Paracelsus was a sage of this kind. He immersed himself in all aspects of nature and transformed his knowledge into vigorous inner forces. Every plant spoke to him, revealing the wisdom inherent in nature.

Animals have wisdom of a certain kind; their instincts are wise. However, they do not individually possess a soul. Animals share a group soul that influences them from outside as spiritual wisdom. All animals whose blood can be mixed without ill effect have a common soul, that is, a group soul. Wisdom thus acting from outside has become individualized in humans. Every human being has a personal individual soul whose influence comes from within. The price human beings pay is loss of certainty. Uncertainty is characteristic of human knowledge and scientific pursuit. Human beings are obliged to grope their way; they must search, select and experiment. However, they have the possibility to evolve, to reach higher stages; they can transform the knowledge they are obliged to attain through effort, through trial and error, so that it becomes wisdom once more. What is already in existence must, as it were, become recast within human beings, must become color-filled, light-filled, sound-filled Imagination; then they attain wisdom.

Paracelsus had attained such wisdom; he approached every plant, every chemical substance, and instantly recognized its healing properties. An animal immediately knows, through its unconscious instincts, what is beneficial for it. Paracelsus knew through conscious wisdom that illness would benefit from a particular substance.

The Therapeutae and Essenes had the same kind of wisdom. It is insight that cannot be attained through experiments; knowledge is transformed into imaginative wisdom. The plant then discerns its own image in the human soul and changes it; in that instant the human being not only senses, but also knows, the healing properties the plant possesses. Spiritual science does not object to natural science; in fact, those who are serious in spiritual scientific striving will not neglect to acquaint themselves with ordinary science's achievements . But they will go further; they will transform such knowledge into creative wisdom. We know the human being consists of physical body, etheric body, astral body, and the "I." Ordinary knowledge penetrates only as far as the astral body, of which it becomes a part, whereas imaginative knowledge reaches the etheric body, filling it with the Life Spirit, making human beings powerful healers.

The immense difference between the effect of abstract concepts and that of imaginative knowledge is easiest to see in an incident in which the effect was painful in nature: A man was present when his brother had a leg amputated. As the bone was cut it made a strange sound; at that moment the man felt a fierce pain in his leg at the place corresponding to where his brother's operation was taking place. For a long time he could not rid himself of the pain, even when his brother no longer felt any. The sound emitted from the bone had, through the power of Imagination, impressed itself deeply into the man's etheric body and produced the pain.

A physician in Bern once made an interesting experiment. He took an ordinary horseshoe and connected to it two wires of the type used in electrical machinery. Everyone thought the gadget must be electrified, and those who touched it were certain they felt an electric current; there were even some who were convinced they experienced a violent shock. All these effects were produced simply by what the persons concerned imagined to themselves; no remonstration convinced them otherwise. People became rich by manufacturing pills from ordinary bread. The pills were supposed to cure all kinds of illnesses, but were especially popular for curing sleeplessness. A lady, a patient in a sanatorium, took such a pill regularly every evening and enjoyed sound sleep. One night she decided to take her own life and swallowed as many of these pills as she could lay her hands on. It was discovered, and the doctors were greatly alarmed; she showed all the signs of someone dying. One doctor remained calm, the one who had manufactured the pills.

Human beings have a natural ability to turn the merely known into vivid images. Hypnotism relies on this fact; hypnotists exclude the astral body and introduce a pictorial content directly into the etheric body, but this is an abnormal process. The pictures we ourselves produce are imprinted on the etheric body. If they are derived from the spiritual world they have the power to eradicate unhealthy conditions, which means harmony is brought about with universal spiritual currents. This brings about healing because unhealthy conditions always originate from egoism, and we are now lifted above our ordinary mental life, which is dimmed. This process must occur every so often, for example during sleep; then the astral body, together with the "I," separates from the physical and etheric bodies and unites with the spirit of the Earth. From this spiritual region the astral body imprints health-giving pictures into the etheric body. This process is unconscious except in highly evolved human beings.

Plato said that eternal ideas are behind everything. The clairvoyant sees the spiritual in every plant, whose very form is built up from such spiritual images. Human beings are able to absorb these eternal ideas, these spiritual images, and thus become creative. Their health-giving effect acts throughout nature. Strictly speaking, it is only human beings that become ill; only human beings take the spirit into their inner being and have to bring it to life once more. Imaginative wisdom will bring a person health. When knowledge is transformed into wisdom, the spirit creates the Imagination. Spiritual science is such wisdom, and it has the ability more than anything else to be a healing force, especially in the sense of preventing illness. This, admittedly, is not easy to prove. However, through spiritual science, life-giving forces flow into human beings, keeping them youthful and strong.

Wisdom makes a person open and receptive because it is a foundation from which love for all things grows. To preach love is useless. (The Therapeutae and Essenes were wise; they were also most compassionate and loving.) When wisdom warms the soul, love streams forth; thus we can understand that there are people who can heal through the laying on of hands. Wisdom pours forces of love through their limbs. Christ was the wisest, and therefore also the greatest, healer. Unless love and compassion unite with wisdom, no genuine help can be forthcoming. If someone lying in the street with a broken leg is surrounded by people full of compassion, but without knowledge, they cannot help. The doctor who comes with knowledge of how to deal with a broken leg can help, for his wisdom transforms his compassion into action. Basic to all help provided by human beings is knowledge, insight, and ability.

We are always surrounded by wisdom because wise beings created the world. When this wisdom has reached its climax it will have become all-encompassing love. Love will stream toward us from the world of the future. Love is born of wisdom, and the wisest spiritual being is the greatest healer. From Christ is born the Holy, that is, the Healing Spirit.

3

The Nature of the Virgin Sophia

and of the Holy Spirit

Hamburg, May 1908

We have reached the point of discussing the change that takes place in the human astral body through meditation, concentration, and other practices given in the various methods of initiation. We saw that these affect the astral body in such a way that it develops within itself the organs it needs for perceiving in the higher worlds. We said that up to this point the principle of initiation is everywhere really the same, though the forms of its practices conform to the respective cultural epochs. The chief difference appears with what follows. In order for a pupil to be able to actually perceive in the higher worlds, the organs that have been formed out of the astral part must impress or stamp themselves upon the etheric body. They must be impressed into the etheric element.

We may call the refashioning of the astral body indirectly through meditation and concentration by the ancient name *katharsis*, or purification. Katharsis, or purification, seeks to discard from the astral body all that hinders it from becoming harmoniously and regularly organized and so able to acquire higher organs. The astral body is endowed with the germ of these higher organs. It is only necessary to bring forth the forces present in it. We have said that the most varied methods can be employed for bringing about katharsis. You can advance quite far in this matter of katharsis if, for example, you have gone through and inwardly experienced everything in my book *Intuitive Thinking as a Spiritual Path*. Having gone through it, you may feel that it has stimulated you to the point where you can actually reproduce the thoughts exactly as they are presented. If you have the same relationship to this book that a virtuoso playing a selection on the piano has to the composer, that is, if you can reproduce the whole thing in yourself, katharsis will be developed to a high degree. . . .

Something else must be considered. When this katharsis has taken place and the astral organs have been formed in the astral body, it must all be imprinted on the etheric body. In pre-Christian initiation, this was done as follows. After pupils had undergone the appropriate preparatory training, which often lasted for years, they were told, "The time has now come when the astral body has developed far enough to have astral organs of perception. These can now become aware of their counterpart in the etheric body." Then pupils were subjected to a procedure that is today—at least for our cultural epoch—not only unnecessary, but is not really feasible. They were put into a lethargic condition for three and a half days. During this time they were treated in such a way that not only did the astral body leave the physical and etheric bodies, which occurs every night in sleep, but to a certain degree the etheric body also was lifted out. Care was taken that the physical body remained intact and that the pupils did not die in the process. The etheric body was then liberated from the forces of the physical body that act upon it. It became, as it were, elastic and plastic, and when the sensory organs that had been formed in the astral body sank down into it, the etheric body received an imprint from the whole astral body. When the pupils were returned to a normal condition by the hierophant, when their astral body and "I" were reunited with the physical and etheric bodies—a procedure the hierophant understood—then the pupils experienced not only katharsis, but also what is called illumination, or *photismos*. They could then not only perceive in the world around them all those things that were physically perceptible, but could also employ spiritual organs of perception, which means that

they could see and perceive the spiritual. Initiation therefore consisted essentially of these two processes, purification, or *katharsis*, and
illumination, or *photismos*.

Then the course of human evolution entered a phase in which it
gradually became impossible to draw the etheric body out of the
physical without disturbing all its functions. This was because the
whole tendency of the post-Atlantean evolution was to cause the
etheric body to be attached more and more closely to the physical
body. Therefore other methods of initiation had to be instituted.
These had to proceed in such a way that, without separating the
physical and etheric bodies, the astral body, sufficiently purified
through katharsis and able to return to the physical and etheric bodies by itself, could imprint its organs on the etheric body despite the
physical body's hindrance. Stronger forces had therefore to become
active in meditation and concentration to provide a strong impulse
in the astral body for overcoming the power of resistance of the
physical body.

In the first place there was the actual specifically Christian initiation in which it was necessary for pupils to undergo the procedure
described yesterday as the seven steps. The astral body of one who
had undergone these feelings and experiences was so intensely
affected that it formed its organs of perception plastically—perhaps
only after years, but still sooner or later—and then impressed them
upon the etheric body, thus making the pupil one of the Illuminati.
I could only fully describe this kind of initiation, which is specifically Christian, if I were able to lecture about its particular aspects
every day for about a fortnight instead of for only a few days. But
that is not the important thing. Yesterday you were given certain
details of the Christian initiation. We wish to become acquainted
only with its principle.

By continually meditating upon passages of the Gospel of St.
John, students of Christian initiation are actually in a condition to
reach initiation without the three-and-a-half-day continued lethargic sleep. If students allow the first verses of the Gospel of St. John,

from "In the beginning was the Word" to the passage "full of grace and truth" to work on them every day, this text becomes a very powerful meditation. The words contain power. John's Gospel is not there simply to be read and understood with the intellect; it must be fully experienced and felt inwardly. It is a force that aids and works for initiation. Then the "Washing of the Feet," the "Scourging," and the other inner processes will be experienced as astral visions, wholly corresponding to the description, beginning with Chapter 13, in the Gospel itself.

Rosicrucian initiation, although resting upon a Christian foundation, works more with other symbolic ideas, chiefly imaginative pictures, that produce katharsis. That is another modification that had to be used, because humankind had progressed a step further in its evolution. Methods of initiation must conform to what has gradually been evolved.

We must understand that when people have attained this initiation they are fundamentally quite different from what they were before. While formerly they were associated only with things of the physical world, they now acquire the possibility of association with events and beings of the spiritual world. This presupposes that we acquire knowledge in a much more real sense than in the abstract, dry, prosaic sense in which we usually speak of it. For a person who acquires spiritual knowledge finds the process of coming to know to be something quite different. It is a complete realization of that beautiful expression "Know thyself." But the most dangerous thing in the realm of knowledge is to grasp these words falsely. Today this occurs only too often. Many people construe these words to mean that they should no longer look about the physical world, but should gaze into their own inner being and seek there for everything spiritual. This is a very mistaken understanding. It is not at all what is meant. We must clearly understand that true higher knowledge is also an evolution from one standpoint, which the human being has attained, to another that has not been attained previously. If we practice self-knowledge only by brooding upon ourselves, we see only what we already possess. We acquire nothing new, but only knowledge of the lower self in the present meaning of the word. This inner nature is only one part of what is necessary for knowledge; the other part must be added. Without the two parts, there is no real knowledge. By means of our inner nature, we can develop organs through which we can gain knowledge. But just as the eye, as an external sense organ, would not perceive the Sun by gazing into itself, but only by looking outward at the Sun, so the inner perceptive organs must gaze outwardly, in other words, gaze into an *external spiritual*, in order to actually perceive. The concept "knowledge" had a much deeper, a more real meaning in those ages when spiritual things were better understood than at present. Read in the Bible the words "Abraham knew his wife!" or this or that patriarch "knew his wife." One does not need to seek very far in order to understand that this expression meant fructification. When one considers the words "Know thyself" in the Greek, they do not mean that you stare into your own inner being, but that you fructify yourself with what streams into you from the spiritual world. "Know thyself" means "Fructify thyself with the content of the spiritual world!"

Two things are needed for this: that one prepare oneself through katharsis and illumination, and then that one open one's inner being freely to the spiritual world. In this connection we may liken our inner nature to the *female* aspect, the outer spiritual to the male. The inner being must be made susceptible of receiving the higher self. When this has happened, the higher human self streams into us from the spiritual world. You may ask, "Where is this higher human self? Is it within us in a personal sense?" No, it is not there. On Saturn, Sun, and Moon, the higher self was diffused over the entire cosmos. At that time the cosmic "I" was spread out over all humankind, but now we have to permit it to work upon us. We must allow this "I" to work upon our previously prepared inner natures. This means that human inner nature, in other words, the astral body, must be cleansed, purified, ennobled—subjected to katharsis. If that is done, the outer spirit will stream in to illumine us. This happens if we have been so well prepared that we have subjected our astral body to katharsis—thereby developing inner organs of perception. The astral body, in any case, has progressed so far that now when it dips down into the etheric and physical bodies, illumination, or *photismos*, results. What actually occurs is that the astral body imprints its organs upon the etheric body, making it possible for the human being to perceive a spiritual world about us. This makes it possible for the inner being, the astral body, to receive what the etheric body is able to offer it, what the etheric body draws out of the entire cosmos, out of the cosmic "I."

This cleansed, purified astral body, which bears within it at the moment of illumination none of the impure impressions of the physical world, but only the organs of perception of the spiritual world, is called in esoteric Christianity "the pure, chaste, wise Virgin Sophia."

By means of everything received during katharsis, the student cleanses and purifies the astral body so that it is transformed into the Virgin Sophia. And when the Virgin Sophia encounters the cosmic "I"—the universal "I" that causes illumination—the student is surrounded by light, spiritual light.

This second power that approaches the Virgin Sophia is called in esoteric Christianity (and is also so called today) "the Holy Spirit."

Therefore, according to esoteric Christianity it is correct to say that through this process of initiation the Christian esotericist attains the purification and cleansing of the astral body. One makes one's astral body into the Virgin Sophia and is illuminated from above—if you wish, you may call it "overshadowed"—by the "Holy Spirit," the cosmic, universal "I." Those who are thus illuminated, who, in other words, according to esoteric Christianity have received the "Holy Spirit," speak in a new, different manner. How? When they speak about Saturn, Sun, and Moon, about the different members of the human being, about the processes of cosmic evolution, they do not express their own opinion. Their own views do not come into consideration at all. When they speak about Saturn, it is

Saturn itself that speaks through them. When they speak about the Sun, the spiritual being of the Sun speaks through them. They are instruments. Their personal "I" has been eclipsed, which means that at such moments it has become impersonal and the cosmic, universal "I" is using their "I" as its instrument through which to speak. Therefore, in the true esoteric teaching that proceeds from esoteric Christianity, one should not speak of *views* or *opinions*, for in the highest sense of the word this is incorrect; there are no such things. According to esoteric Christianity, whoever speaks with the right attitude of mind toward the world will reflect, for instance, as follows: If I tell people that there were two horses outside, the important thing is not that one of them pleases me less than the other and that I think one is a worthless horse. The important point is that I describe the horses to the others and give the facts. Similarly, what has been observed in the spiritual worlds must be described irrespective of personal opinions. In every spiritual-scientific system of teaching, only the facts must be related and this must have nothing to do with the opinions of the one who relates them.

Thus we have acquired two concepts in their spiritual significance. We have learned to know the nature of the Virgin Sophia, which is the purified astral body, and the nature of the "Holy Spirit," the cosmic, universal "I," which is received by the Virgin Sophia and can then speak out of this purified astral body. There is something else to be attained, a still higher stage. This is the ability to help someone else, the ability to give someone the impulse to accomplish these. Human beings today can receive the Virgin Sophia (the purified astral body) and the Holy Spirit (illumination) as I have described, but only Jesus Christ could give to the Earth what was necessary to accomplish this. He has implanted in the spiritual part of the Earth those forces that make it possible for what has been described in Christian initiation to happen at all. How did this come about?

Two things are necessary to understand this. First, we must acquaint ourselves with something purely historical, that is, with the way of giving of names when the Gospels were written, which was quite different from the way it is done today.

Those who interpret the Gospel today do not understand the principle of how names were given at the time the Gospels were written. Therefore they are wrong in what they say. It is, in fact, very difficult to describe the principle of giving names at that time, yet we can make it comprehensible, even though only in rough outline. Let us suppose that, in the case of a man we meet, instead of holding to the name that does not at all fit him—which was given to him in the abstract way customary today—we were to notice and hearken to his most distinguishing characteristics. Let us say we would instead notice the most prominent attribute of his character and were in a position to discern clairvoyantly the deeper foundations of his being. Let us say we would then give him a name in accordance with the most important qualities we believe should be attributed to him. If we followed such a method of giving names, we would be doing something similar—at a lower, more elementary level—to what was done at that time by those who gave names as the writer of the Gospel of St. John did.

To make his manner of giving names very clear, consider the following: The author of St. John's Gospel regarded the physical, historic mother of Jesus in her most prominent characteristics and asked himself, Where shall I find a name for her that will express most perfectly her real being? Then, because she had, through her earlier incarnations, reached the spiritual heights upon which she stood, and because she appeared in her external personality to be a counterpart, a revelation, of what was called in esoteric Christianity the Virgin Sophia, he called the mother of Jesus "the Virgin Sophia." This is what she was always called in the esoteric places where esoteric Christianity was taught.

Exoterically John leaves her entirely unnamed in contradistinction to those who have chosen the secular name Mary for her. He could not take the secular name; he had to express in the name the profound, historic world evolution that was taking place. He does this by indicating that she cannot be called Mary, and, what is more, he places by her side her sister Mary, wife of Cleophas, and calls her simply the "mother of Jesus."

John shows that he does not wish to mention her name, that it cannot be publicly revealed. In esoteric circles, she is always called the "Virgin Sophia." It was she who represented the "Virgin Sophia" as an external historical personality.

If we now wish to penetrate further into the nature of Christianity and its founder, we must consider yet another mystery. We should understand clearly how to distinguish between the personality who in esoteric Christianity was called "Jesus of Nazareth" and he who was called "Jesus Christ," the Christ dwelling in Jesus of Nazareth.

Now what does this mean? It means that in the historical personality of Jesus of Nazareth we have to do with a highly developed human being who had passed through many incarnations and after a cycle of high development was again reincarnated. This was a person who, because of this, was attracted to a mother so pure that the writer of the Gospel could call her the "Virgin Sophia." Thus we are dealing with a highly developed human being, Jesus of Nazareth, who had progressed far in his evolution during previous incarnations, and in this incarnation had entered a highly spiritual stage.

The other evangelists were not illuminated to such a high degree as the writer of John's Gospel. What was revealed to them was more the actual sense world, a world in which they saw their Master and Messiah moving about as Jesus of Nazareth. The mysterious spiritual relationships, at least those of the heights into which the writer of the Gospel of St. John could peer, were concealed from them. For this reason they especially emphasized the fact that the Father, who had always existed in Judaism and was transmitted down through the generations as the God of the Jews, lived in Jesus of Nazareth. And they expressed this when they said, "If we trace back the ancestry of Jesus of Nazareth through generation after generation, we are able to prove that the same blood flows in him that has flowed down through these generations." The evangelists give the genealogical tables and show precisely according to them at what different stages of evolution they stand. For Matthew, the important thing is to show that in Jesus of Nazareth we have a person in whom Father Abraham is living. The blood of Father Abraham has flowed down through the generations as far as Jesus. Matthew thus traces the genealogical tables back to Abraham. He has a more materialistic point of view than Luke. The important thing for Luke was to show not only that the God who lived in Abraham was present in Jesus, but that the ancestry, the line of descent, can be traced back still further, even to Adam, and that Adam was a son of the very Godhead. This means that Adam belonged to the time when humanity had just made the transition from a spiritual to a physical state. Both Matthew and Luke wished to show that this earthly Jesus of Nazareth has his being only in what can be traced back to the divine Father-power.

This was not a matter of importance for the writer of the Gospel of St. John, who could gaze into the spiritual world. The important thing for John was not the words "I and Father Abraham are one," but that at every moment of time something eternal exists in human beings that was present in them before Father Abraham. This is what John wished to show. In the beginning was the Word that is called the "I am." Before all external things and beings, he was. He was in the beginning. For those who wished rather to describe Jesus of Nazareth and were able to describe only him, it was a question of showing how from the beginning the blood flowed down through the generations. It was important to them to show that the same blood flowing down through the generations flowed also in Joseph, the father of Jesus.

If we could speak quite esoterically, it would naturally be necessary to speak of the idea of the so-called virgin birth, but this can be discussed only in the most intimate circles. It belongs to the deepest mysteries that exist, and the misunderstanding connected with this idea arises because people do not know what is meant by the "virgin birth." They think that it means there was no fatherhood. But it is not that. Something much more profound, more mysterious, lies behind it that is quite compatible with what the other disciples wish to show—hat is, that Joseph is the father of Jesus. If they were to deny this, then all the trouble they take to show this to be a fact would be meaningless. They wish to show that the ancient God exists in Jesus of Nazareth. Luke especially wished to make this very clear; therefore he traces the whole ancestry back to Adam and then to God. How could he have come to this conclusion, if he really wished to say, "I am showing you that this genealogical tree exists, but Joseph, as a matter of fact, had nothing to do with it"? It would be very strange if people were to take the trouble to represent Joseph as a very important personality and then were to shove him aside out of the whole affair.

In the event of Palestine, we have to do not only with this highly developed personality, Jesus of Nazareth, who had passed through many incarnations and had developed himself so highly that he needed such an extraordinary mother as the Virgin Sophia. We also have to do with a second mystery.

When Jesus of Nazareth was thirty years of age, he had advanced to such a stage through what he had experienced in his present incarnation that he could perform an action it is possible to perform in exceptional cases. We know that the human being consists of physical, etheric, and astral bodies and an "I." This fourfold human being is the human being as he or she lives here among us. It is possible for a person who stands at a certain high stage of evolution to draw the "I" out of the three bodies and abandon them at a particular moment, leaving them intact and entirely uninjured. This "I" then goes into the spiritual worlds and the three bodies remain behind. We meet this process at times in cosmic evolution. At some especially exalted, enraptured moment, a person's "I" departs and enters the spirit world. Under certain conditions this can be extended over a long period. And because the three bodies have been so highly developed by the "I" that lived in them, they have become fit instruments for a still higher being who now takes possession of them. In the thirtieth year of Jesus of Nazareth, that Being we have called the Christ, took possession of his physical, etheric, and astral bodies. This Christ Being could not incarnate in an ordinary child's body, but only in one that had first been prepared by a highly developed "I," for this Christ Being had never before been incarnated in a physical body. Therefore, from the thirtieth year on, we are dealing with the Christ in Jesus of Nazareth.

What in reality took place? The fact is that the corporality of Jesus of Nazareth that he had left behind was so mature, so perfect, that the Sun Logos, the Being of the six Elohim, which we have described as the spiritual Being of the Sun, was able to penetrate into it. It could incarnate for three years in this bodily nature. It could become flesh. The Sun Logos who can shine into human beings through illumination, the Sun Logos himself, the Holy Spirit, entered. The universal "I," the cosmic "I," entered, and from then on for three years the Sun Logos spoke through the body of Jesus. The Christ speaks through the body of Jesus during these three years. This event is indicated in the Gospel of St. John and also in the other Gospels as the descent of the dove, of the Holy Spirit, upon Jesus of Nazareth. In esoteric Christianity it is said that at that moment the "I" of Jesus of Nazareth left his body. From then on the Christ is in him, speaking through him in order to teach and work. This is the first event that happens, according to the Gospel of St. John. We now have the Christ within the astral, etheric, and physical bodies of Jesus of Nazareth. There he worked as described until the Mystery of Golgotha occurred.

What occurred on Golgotha? Let us consider that important moment when the blood flowed from the wounds of the crucified Savior. In order that you may understand me better, I shall compare what occurred with something else.

Let us suppose we have here a vessel filled with water. In the water, salt is dissolved, and the water becomes quite transparent. Because we have warmed the water, we have made a salt solution.

Now let us cool the water. The salt precipitates, and we see how the salt condenses below and forms a deposit at the bottom of the vessel. That is the process for one who sees only with physical eyes. But for a person who can see with spiritual eyes, something else is happening. While the salt is condensing below, the spirit of the salt streams up through the water, filling it. The salt can condense only when the spirit of the salt has departed from it and become diffused into the water. Those who understand these things know that wherever condensation takes place, spiritualization also always occurs. What thus condenses below has its counterpart above in the spiritual, just as when the salt condenses and is precipitated below, its spirit streams upward and disseminates.

Therefore, when the blood flowed from the wounds of the Savior not only did a physical process take place, but it was also actually accompanied by a spiritual process. That is, the Holy Spirit, which was received at the Baptism, united itself with the Earth. The Christ himself flowed into the very being of the Earth. From then on, the Earth was changed, and this is the reason for saying that if a person had viewed the Earth from a distant star, he or she would have observed that its whole appearance was altered with the Mystery of Golgotha. The Sun Logos became a part of the Earth, formed an alliance with it and became the Spirit of the Earth. This he achieved by entering the body of Jesus of Nazareth in his thirtieth year, and by remaining active on the Earth for three years after that.

Now, the important thing is that this event must produce an effect upon true Christians. It must give something by which one may gradually develop the beginnings of a purified astral body in the Christian sense. There had to be something there for Christians whereby they could make the astral body gradually more and more like a Virgin Sophia, and through it receive into themselves the Holy Spirit, which was able to spread out over the entire Earth but could not be received by anyone whose astral body did not resemble the Virgin Sophia. There had to be something that possesses the power to transform the human astral body into a Virgin Sophia.

What is this power? It consists in the fact of Jesus Christ's entrusting to the disciple whom he loved—to the writer of the Gospel of St. John—the mission of describing truly and faithfully through his own illumination the events of Palestine in order that people might be affected by them. If you permit what is written in the Gospel of St. John to work sufficiently upon you, your astral body is in the process of becoming a Virgin Sophia, and it will become receptive to the Holy Spirit. Gradually, through the strength of the impulse emanating from this Gospel, it will become able to feel the true spirit and later to perceive it. This mission was given to the writer of the Gospel by Jesus Christ.

You need only read the Gospel. The mother of Jesus—the Virgin Sophia in the esoteric meaning of Christianity—stands at the foot of the cross, and from the cross the Christ says to the disciple whom he loved: "Henceforth, this is thy mother," and from this hour that disciple took her unto himself. The meaning of this is: "That force which was in my astral body and made it capable of becoming a bearer of the Holy Spirit, I now give to you; you will write down what this astral body has been able to acquire through its development."

"And the disciple took her unto himself." That means he wrote the Gospel of St. John. And this Gospel of St. John is the Gospel in which the writer has concealed powers that develop the Virgin Sophia. At the cross the mission was entrusted to him of receiving that force as his mother and of being the true, genuine interpreter of the Messiah. This really means that if you live wholly in accordance with the Gospel of St. John and understand it spiritually, it has the force to lead you to Christian katharsis. It has the power to give you the Virgin Sophia. Then the Holy Spirit, united with the Earth, will grant you illumination, or *photismos*, in the Christian sense.

What the most intimate disciples experienced was so powerful that from that time on Christian esotericists possessed at least the capacity of perceiving in the spiritual world. The most intimate disciples had taken this capacity into themselves. Perceiving in the spirit, in the Christian sense, means that one transforms the astral body to such a degree through the power of the event in Palestine that what one sees need not be before one externally, or sensorially. One possesses something by means of which one can perceive in the spirit. There were such intimate pupils. The woman who anointed the feet of Jesus Christ in Bethany had received such perception. For example, she is one of those who first understood that what had lived in Jesus was present after his death, that is, had been resurrected. She possessed this faculty of seeing.

Where did this possibility come from? It came from the development of her inner sense organs. Are we told this in the Gospel? Indeed we are. We are told that Mary Magdalene was led to the grave, that the body had disappeared, and that she saw two spiritual forms. These two spiritual forms are always to be seen for a certain time when a corpse is present: on the one side, the astral body, on the other, what gradually separates from it as etheric body, which then passes over into the cosmic ether. Wholly separate from the physical body, two spiritual forms are present that belong to the spiritual world.

Then the disciples went away again unto their own home. But Mary stood without at the sepulchre weeping: and as she wept, she stooped down and looked into the sepulchre, and seeth two angels in white sitting.

She saw this because she had become clairvoyant through the force and power of what had taken place—the event in Palestine. But she saw something more: she saw the Risen Christ. Did she have to be clairvoyant to be able to see the Christ? If you have seen a person in physical form a few days ago, don't you think you would recognize him again if he should appear before you?

And when she had thus said, she turned herself back, and saw Jesus standing, and knew not that it was Jesus.

Jesus saith unto her, Woman why weepest thou? whom seekest thou? She, supposing him to be the gardener . . .

So that it might be told us as exactly as possible, it was said not only once, but again at the next appearance of the Risen Christ, when Jesus appeared at the sea of Gennesareth.

But when the morning was now come, Jesus stood on the shore: but the disciples knew not that it was Jesus.

His esoteric pupils find him there. Those who had received the full force of what had happened could grasp the situation and see that it was the Risen Jesus who could be perceived spiritually. Although the disciples and Mary Magdalene saw him, there were some among them who were less able to develop clairvoyant power. One of these was Thomas. It is said that he was not present the first time the disciples saw the Lord. He said he would have to lay his hands in his wounds—he would have to touch physically the body of the Risen Christ—if he were to believe. The effort was then made to assist him to develop spiritual perception.

And after eight days again his disciples were within, and Thomas with them: then came Jesus, the doors being shut, and stood in the midst, and said, Peace be unto you.

Then saith he to Thomas, Reach hither thy finger, and behold my hands; and reach hither thy hand, and thrust it into my side: and be not faithless, but believing. And thou shalt behold something if thou dost not rely upon the outer appearance, but art impregnated with inner power.

This inner power that should follow from the event of Palestine is called "Faith." It is no ordinary force, but an inner clairvoyant power. Permeate yourself with inner power, then you need no longer hold as real only what you see externally. Blessed are those who are able to know what they do not see outwardly! Thus we see that we have to do with the full reality and truth of the Resurrection and that only those who have first developed the inner power to perceive in the spirit world are fully able to understand it. This will make the last chapter of the Gospel of St. John comprehensible to you. Here again and again it is pointed out that the closest followers of Jesus Christ have reached the stage of the Virgin Sophia, because the event of Golgotha had been consummated in their presence. But when they had to stand firm for the first time, and had actually to behold a spiritual event, they were still blinded and had first to find their way. They did not know that he was the same who had earlier been among them.

Here is something that we must grasp with the subtlest concepts. The materialistic person would say, "Then the Resurrection is undermined!" But the miracle of the Resurrection must be taken literally. Remember he said, "Lo, I remain with you always, even unto the end of the age, unto the end of the cosmic age."

He is there and he will come again, although not in a form of flesh. He will come again in a form that can actually be perceived by those who have been sufficiently developed through the power of the Gospel of St. John. Possessing the power to perceive him, they will no longer be unbelievers.

Our mission is to prepare those who have the will to allow themselves to be prepared for the return of Christ on Earth. This is the cosmic, historical significance of spiritual science. It is to prepare humankind and to keep its eyes open for the time when Christ will come again among human beings in the sixth cultural epoch. It is to do so in order that what was indicated to us in the marriage at Cana may be accomplished for a great part of humanity.

Therefore the ideas that we receive from spiritual science seem like a witness to the testament of Christianity. To be led to real Christianity, people in the future will have to receive the spiritual teaching that spiritual science can give. Many people may still say today that spiritual science is something that really contradicts true

Christianity. But those are the "little popes" who form opinions about things they know nothing of and who make "What I do not know does not exist" into a dogma.

This intolerance will become greater and greater in the future. Christianity will run the greatest danger from those who at present believe they can be called good Christians. The Christianity of spiritual science will experience serious attacks from such nominal Christians, for all our concepts must change if a true spiritual understanding of Christianity is to come about. Above all, the soul must become more and more conversant with and develop understanding of the legacy of the writer of the Gospel of St. John. This is the great school of the Virgin Sophia, the St. John's Gospel itself. Only spiritual science can lead us deeper into this Gospel. In these lectures, I could give only examples to show how spiritual science can introduce us into the Gospel of St. John. It is impossible to explain the whole of it. Indeed, we read in the Gospel itself:

> And there are also many other things that Jesus did; and I suppose that were they all written down one after the other, the world could not contain all the books that would have to be written.

Just as the Gospel itself cannot go into all the details of the event of Palestine, so too is it impossible for even the longest course of lectures to present the full spiritual content of the Gospel. Therefore we must be satisfied with the indications that can be given at this time. We must content ourselves with the thought that the true testament of Christianity is carried out through just such indications in the course of human evolution. Let us allow all this to have such an effect upon us that we may possess the power to hold fast to the foundation we recognize in the Gospel of St. John when others come to us and say, You are giving us too complicated concepts, too many concepts that we must first make our own in order to comprehend this Gospel; the Gospel is for the simple and naive, and one dare not approach it with many concepts and thoughts. Many say this today. They perhaps refer to another saying, "Blessed are the poor in spirit, for theirs is the kingdom of heaven." One can merely quote such a saying as long as one does not understand it, for it really says, "Blessed are the beggars in spirit, for they shall reach the kingdom of heaven within themselves." This means that those who are like beggars of the spirit, who desire to receive more and more of the spirit, will find in themselves the kingdom of heaven!

At the present time the idea is all too common that everything religious is identical with all that is primitive and simple. People say: We acknowledge that science possesses many and complicated ideas, but we do not grant the same to faith and religion. Faith and religion must be simple and naive! Many "Christians" demand this. And many rely upon a conception that is little quoted perhaps, but is haunting the minds of people in the present, which Voltaire, one of the great teachers of materialism, expressed in the words "Whoever wishes to be a prophet must find believers, for what he asserts must be believed, and only what is simple and is always repeated in its simplicity finds believers."

This is often so with prophets, both true and false. They take the trouble to say something and to repeat it again and again, and people learn to believe it because it is constantly repeated. The representative of spiritual science has no desire to be such a prophet. . . .

Spiritual science has no desire to lead to *belief,* but to *knowledge.* . . . Let us try to understand more and more that spiritual science is something many-sided—not a creed, but a path to knowledge. Consequently it bears within it many facets. Therefore let us not shrink from collecting a great deal in order that we may understand one of the most important Christian documents, the Gospel of St. John. We have tried to assemble the most varied material, placing us in the position of being able to understand more and more the profound truths of this Gospel. We can begin to be able to understand how the physical mother of Jesus was an external manifestation, an external image of the Virgin Sophia. We can begin to understand what spiritual importance the Virgin Sophia had for the pupil of the Mysteries whom the Christ loved. Again we can begin to understand how, for the other Evangelists—who view the bodily descent of Jesus as important—Jesus' physical father plays a significant part when it was a question of the external imprint of the God idea in the blood. Further, we can begin to understand the significance for John of the Holy Spirit—symbolized for us in the descent of the dove at the Baptism. Through it the Christ was begotten in the body of Jesus and dwelt there for three years.

The Father of Jesus Christ is the Holy Spirit, who begot the Christ in the bodies of Jesus. If we understand this—and if we can comprehend a thing from all sides—we shall find it easy to understand that the less highly initiated disciples could not give us as profound a picture of the events of Palestine as the disciple whom the Lord loved. And if people speak of the Synoptic Gospels as the only authoritative Gospels, this only shows that they do not have the will to rise to an understanding of the true form of the Gospel of St. John. For each person resembles the God he or she understands. If we try to make what we can learn from spiritual science about the Gospel of St. John into a feeling, into an experience, we shall then find that this Gospel is not a textbook, *but a force that can be active within our souls.*

If these short lectures have aroused in you the feeling that this Gospel contains not only what we have been discussing here, but that indirectly, through the medium of words, it contains the force that can develop the soul itself further, then what was really intended in these lectures has been rightly understood. Because in them, not only was something intended for the understanding, for the intellectual capacity of understanding, but also that what takes its roundabout path through this intellectual capacity of understanding should condense into feelings and inner experiences, and these feelings and experiences should be a result of the facts presented here. If, in a certain sense, this has been rightly understood, we shall also comprehend what is meant when it is said that the movement for spiritual science has the mission of raising Christianity into Wisdom, of rightly understanding Christianity, indirectly through spiritual wisdom. We shall understand that Christianity is only in the beginning of its activity, and its true mission will be fulfilled when it is understood in its true spiritual form. The more these lectures are understood in this way, the more have they been comprehended in the sense in which they were intended.

4

Isis and Madonna

Berlin, April, 29, 1909

Goethe repeatedly pointed out how a person who approaches the secrets of nature also longs for the worthiest interpreter of these secrets—art. In all his works throughout his long life Goethe showed that for him art was the interpreter of truth. It may be said, in fact, that in exemplifying this view Goethe discovered something that has always been a basic conviction, a fundamental theme, in all ages and epochs of human evolution.

More or less consciously or unconsciously the different arts present us with different "languages" that express certain truths living in the human soul. These are often the most *secret* truths, the most secret insights, which cannot be easily reduced to rigid concepts or abstract formulae but seek artistic expression.

Today we shall consider just such a secret truth, one that for centuries has sought expression in art. This truth has always found scientific formulation in certain narrow circles, but it will become a matter of popular knowledge for a wider public in the future only through spiritual science. Goethe was able to approach this truth with his soul from the most varied points of view. In one of my lectures here I pointed to a significant moment in his life that was an experience of this kind of mystery. I told how Goethe, while reading the Roman writer Plutarch, came across the remarkable story of Nikias, who wanted to reconquer for Rome a certain town in Sicily that belonged to the Carthaginians. On that account, he was being pursued.

In his flight Nikias feigned insanity, and by his strange cry "The Mothers, the Mothers are pursuing me!" it was recognized that this insanity was of no ordinary kind. For in that region there was a so-called Temple of the Mothers, set up in accordance with ancient Mysteries. Hence the meaning of the expression "the Mothers" was known. Goethe let the full meaning of "the Mothers" sink meditatively into his soul and feeling. Then he knew that if he wished to present something very high with awe-inspiring beauty, there was no better way of doing this than by sending Faust himself to the Mothers. This was in the second part of his *Faust*.

What does this journey to the Mothers represent? I spoke of this briefly before. Mephistopheles can give Faust the key, but he cannot himself go to the realm where the Mothers sit in majesty. Mephistopheles is the spirit of materialism—the spirit contained, as it were, in the forces and powers of human material existence. For Mephistopheles, the realm of the Mothers is the realm of *nothingness*. But Faust, the spiritual human being—who is inclined to the spirit—can answer, "In your nothingness, I hope to find the All."

After this, we have the most remarkable, deeply meaningful description of the realm of the Mothers. We are told how the Mothers weave and live in a region where the forms of the visible world are fashioned. And we learn how we must transcend everything that lives in space and time if we wish to penetrate to these Mothers. Formation, transformation, is the essence of their realm. They are mysterious goddesses who rule in a spirit realm behind sensible reality. Faust must penetrate to them if he would obtain knowledge of what transcends the sensory, the physical. Only by opening his soul to this realm of the Mothers can Faust worthily unite the eternal in Helen with the temporal.

Goethe fully understood how in this realm of the Mothers one has to do with a sphere into which we can penetrate when we awaken the slumbering spiritual forces in our souls. For Goethe, this is the great moment when the spiritual beings and facts that are always around us—but which we see as little as the blind man sees color and light—reveal themselves to him. It is the moment when his spiritual eyes and ears are opened to a world behind the physical. Entrance into this realm is portrayed by the journey to the Mothers.

I have told you often that when human beings impress certain inner process in the soul, certain precisely prescribed methods for absorption into the world of conceptions, feelings, and will, then their spiritual eyes and ears actually open and new realms unfold around them. I have also shown you that those who enter this realm are confused by all the impressions that work upon them. Whereas in the physical world there are objects with sharp outlines from which we take our bearings, in the spiritual world we have a confused feeling of interweaving, hovering form—just as Goethe describes it in the second part of *Faust*. All that is given to our senses is born, however, out of this realm of the Mothers, just as metals are born out of the mother ore in the mountains. This mysterious mother realm of all earthly and physical things—the realm of the divine substance of all things—sounds a deep note in Goethe. This is why the expression "the Mothers" works such fascination and awesome beauty in him. This also explains why, when he read in Plutarch that someone cried, "The Mothers, the Mothers," he recognized that this was not a mad vision into an insane and unreal world, but a vision into a world of spiritual reality. The cosmic problem posed by the Mothers stood before Goethe while he was reading Plutarch, and, as was his habit, he inserted this Mother problem as a mystery into the second part of his *Faust*.

Now, whoever wishes to enter this realm of the Mothers, the realm of the spiritual world, has always had to undertake—besides other exercises described in *How to Know Higher Worlds*—what has always been called the "preparatory purification (katharsis) of the heart." We must so prepare ourselves that our souls, from which the higher spiritual forces are to be drawn, no longer have the slightest compulsion or passion for the ordinary world of the senses. Our souls must be purified and purged of all that attracts us sensuously, feeds our senses, and holds the understanding captive to the physical body. Our souls must be free of such attachments. Then they will awaken within themselves our spiritual eyes and penetrate the spiritual realm. Wherever knowledge of this mystery has existed, the purified soul that has passed through katharsis and is no longer turned toward the physical world has always been called *the higher inner being*. It has been said that this inner being does not stem from anything that outer eyes can investigate. It stems from higher soul-spiritual sources. It has no earthly home but a heavenly one.

This ennobled, purified soul was always considered to be connected with humanity's true origin. Spiritual science has never spoken of a purely *material* evolution—of perfection or imperfection determined by the senses. Spiritual science does not condemn as false what we call evolution today—the ascent from the lowest to the most perfect earthly physical being, the physical human being. I have often emphasized that we fully recognize the fact of evolution. Spiritual science fully recognizes the scientific theory of evolution and the descent of species. At the same time, however, we always point out that this "evolution" does not include what we call "humanity." The scientific theory of evolution applies only to the outer side of human development.

When we trace humanity back through time we find that the further back we go to ever more imperfect physical forms, the more we discover humanity's origin as a soul-spiritual being. We have often gone back to periods of human evolution when the being we now call human did not yet have any physical existence and was still concealed in soul-spirit existence. I have often drawn your attention to how, in spiritual science, we consider the material form, the human physical body, as a densification, as water is solidified into ice, of an originally soul-spiritual being. I have often used this image of a body of water condensing to ice so that what we are left with is a certain quantity of water together with the part that is changed into ice. Here we have an image of humanity's origin. As soul-spiritual beings, we had nothing of the physical, material bodily nature that we perceive today with our eyes and touch with our hands. Human beings gradually became more and more physical, until we acquired our present physical form. Conventional science can indeed look back to a time that shows human beings in the physical form we still see today. Spiritual science however looks back to a primordial past when humanity was born out of the spiritual world and was still of a soul-spiritual nature. When we contemplate the human soul today we can say that the soul element in us is the last remnant, so to speak, of the soul-spiritual nature that was once ours. When we look at our inner nature, we learn to know soul-spiritual being. In doing so, we come to realize that as we are in our inner being, so we once were long ago when we were born out of the womb of the spiritual world. And this soul being who we are, sheathed outwardly in the lower elements of the sense world, can be purified and cleansed. We can raise ourselves to sense-free perception, and thereby regain the spiritual nature from which we were born. Such is the process of acquiring spiritual knowledge through purgation and purification. Then in the spirit we can gaze into our soul being. And, speaking not just in images but also in reality, we can say the following: *Truly knowing this soul being, we see that it is not of this world. For behind it we see a divine spiritual world from which it was born.*

Let us now try to translate what I have just said into a sensible image. In fact, don't we already have an image of what I have described, one in which the spiritual world is represented to the senses, in cloud formations, out of which—to render the human soul itself sensible—spiritual forms like angels' heads are born? Don't we have a picture, an image, born of the divine spiritual world, in the figure of the Virgin in Raphael's *Sistine Madonna?*

Let us go on to ask, What happens to those souls that have been cleansed and purified and have ascended to higher knowledge and unfolded the spiritual images within themselves that give life to the same divine that lives and weaves through the world? Such people who give birth in themselves to a higher being representing a little world in the great world, who out of their purified souls bring forth the true higher being—what are they? They cannot be described other than by the word "clairvoyant." If we want to create an image of the soul that gives birth out of itself—out of the spiritual universe—to the higher human being, we need only recall the painting of the *Sistine Madonna:* the Madonna with the wonderful child in her arms!

In the *Sistine Madonna,* then, we have a painting depicting the human soul born of the spiritual universe. Springing from this soul is the highest that a human being can bring forth: *our own spiritual birth,* the birth of what in us is a begetting of cosmic creative activity.

Once the structure of the world was founded on divine spirituality. Indeed, it would be senseless to seek in the world for spirit if spirit had not originally built the world. What surrounds us in the world came from the spirit that we seek in our souls. Our souls have sprung from the divine Father Spirit that lives and weaves through the universe, bearing the Son of Wisdom who is like his Father Spirit, whose "reiteration" in fact he is.

Goethe approached this problem in all its mystical significance when he tried to gather the whole content of *Faust* together in the final "Chorus Mysticus." Here he speaks of the human soul as the "eternal feminine" that draws us onward to the universal spirit of the world. Such was still Goethe's attitude to the Madonna at the very end of *Faust.* From the form that the portrayal of the Madonna has assumed today it is almost impossible to recognize fully what is here expressed as in a picture—though it is founded on a profound truth. If, however, we trace the Madonna back to its origin, we will realize that truly the mightiest human problem, though closely veiled, still confronts us in the figure of the Madonna today. Certainly the Madonna images have greatly changed from the simple figure of the catacombs in the first Christian centuries, where we find Madonnas portrayed with the child groping for the mother's breast. It is a long way from this first simple figure, having little artistic about it, to the fifteenth century, to Michelangelo and Raphael, where after many transformations the Madonna and Child have become artistic, painterly in the modern sense.

It is certainly the case that these supreme artists, even if they proceeded from no great knowledge, worked nevertheless out of a definite feeling of the deeper truth of the Madonna.

When we stand before Michelangelo's *Pieta* in St. Peter's in Rome, the most beautiful sensations arise in us. We see the Madonna sitting with her dead son across her knees; she is therefore at the age when Christ had already passed through death, and yet she is portrayed with all the beauty of youth. It was much discussed in Michelangelo's day why he had given the Madonna this youthful beauty. When asked about it, he replied that it was his experience—not belief, but knowledge!—that virgins long preserve the freshness of youth. Therefore surely he was right to represent the Mother of God at this age still with all the freshness of youth? Michelangelo expresses something remarkable here! And although Raphael does not openly express it, we feel it to be there in his pictures too.

We can understand this idea only if we go back to ancient times when what we find expressed unconsciously by art in the representations of the Madonna still lived outwardly in the world. If we go back far enough, we find such representations everywhere. For instance, if we go back to ancient India, we find there the goddess with the child Krishna at her breast. We could find similar pictures in China.

We will not, however, go back to those distant regions. Rather, we will turn to those ancient Egyptian representations that so impressively recall what is represented with such beauty in the Christian Madonna—the images of Isis with the child Horus. These images, which grew wholly out of Egyptian wisdom, will in a certain way provide the key for understanding the Madonna image correctly. To do so, we will have to direct our attention a little to the nature of the wisdom that led to this remarkable figure of the Egyptian goddess. We will have to fix our attention on what this wisdom, expressed in the myth of Isis and Osiris, means to us

Understood correctly, the myth of Isis and Osiris leads us deep into humanity's present problems. The myth of Osiris—the story of the king who ruled as if in a golden age in primordial times and married his sister, Isis, who brought happiness and blessing to humankind—is still the deepest and most significant thing for us in Egyptian religion. In the eyes of ancient Egypt, Osiris was a human king of divine power and virtue who ruled until his evil brother, Set, killed him.

Osiris was killed in a special way. For a banquet, Set (later called Typhon) had a chest made. Then with great cunning he induced Osiris to lie down in it—and quickly closed the lid. The chest was then thrown into the water and swept away to the unknown. Osiris's sorrowing wife, Isis, looked for her husband everywhere. After a long search, she finally found him in Asia. After she brought him back to Egypt, Set dismembered him and the pieces were buried in many graves. This is the reason for the great number of tombs of Osiris in Egypt. Osiris now became King of the Dead. Previously, he was King of the Living. Then, from the other world, a ray pierced the head of Isis and she gave birth to Horus, who became the ruler of this world.

According to Egyptian legend, Horus is the posthumous son of Osiris. Horus, who entered existence as the result of impregnation from the other world—the world beyond—is ruler of the earthly world of the senses. Osiris is ruler of the realm of the dead. The soul in the body is subject to the rulership of Horus. When it leaves the body—so *The Egyptian Book of the Dead* testifies—it enters the realm of Osiris and itself becomes an "Osiris." *The Egyptian Book of the Dead* describes in a deeply impressive way how the soul is arraigned before the tribunal. It says, "And you, O Osiris, what have you done?" Thus the soul, by passing through the gate of death, itself becomes an Osiris.

According to the ancient Egyptians, then, there are two realms: the realm perceived by the senses, the realm of Horus, and the realm the soul enters after death, where Osiris holds sway. But at the same time, according to the Egyptian initiates, we know that an initiate who has acquired the faculty of clairvoyance enters *in this lifetime* the region that otherwise can be entered only after death. Such initiates can be united with Osiris in this life. The initiates therefore become Osiris. They tear themselves from the physical and renounce all habits of the physical plane, all passions and desires. Cleansing themselves of the physical, they become purified souls and as such unite with Osiris.

Now what does the myth of Isis, Osiris, and Horus tell us? It is childish to maintain that this story represents the yearly course of the Sun around the Earth. Ivory-towered scholars have created the legend that Osiris is the Sun and that his disappearance indicates the Sun's conquest by nature's wintry powers. These are said to be Set, or Typhon, Osiris's evil brother. In this view, Isis represents the Moon, who seeks the Sun in order to be irradiated by its light. Only those who spin nature myths out of their own heads can make such statements. The truth is that the myth of Isis is the external, pictorial expression of a most profound truth.

What is this age when Osiris ruled over human beings? It was the time when human beings were still beings of soul and spirit, and still dwelt in the world of soul and spirit among beings who also had their being in soul and spirit. Therefore, the realm of Osiris does not refer to the physical realm but to a past realm when human beings lived as beings of soul and spirit. And the brother, the enemy of Osiris, is that being who surrounded human beings in a physical body, who densified part of this spirit and soul being into the physical body. This reveals how the once purely spiritual Osiris was laid in a chest. The chest is simply the human physical body. And because Osiris is a being whose whole nature cannot descend as far as the physical world—who is meant to remain in the divine spiritual world—laying him in a chest, which is the human body, means the same as death.

Osiris thus represents in a wider sense the passage from the evolutionary realm of soul and spirit to the evolutionary epochs of physical humanity. Osiris, however, could not enter this physical realm. He died to the external physical world and became king in the realm that the soul enters when it leaves the physical world of the senses or develops clairvoyant powers. In other words, the soul of an initiate is united with Osiris.

What has remained of the realm of soul and spirit for those who did not withdraw like Osiris from the physical world of the senses but entered into it? The soul remains—one's being of spirit and soul. This soul will always draw us to our original source of spirit and soul, to Osiris. This human soul dwelling within us is, in a certain sense, Isis, the eternal feminine in us that draws us onward to the realm out of which we are born.

This Isis, when she is purified and has laid aside all she has received from the physical, is impregnated from the spiritual world and gives birth to Horus, the higher human, who is to be victorious over the lower human being. Thus we see Isis as the representative of the human soul, as the divine spiritual in us that is born of the universal Father and has remained within us, seeking Osiris and only finding him through initiation or death. By conjuring this Osiris and Isis saga in a picture before our souls, we are looking into the realm that lies behind the physical world of the senses. We are looking into a time when we were still among the Mothers, the primordial grounds of existence. This was the time when Isis was not yet enclosed in the physical body but still united in the golden age with her spouse, Osiris.

All this reveals to us the most beautiful flower of humanity, the highest human ideal, which is born out of the human body by impregnation by the eternal World Spirit itself. How could this be other than the most sublime ideal, the highest peak of humanity, Christ himself? He is this ideal represented here. Who else could naturally enter the realm of the Mothers? In Goethe's *Faust* we find three Mothers seated on golden tripods. Our souls have evolved through the ages when they were not yet in a human body. What appears as human conception and birth today is the last image and symbol of the earlier form of the same thing. In a physical mother we see, as it were, the last physical form of a spiritual Mother who is behind her. This spiritual Mother is not impregnated as we are on Earth today, but out of the cosmos itself—just as in higher knowledge our souls are fructified out of the cosmos. In other words, we can look back to ever more spiritual forms of fructification and reproduction.

Therefore in the true sense of spiritual science we do not speak of only *one* Mother but of the *Mothers*, realizing that the physical mother is but the last development out of the spiritual realm of the soul-spiritual figure of the Mother. There are in fact images of Isis representing not one Mother but Mothers—three Mothers. First, in front, as it were, we have the figure of Isis with the Horus child at her breast. This image resembles the oldest representations of the Madonna. Behind this figure in certain Egyptian representations, however, we have another Isis. This one bears on her head the two familiar cow horns and the wings of the hawk. She offers her child the ankh or cross of life. What is physical or human in the first figure is more spiritualized here. Behind this second figure there is yet a third figure, this one bearing a lion's head and representing the third stage of the human soul. This is how these three Isis figures appear, one behind the other. It is an actual fact that our human soul bears in it three natures—a *will* nature, found in the inmost depths of the being, a *feeling* nature, and a *wisdom* nature. These are the three soul Mothers we meet in the three figures of the Egyptian Isis.

Thus, behind the physical Mother we have the supersensible Mother, the spiritual Mother, the Isis of spiritual antiquity, with the hawk's wings and the cow horns with the globe of the world between them. The symbolism here is profound. Those who understand something of the ancient theory of numbers have always said—and this corresponds with a deep truth—that the sacred number three represents the divine masculine in the cosmos. This sacred number three is pictorially expressed by the globe of the world and the two cow horns, which are, if you like, a kind of image of the Madonna's crescent, but actually represent the fruitful working of the forces of nature.

The globe represents the creative activity of the cosmos. I would have to speak for hours to give a picture of the masculine element in the world. Thus, behind the physical Isis stands her representative, the superphysical Isis, who is not impregnated by one of her own kind but by the divine masculine living and weaving through the world. The process of fructification is still portrayed as being akin to the process of cognition. The consciousness that the process of cognition is a kind of fructification was still lived in those ancient times. Thus you may read in the Bible, "Adam knew his wife and she brought forth." What we receive as spiritual today gives birth to the spiritual in the soul. This represents a last remnant of the ancient mode of fructification. It shows us how today we are fructified by the Spirit of the World and receive this spirit into the human soul in order to acquire human knowledge, human feeling, and human will.

This is what is represented in the second Isis. She is fructified by the divine male element, so that her head is fructified. She does not offer material substance to the child, as in the case of the physical Isis, but the *ankh*, which is the sign of life. Thus, behind the physical Mother Of Life appears the spiritual Mother of Life; and behind her again the primal force of all life, represented by the life force. Just so, the will dwells behind everything in the still spiritual, far distant past. Here we have the three Mothers, and also the way in which these three Mothers impart the vitalizing force of the cosmos to the Sun. What we have here is not just artistic expression, but a symbolic expression of a profound cosmic truth.

What persisted throughout the Egyptian period of evolution as the symbol of Isis was transformed by the appearance of Jesus Christ on Earth. In Jesus Christ we have the great prototype of all that the human soul is destined to bring forth out of itself. The human soul in its fructification out of the Spirit of the World is given tangible form therefore in the Madonna. In the Madonna we meet, as it were, with Isis reborn and in an appropriate way enhanced, transfigured.

What I spoke of in images at the beginning of the lecture now comes before our souls as bound up with the evolution of humanity, streaming forth from hoary antiquity. It is artistically transfigured and given new form in modern pictures presented throughout the world to the human souls thirsting for art. Here we see how in very truth art, in Goethe's words, becomes the exponent of Truth. We see how in reality when our gaze falls on the Madonna and is permeated with deep feeling, the soul partakes in certain knowledge of the mighty riddle of the world. We realize that in such surrender our soul, seeking in itself the eternal feminine, yearns for the divine Father Spirit born out of the cosmos, to whom we give birth as the Son in our own soul.

What we find in the Madonna is what we are as human beings and how we are related to the universe. That is why the pictures of the Madonna are such holy things, apart altogether from any religious stream, any religious dogma. Hence when the hazy masses of cloud form themselves into the heads of angels, and out of the whole the representative of the human soul comes into being, we can feel it as something born out of the cosmos. The Madonna of course also includes what can be born out of the human soul: the true higher being slumbering in every human being, that which is best in us and flows and weaves through the world as spirit.

Goethe felt this when he gave final form to his *Faust*. Faust had been led through the different stages up to higher knowledge and the higher life. This is why Goethe makes Faust go to the Mothers and why the name "Mothers" sounds to Faust so awe-inspiring and so beautiful, instilling in him a feeling for the wisdom echoing down from ancient times. Goethe felt that he had to send Faust to the Mothers, for only there could Faust seek and find the eternal through which the Euphorion—the child of Faust and Helen—can come into being. Because the human soul appeared to him to be represented by the Madonna, Goethe expressed the riddle of the soul in the words of the "Chorus Mysticus" that concludes *Faust*: "The eternal feminine draws us upward."

Whatever modern times may have to say, this is the reason why Raphael's wonderful picture of the Madonna succeeds so well in leading us back to the realms to which the old figures of Isis belong. From what is spiritual, from what can no longer be expressed in a human figure because it would be too material, from that Isis whose force can be represented symbolically only by the lion's head, we descend to the human Isis who transmits her force to Horus through physical substance. Raphael unconsciously expressed this in his *Sistine Madonna*. Spiritual science, however, will lead humanity consciously back to the spiritual realm from which it has descended. Two lectures that I shall be giving here will furnish examples of how humanity has descended out of spiritual heights and will ascend again to this higher existence.

In the words of Plato, "Once humans were spiritual beings; they descended to Earth only because they were robbed of their spiritual wings, and were enveloped in a physical body. But they will struggle out of this physical body again and reascend to the world of spirit and soul." Pictures of the Madonna proclaim the same, for in the most beautiful sense they are what Goethe wished to express in the words "Art is the worthiest exponent of the known mysteries of the world." We need not fear that art will become abstract or wholly allegorical if it is once again compelled, I repeat compelled, to recognize the higher spiritual realities; nor need we fear that it will become stiff and lifeless when it finds itself unable to continue using outer, crude physical models.

Because we have forgotten the spiritual, our art has become bound up with the outer senses. But when we find the way back to spiritual heights and spiritual knowledge, we will realize that true reality lies in the spiritual world. Those who perceive this reality will create in a living way, without being slavishly bound to physical models. Goethe will be understood only when it is more widely recognized that art and wisdom go hand in hand, only when art becomes again a representation of the spiritual. Science and art will then again be one; in their union they will become religion, for the spiritual will work in this form as divinity in the human heart and give birth to what Goethe called true, genuine piety. "Whoever has both science and art also has religion," says Goethe. "If anyone does not possess these two, then let him have religion."

Whoever knows the spiritual secrets of the world and knows what speaks through Isis and Madonna sees in them something of primeval life, something much more alive than whatever one can express in any slavish imitation of a physical human model. A person of this kind whose gaze penetrates to the living quality of these Madonnas as through a veil, beholding the spiritual behind them, can feel piety in complete spiritual freedom, free from all dogma and prejudice. Such a person will unite science, or wisdom, with art in his or her soul and give new birth to genuine free religious feeling—to genuine piety.

5

WISDOM AND LOVE IN COSMIC

AND HUMAN EVOLUTION

from An Outline of Esoteric Science

. . . JUST AS GREATER COSMIC EVOLUTION can be presented as a succession of states from Saturn through the Vulcan phases, it is also possible to present shorter spans of time, such as those making up the Earth phase of evolution. The enormous upheaval that brought an end to life on Atlantis was followed by the stages in human evolution that have been described as the ancient Indian, ancient Persian, Egypto-Chaldean, and Greco-Latin cultural periods. The fifth period is where we stand now—the present. This period began gradually around the twelfth, thirteenth, and fourteenth centuries C.E., after having been prepared since the fourth and fifth centuries. It has been clearly evident since the fifteenth century. The Greco-Latin period that preceded it began around the eighth century B.C.E., and at the end of its first third the Christ event took place.

The disposition and faculties of the human soul changed during the transition from the Egypto-Chaldean period to the Greco-Latin. During the Egypto-Chaldean period, what we now know as logical thinking or grasping the world through reason did not yet exist. At that time, the knowledge we now make our own through our intellect was acquired in a way that was appropriate then—directly, through an inner knowledge that was supersensible in a certain respect. While people perceived things, the necessary concept or image of those things simply appeared in their souls. When the faculty of cognition is like this, not only do images of the physical world of the senses appear, but a certain knowledge of nonsensory realities and beings also rises out of the soul's depths. This was a remnant of the ancient, dusklike supersensible consciousness that all of humankind had formerly possessed.

In the Greco-Latin age, there were more and more people who lacked this faculty. In its place, the capacity for intellectual reflection appeared. People became more and more removed from direct dreamlike perception of the world of soul and spirit and ever more dependent on their intellect and feelings to provide an image of that world. In some respects, this state of affairs continued throughout the fourth post-Atlantean period. Only those individuals who had retained the legacy of the former soul disposition, so to speak, were able to admit the spiritual world into their consciousness directly. These people, however, were holdovers from an earlier age. Their type of cognition was no longer suited to the new age because, as a result of the laws of evolution, an old soul capacity loses its full significance when new faculties appear. Human life adapts to these new faculties and no longer knows what to do with the old ones.

There were also individuals, however, who quite consciously began to develop other, higher, powers in addition to the powers of intellect and feeling they had acquired. These powers made it possible for them to break through into the world of soul and spirit again. The way they had to begin to do this was quite different from how it had happened among the students of the ancient initiates, who had not had to consider the soul faculties that developed only during the fourth post-Atlantean period. This fourth period saw the first beginnings of the type of modern spiritual training that has been described in this book [*An Outline of Esoteric Science*]. However, at that time it was only in its beginning stages; it could only be fully developed in the fifth post-Atlantean period beginning with the twelfth and thirteenth centuries, and especially since the fifteenth century. People who attempted to ascend into supersensible worlds in this way were able to experience something about higher realms of existence through their own Imagination, Inspiration, and Intuition. To those who were content with the faculties of intellect and feeling that had developed, what ancient clairvoyance had known was accessible only through oral or written traditions that were passed down from generation to generation.

For people born after the Christ event who did not make their way up into supersensible worlds, such traditions were also their only means of knowing anything about the essential nature of this event. However, there were certain initiates who still possessed the old natural ability to perceive the supersensible world and whose development allowed them to enter a higher world in spite of the fact that they disregarded humankind's new intellectual and emotional powers. They created a transition from the old form of initiation to the new one. People like this were also present in subsequent periods. However, the essential characteristic of the fourth post-Atlantean period was that human powers of intellect and feeling were strengthened by being cut off from direct interaction with the world of soul and spirit. The souls who incarnated then and greatly developed these powers then carried the results of their development over into their incarnations during the fifth period. As compensation for having been cut off from the spiritual world, the mighty traditions of ancient wisdom were available, especially those having to do with the Christ event. Through the very power of their content, these traditions provided human souls with a confident knowledge of the higher world.

There were also always human souls, however, who developed their powers of higher cognition in addition to their faculties of intellect and feeling. It was incumbent upon them to experience the realities of the higher world and especially the mystery of the Christ event by means of direct supersensible knowledge. They always allowed as much of this to flow into other human souls as was comprehensible to them and good for them.

In harmony with the purpose of Earth's evolution, the first expansion of Christianity was meant to take place at a time when most of humankind had not developed faculties of supersensible cognition. This is why the force of tradition was so powerful at that time. An extremely powerful force was needed to make people confident in the supersensible world if they themselves were not able to behold this world. With the exception of a brief time during the thirteenth century, there were almost always individuals who were capable of lifting themselves up into the higher worlds through Imagination, Inspiration, and Intuition. In the Christian era, these people were the successors of the initiates of antiquity who had been leaders and members of the centers of Mystery wisdom. The task of these new initiates was to recognize once again, through their own faculties, what had once been comprehended through ancient Mystery wisdom and to add to this a knowledge of the essential nature of the Christ event.

Thus the knowledge arising among the new initiates encompassed all the subject matter of ancient initiation, but from its center radiated the higher knowledge of the mysteries of the Christ event. As long as the human souls of the fourth post-Atlantean period were meant to be consolidating their faculties of intellect and feeling, this knowledge was only able to flow into general life to a limited extent, so during that time it was really quite hidden. Then the new age of the fifth cultural period dawned. Its main feature was the further development of intellectual abilities, which blossomed exuberantly then and will continue to unfold in the present and future. A gradual buildup to this period began in the twelfth and thirteenth centuries, and its progress accelerated from the sixteenth century to the present.

Under these influences, cultivating the forces of reason became the chief concern of evolution in the fifth cultural period. In contrast, traditional knowledge of and confidence in a supersensible world lost more and more of its power over human souls. However, it was replaced by what we may call an increasingly strong influx into human souls of knowledge derived from modern supersensible consciousness. "Hidden" knowledge was now flowing, although imperceptibly to begin with, into people's ways of thinking. It is self-evident that intellectual forces have continued to reject this knowledge right into the present. But what must happen will happen in spite of any temporary rejection. Symbolically, this hidden knowledge, which is taking hold of humanity from the other side and will do so increasingly in the future, can be called "the knowledge of the Grail." If we learn to understand the deeper meaning of this symbol as it is presented in stories and legends, we will discover a significant image of what has been described above as the new initiation knowledge with the Christ Mystery at its center. Therefore, modern initiates can also be known as "Grail initiates."

The path to supersensible worlds whose first stages have been described in this book leads to "the science of the Grail." A unique feature of this knowledge is that its facts can be investigated only by those who acquire the means of doing so that are described in this book. Once these facts have been discovered, however, they can then be understood by means of the soul forces that have been developing during the fifth cultural period. In fact, it will become increasingly evident that these forces will find their satisfaction in this knowledge to an ever greater extent. At present, we are living in a time when more of this knowledge ought to enter common consciousness than was formerly the case. This book hopes to convey the information it contains from this point of view. To the extent that human evolution will absorb Grail knowledge, the impulse supplied by the Christ event can become ever more significant. Increasingly, an inner aspect will be added to the external aspect of Christian evolution. What we can recognize through Imagination, Inspiration, and Intuition about the higher worlds in conjunction with the Christ Mystery will increasingly permeate our life of thinking, feeling, and will. "Hidden" Grail knowledge will become evident; as an inner force, it will increasingly permeate the manifestations of human life.

For the duration of the fifth cultural period, knowledge of supersensible worlds will continue to flow into human consciousness;

when the sixth period begins, humanity will have been able to reacquire the nonsensory perception it possessed in a dusklike way in earlier times—but now on a higher level and in a form that is quite different from the old perception. In ancient times, what our souls knew about the higher worlds was not imbued with our own forces of reason and feeling; it was received as inspiration from above. In the future, our souls will not only receive these flashes of Inspiration, but will also comprehend them and experience them as the essence of human soul-nature. In the future, when a soul receives knowledge about a certain being or thing, the very nature of the intellect will find this justified. If knowledge of a different sort asserts itself—knowledge of a moral commandment or a human behavior—the soul will tell itself: My feelings will only be justified if I act in accordance with this knowledge. A sufficiently large number of human beings are meant to develop this state of mind during the sixth post-Atlantean cultural period.

In a certain way, what the third or Egypto-Chaldean period contributed to humanity's evolution is being repeated in the fifth. At that time, the human soul still perceived certain realities of the supersensible world, although this perception was waning as intellectual faculties prepared to emerge. These faculties were to temporarily exclude human beings from the higher world. In the fifth cultural period, the supersensible realities that had been perceived in a dusklike state of consciousness are becoming evident again but are now being imbued with our personal forces of intellect and feeling and with what human souls can gain through knowledge of the Christ Mystery. This is why they are assuming different forms than they did previously. In ancient times, impressions from the supersensible worlds were experienced as forces that urged human beings on but emanated from an outer spiritual world that did not include them. In contrast, more recent evolution allows us to perceive these impressions as coming from a world we human beings are growing into and are increasingly a part of. No one ought to believe that the Egypto-Chaldean cultural period will be repeated in such a way that our souls will simply be able to take up what was then present and has come down to us from those times. If understood correctly, the effect of the Christ impulse is to make the human souls that receive it feel, recognize, and conduct themselves as members of a spiritual world, whereas formerly they were outsiders.

While the third cultural period is revived in the fifth in order to be imbued with the totally new element in human souls provided by the fourth period, something similar will happen in the sixth cultural period with regard to the second and in the seventh with regard to the first or ancient Indian cultural period. All the wonderful wisdom that the great teachers of ancient India could proclaim will be able to reappear as life truths in human souls in the seventh cultural period.

Now, any transformations in things in the earthly world outside of human beings also have a certain relationship to humanity's own evolution. When the seventh cultural period has run its course, the Earth will be struck by an upheaval comparable to the one that took place between the Atlantean and post-Atlantean ages. After this, evolution will continue under transformed earthly circumstances through seven more time periods. On a higher level, the human souls incarnating then will experience the same fellowship with a higher world that the Atlanteans experienced on a lower level.

However, only human beings embodying souls that have become all that they could under the influence of the Greco-Latin cultural period and the subsequent fifth, sixth, and seventh periods of post-Atlantean evolution will be able to cope with these reconfigured earthly circumstances. The inner nature of these souls will correspond to what the Earth has then become. Other souls will have to remain behind at this stage, although earlier they could still have chosen to create the prerequisites for participation in it. The souls mature enough to face the conditions that will exist after the next great upheaval will be the ones who succeeded in imbuing supersensible knowledge with their own forces of intellect and feeling at the transition from the fifth post-Atlantean period to the sixth. The fifth and sixth periods are the decisive ones, so to speak. In the seventh period, although the souls who have achieved the goal of the sixth will continue to develop accordingly, the changed circumstances in their surroundings will provide little opportunity for the others to make up for lost time. The next opportunity will present itself only in the distant future.

This is how evolution is proceeding from one age to the next. Supersensible cognition observes not only future changes involving the Earth alone, but also ones that occur in interaction with the neighboring heavenly bodies. A time will come when both the Earth and humanity have made such progress in evolution that the forces and beings that had to separate from the Earth during Lemurian times to enable earthly beings to continue to progress will be able to reunite with the Earth. At that time, the Moon will reconnect with the Earth. This will happen because sufficient numbers of human souls possess enough inner strength to make these Moon forces fruitful for further evolution. This will take place at a time when another development that has turned toward evil will be taking place alongside the high level of development reached by the appropriate number of human souls. Souls whose development has been delayed will have accumulated so much error, ugliness, and evil in their karma that they will temporarily form a distinct union of evil and aberrant human beings who vehemently oppose the community of good human beings.

In the course of its development, the good portion of humankind will learn to use the Moon forces to transform the evil part so that it can participate in further evolution as a distinct earthly kingdom. Through the work of the good part of humanity, the Earth, then reunited with the Moon, will become able to reunite with the Sun after a certain period of evolution, and also with the other planets. After an interim stage that resembles a sojourn in a higher world, the Earth will transform itself into the Jupiter state.

During the Jupiter stage, what is now called the mineral kingdom will not exist; mineral forces will have been transformed into plant forces. The lowest kingdom appearing during the Jupiter stage will be the plant kingdom, which will have a form entirely different from what it has now. Above that will be the animal kingdom, which will have undergone a comparable transformation, followed by a human kingdom consisting of the descendants of the evil union that came about on Earth. Above these, there will be a higher human kingdom consisting of the descendants of the community of good human beings on Earth. A great deal of the work of this second human kingdom will consist in ennobling the fallen souls in the evil union so that they will still be able to find their way back into the actual human kingdom.

At the Venus stage, the plant kingdom will also have disappeared, and the lowest kingdom will be the animal kingdom, transformed once more. Above that will be three human kingdoms of different degrees of perfection. During the Venus stage, the Earth will remain united with the Sun; in contrast, as evolution proceeds on Jupiter, the Sun will once again break away from Jupiter and influence it from outside. Then a reunification of the Sun and Jupiter will take place, and the transformation into the Venus stage will gradually continue. During the Venus stage, a distinct cosmic body will break away, containing all the beings who have resisted evolution and constituting an "unredeemable moon," so to speak. It will move toward an evolution that is so different in character from anything we can experience on Earth that there are no words that can possibly express it. The part of humanity that has continued to evolve, however, will move on to the Vulcan phase of evolution in a fully spiritualized form of existence. Describing this state falls outside the scope of this book.

We see that the highest imaginable ideal of human evolution results from Grail knowledge—that is, the spiritualization that we achieve through our own work. Ultimately, this spiritualization will appear as the result of the harmony that human beings were able to bring about in the fifth and sixth cultural periods between their forces of intellect and feeling and their knowledge of supersensible worlds. What they produced there in their inmost souls will ulti-mately become the outer world. The human spirit raises itself up to the mighty impressions of its outer world, first divining and later recognizing the spiritual beings behind these impressions, while the human heart senses the infinite loftiness of this spiritual element. However, human beings can also recognize their own inner experi-ences of intellect, feeling, and morality as the seeds of a future spiri-tual world.

If we believe that human freedom is incompatible with fore-knowledge and with predestination of the shape of things to come, we should think of it like this: Our free action in the future will depend as little on what predestined things will be like then as it does on our intention to be living a year from now in a house we design today. To the extent that our inner nature permits, we will be free in the house we have built for ourselves, and we will also be free in the circumstances that come about on Venus and Jupiter to the extent that our own inner nature permits. Our freedom will not depend on what is predestined by prior circumstances, but on what our souls have made of themselves.

The Earth stage contains what evolved during the preceding Sat-urn, Sun, and Moon phases of evolution. Earthly human beings find wisdom in the events taking place around them; it is there as the result of what happened previously. The Earth is the descendant of the old Moon, which shaped itself and everything belonging to it into the cosmos of wisdom. The Earth, which is the beginning of an evolution that will inject new force into this wisdom, brings human beings to the point where they experience themselves as independent members of a spiritual world. This is due to the fact that the human "I" was fashioned by the Spirits of Form during the Earth phase of evolution, just as the physical body was shaped by the Spirits of Will on Saturn, the life body by the Spirits of Wisdom on the Sun, and the astral body by the Spirits of Motion on the Moon. That which manifests as wisdom does so through the interaction of the Spirits of Will, Wisdom, and Motion. In wisdom, earthly beings and processes can exist in harmony with the other beings of their world through the work of these three orders of spiritual beings.

In the future, the independent human "I," which was received through the Spirits of Form, will exist in harmony with the beings of Earth, Jupiter, Venus, and Vulcan because of the power that the Earth stage injects into wisdom. This is the power of love, which must begin in human beings on Earth. The "cosmos of wisdom" is developing into a "cosmos of love." Everything that the "I" can develop within itself must turn into love. The exalted Sun Being we were able to characterize in describing Christ's evolution manifests as the all-encompassing example of love, planting the seed of love in the innermost core of the human being. From there, it is meant to flow out into all of evolution. Just as wisdom, which formed earlier, discloses itself in the forces of the sense-perceptible earthly world, in present-day forces of nature, love itself will appear as a new natural force in all phenomena in the future. This is the mystery of all future evolution: that our knowledge and everything we do out of a true understanding of evolution sow seeds that must ripen into love. The greater the power of the love that comes into being, the more we will be able to accomplish creatively on behalf of the future. The strongest forces working toward the end result of spiritualization lie in what will come from love. The more spiritual knowledge flows into the evolution of humanity and the Earth, the greater the number of viable seeds there will be for the future. Through its very nature, spiritual knowledge transforms itself into love.

The whole process that has been described, beginning with the Greco-Latin cultural period and extending throughout the present time, shows how this transformation is to proceed. It also shows us the purpose of this future evolution that is now in its beginning stages. The wisdom for which the groundwork was laid on Saturn, Sun, and Moon works in the human physical, etheric, and astral bodies, presenting itself as cosmic wisdom. In the "I," however, it becomes inner wisdom. Beginning with the Earth phase of evolution, the wisdom of the outer cosmos becomes inner wisdom in the human being. Internalized in this way, it becomes the seed of love. Wisdom is the prerequisite for love; love is the result of wisdom that has been reborn in the "I."

If anyone is misled into believing that evolution as it has been explained above bears a fatalistic stamp, this is a result of having misunderstood the explanations. Anyone who believes that evolution condemns a certain number of people to become members of the kingdom of "evil humanity" has failed to see how the inter-relationship between the sense-perceptible and the soul-spiritual takes shape in the course of this evolution. Within certain limits, each of these worlds, the sense-perceptible and the soul-spiritual, constitutes a separate evolutionary current. Through forces inherent in the sense-perceptible current, the forms of "evil human beings" come about. However, it will only be necessary for any given human soul to incarnate in such a body if it has created the necessary pre-conditions itself. It might also happen that the forms arising out of the forces of the sense-perceptible world find no reincarnating human souls to embody, because these souls have all become too good for such bodies. In that case, the cosmos would have to ensoul these forms with something other than former human souls. Such forms will be occupied by human souls only when those souls have prepared themselves for such an incarnation. In this field, super-sensible cognition is bound to report what it sees—for instance, that at a particular point in the future there will be two human king-doms, one good and one evil. However, this does not mean that the present state of human souls forces supersensible cognition to the rational conclusion that this future state will be the natural and inevitable result. Supersensible cognition's ways of investigating the evolution of human forms and the evolution of the destinies of souls are and must be completely separate, and to confuse the two in our worldview would be a remnant of a materialistic attitude that would seriously impinge on the science of the supersensible.

6

THE BEING ANTHROPOSOPHIA

Berlin, February 3, 1913

... THOSE TRULY SEEKING TO ADVANCE human development must draw what they wish to give from the sources from which the advancing life of humanity itself flows. Such people cannot follow an arbitrarily constructed ideal and steer toward it merely because it pleases them. In any given period, they must follow the ideal that may be said to belong precisely to their time. *The being of Anthroposophy is intimately connected with the being of our time*—not with our own immediate little present moment, of course, but with the whole age within which we stand. The next four lectures and, indeed, all the lectures that I shall deliver in the next few days will really deal with this "being," or essence, of Anthroposophy.[1] All that I will say later about the nature of the Eastern and Western Mysteries will be an amplification of this being of Anthroposophy.

Today I want to point out the character of this being by speaking of the necessity for establishing Anthroposophy in our time. Once again, I do not wish to begin with definitions or abstractions, but with facts and, initially, one particular fact: the fact of a poem that was once—for now I shall say only once—written by a poet. I shall read part of this poem to you, just a few lines, to begin with, to bring out what I want to say.

---

1.   Those four lectures comprise *The Mysteries of the East and of Christianity*, Blauvelt, NY: Spiritual Science Library, 1989.

Love, who commands the chambers of my mind
Discoursing of my lady passionately,
From hour to hour speaks things of her to me
At which my intellect bids me demur.
Sweetly his words make music of such kind
My soul, which hears and feels how they agree,
Exclaims, "Alas, that I can never be
Equal to saying all I hear of her!"

And after the poet has sung further of the difficulty of expressing what the god of love has said to him, he describes the being he loves in the following words:

Such things appear within her fair aspect
As show they bear the joys of paradise
I mean, both in her smile and in her eyes,
Where Love brings them as if he brought them home.

It seems very clear. A poet has written a love poem. And it is certain that, if this poem were published anonymously somewhere today (it could easily be a contemporary poem by one of our better poets), people would say, "What a star he must have found to describe his beloved in such wonderful verses!" And truly the beloved might well feel congratulation at being addressed in this way:

Such things appear within her fair aspect
As show they bear the joys of paradise
I mean, both in her smile and in her eyes,
Where Love brings them as if he brought them home.

This poem was not written in our time. If it had been, and the critics discovered it, they would say, "What a deeply felt, direct, concrete living relation! It is astonishing how someone who can write poetry from the soul's depths, as only our most modern poets can, can say something in which no mere abstraction, but a direct, concrete presentment of the beloved, speaks to us and becomes a manifest reality." A critic today might say such a thing. This poem was not written today, however, but was written by Dante.[2] And the modern critic, knowing that now, would perhaps say, "The poem must have been written by Dante when he was passionately in love with Beatrice (or someone else), and this is another example of how a great figure enters life through immediate experience, far removed from any concepts or ideas." Perhaps we could even find a modern critic who would say, "People should learn from Dante the possibility of rising to the highest celestial spheres, as we do in *The Divine Comedy*, and still being able to feel a direct, living connection between one human being and another." As fortune would have it, however, Dante himself wrote an explanation of this poem and identified the woman about whom he wrote those beautiful words:

> Such things appear within her fair aspect
> As show they bear the joys of paradise
> I mean, both in her smile and in her eyes,
> Where Love brings them as if he brought them home.

Dante himself told us—and I don't think any modern critic will deny that Dante knew what he wanted to say—that the beloved lady, with whom he had so direct and personal a relationship, was none other than *Philosophy*.[3]

Dante says that when he speaks of the lady's eyes and says that what they say is no lie, he means the *evidence of truth;* and by her "smile" he means the art of *expressing the truth* communicated to the soul; and by "love," or *amor,* he means scientific study—the *love of the*

---

2.   "Love who commands the chambers of my mind," poem number 61 in *Dante's Rime*, trans. Patrick S. Diehl, Princeton: Princeton University Press, 1979.

3.   In his *Convivio* ("The Banquet") *III,* Dante explains this canzone as a panegyric to philosophy (see *Dante's Rime*, notes, p. 243).

truth. Dante explicitly says that when his personal beloved, Beatrice, was torn from him, and he was required to continue without a personal relationship, it was the lady Philosophy who drew near to his soul, full of compassion and more human than any human thing. And-feeling in his soul's depths that her "eyes" represent the evidence of truth, her "smile" the truth communicated to his soul, and "love" the love of the truth, cognitive life, or scientific study, Dante could say of this lady, Philosophy:

> Such things appear within her fair aspect
> As show they bear the joys of paradise
> I mean, both in her smile and in her eyes,
> Where Love brings them as if he brought them home.

One thing is clear: a modern poet cannot easily address philosophy with real honesty in such directly human language. If a modern poet were to do so, the critics would seize that poet by the collar and say, "No more formal allegories." Even Goethe had to suffer many people taking the allegories in Part II of *Faust* in the wrong spirit. People who do not know how the times—into which our soul is ever growing with new life—change, lack any idea that Dante was just one among many of those with the capacity for a concrete experience of a passionate and personal relationship, immediate and of the soul, with Lady Philosophy, such as we today can feel only toward a man or woman of flesh and blood. In this sense, Dante's time is past. The modern soul no longer approaches Lady Philosophy, the woman Philosophy, as a being of the same fleshly nature as itself, as Dante did. Or perhaps it is somewhat closer to the honest truth to say that Philosophy was something, or someone, who went around as a being of flesh and blood—someone with whom one could have a relationship, the expression of which could not really be distinguished from the intense words of love one would use in relation to a being of flesh and blood. Whoever enters into the whole relationship Dante had with Philosophy will know that this relationship was concrete, the kind that modern human beings can imagine only between a man and a woman.

In the age of Dante, then, Philosophy appears as a being whom Dante says he loves. And, when we look for it, we certainly find the word "philosophy" also coming to the surface in Greek spiritual life, but we will not find there what we now call "definitions," the presentations of philosophy. When the Greeks present something, it is *Sophia*, not *Philosophia*. And they present her in such a way that, again, we experience her as a living being, an immediate presence. We experience the Greek Sophia as an immediate, living being, just as Dante feels Philosophy to be. Always, however, we feel this Greek Sophia—and I ask you to please go through the descriptions that exist—to be an elemental force, as it were, an active being who intervenes in existence through action.

We find that Philosophia is first represented beginning around the fifth century C.E., initially described by poets in the most varied guises: nurse, benefactor, guide, and so on. Then somewhat later, painters begin to represent her. Thus, we reach the period during the Middle Ages called *Scholasticism*, when many philosophers really felt they were experiencing a directly human relation when they became aware of beautiful, noble Lady Phiosophia, who actually approached them from the clouds. Many medieval philosophers, in fact, felt the same deep, burning feelings for the Lady Philosophia as she bated toward them on the clouds as Dante describes for his Lady. And anyone who can feel such things will find a direct connection between Raphael's *Sistine Madonna* floating on the clouds, and the exalted Lady Philosophia.

I have often described how, in ancient times of human development, the world's spiritual relationships were still perceivable through normal human cognitive capacities. I have tried to describe how a primeval clairvoyance existed, as it were, how in primeval times everyone who developed normally was naturally constituted to see into the spiritual world. Slowly and gradually over the course of human evolution this primal clairvoyance was lost, and our present cognitive situation arose. This occurred slowly and gradually, as I say. And our contemporary life condition—which represents a temporary and very deep entanglement, as it were, in a material kind of perception—also came about gradually and slowly.

For a person such as Dante, as we may gather from his descriptions *in The Divine Comedy*, it was still possible to experience in a natural way, so to speak, the last remnant of an immediate connection with the spiritual worlds. To modern people it is merely foolish nonsense to expect that they might first, like Dante, love the Beatrice of flesh and blood and then later become involved in a second passion with Philosophy, and that these two—the Beatrice of flesh and blood and Philosophy—were very similar beings.

I have heard it said, it is true, that Kant was once in love, and that someone became jealous because Kant loved "Metaphysics" and asked, "Meta *who*?" Nevertheless, it is certainly difficult to bring enough understanding to modern spiritual life to enable people to feel Dante's Beatrice and Philosophy as equally real. But why is this? Because the once direct, immediate relationship of the human soul to the spiritual world has gradually come to what it is today. Those of you who have often heard me speak know very well the high regard I have for nineteenth-century philosophy, but even I would not suggest that anyone pour out feelings for Hegel's *Logic* by saying,

> Such things appear within her fair aspect
> As show they bear the joys of paradise
> I mean, both in her smile and in her eyes,
> Where Love brings them as if he brought them home.

It would be difficult, I think, to say this about Hegel's *Logic*. It would even be difficult, though more possible, to speak this way of the intellectual depth of Schopenhauer's worldview. It would certainly be easier in his case, but even there it would still be difficult to get any concrete idea or feeling that philosophy approaches as a concrete being in the way Dante speaks of. Times have changed.

For Dante, life within the philosophical element, within the spiritual world, was a direct, personal relationship—as personal as any relationship within what is called today the real, material world. And, strange as it may seem—because Dante's century is not so far from our own—it is nonetheless true that anyone who can observe the spiritual life of humanity feels it as almost self-evident that, although we try to know the world, if we assume that human beings have remained the same throughout the centuries, we really cannot see any farther than the ends of our noses! Even as recently as Dante's time, life in general, the whole relation of the soul to the spiritual worlds, was very different. Thus, if philosophers think that the relationship they may have with the spiritual world through the philosophy of Hegel or Schopenhauer is the only one possible, this only means that philosophers can still be very ignorant of the truth.

Let us consider what we have been presenting—that, in our evolution until the present, with the transition from the Greco-Roman epoch to our own fifth post-Atlantean epoch, the intellectual or mind soul, or the "soul of higher feeling," which developed especially during the Greco-Roman period, evolved into the consciousness soul. In light of this observation, we may ask: How in the concrete case of philosophy does the transition from the intellectual soul of the Greco-Roman epoch to the consciousness soul of our time take form? It does so in such a way that we clearly understand that during the development of the intellectual soul human beings still experienced a certain separation between themselves and the spiritual worlds from which they originate. Thus, the Greeks confronted Sophia, or Wisdom, as a being, so to speak, whom they could encounter standing before them in a particular place. Two beings then—Sophia and the Greek—faced each other, as if Sophia were a definite objective entity, to be looked at with all the objectivity of the Greek's way of seeing. At the same time, however, the Greeks, because they still lived in the intellectual soul (the soul of higher feeling), had to express the directly personal relationship of their consciousness to the objectivity of the being facing them. This was necessary to gradually prepare the way for a new epoch, that of the consciousness soul.

How then does the consciousness soul confront Sophia? This is done so that it brings the "I" into direct relationship with Sophia while at the same expressing—much more so than the objective being of Sophia—the activity of the "I" within the relationship between the consciousness soul and this Sophia.

"I love Sophia" was the natural feeling of an age that still had to encounter the being we designate as Philosophy—an age that was preparing the consciousness soul and, out of the relationship between the "I" and the consciousness soul (on which the greatest value must be placed), was working toward representing Sophia as simply as it represented everything else. It was natural for the time of the intellectual soul—which was preparing for the consciousness soul—to express this relationship to Philosophy. And because things came to expression slowly and gradually, this relationship was being prepared during Greco-Latin times. Outwardly, however, we can also see this relationship of human beings to Philosophia developing to a certain height in the pictorial representations of Philosophy floating down on clouds and, later, in Philosophia's *expression* (even if she bears another name) when we see her gaze full of kindly feelings that once again express the relationship to the consciousness soul.

In truth, it was from a specifically human personal relationship, like that of a man to a woman, that the relationship of human beings to philosophy arose during the age when philosophy directly took hold of the whole spiritual life of human evolution. This relationship, if you do not take these words lightly, but take a little time to find the meaning behind them, has grown cold, truly cold. It has even become ice-cold. When we pick up most books on philosophy today, even those by philosophers who struggled and attained the finest possible relation to philosophy, we must really say that the relationship, so ardent when people viewed Philosophy as a personal being, has grown very cold. Philosophy is no longer the "woman" she was to Dante and others who lived in his time. Philosophy meets us today in a shape we may speak of by saying, "The very form of philosophy that confronts us in the nineteenth century, in its highest development—as German idealism, the philosophy of concepts, the philosophy of objects—shows us that its role in the spiritual development of humanity has been played out." It is really very symbolic when we take up Hegel's philosophy, especially *The Encyclopedia*, and find that the last thing presented in this nineteenth-century volume is about how philosophy understands itself. It has comprehended everything else; finally, it grasps itself. What is left for it to understand? This is a symptom of philosophy's end, even though many questions remain unanswered since Hegel's death. The radical thinker Richard Wahle has followed this thought through in his book *The Whole of Philosophy and its End*, and he has ably worked through the thesis that everything achieved by philosophy may be divided among the various departments of physiology, biology, aesthetics, and so forth, and that when this has been done, nothing remains of philosophy. Of course, such books go too far, but they contain a deep truth—that spiritual movements have their time and day, and that, just as a day has its morning and its evening, spiritual movements, too, have their morning and evening in the history of humanity's development.

We know we are living in the age that is preparing the *Spirit Self*. Thus, we know that, though we live in the age of the consciousness soul, the Spirit Self is being prepared. Just as the Greeks lived in the age of the intellectual soul and looked toward the dawn of the consciousness soul, so we live in the age of the consciousness soul and seek to prepare the age of the Spirit Self. The Greeks established philosophy, which, despite Paul Deussen and others, did first exist in Greece during the unfolding of the intellectual soul when human beings still directly experienced the lingering influence of the objective Sophia; and Philosophy then came into being, and Dante could view her as a real, concrete being who brought him consolation when Beatrice was torn from him by death. In the same way, we now live in the age of the consciousness soul and look toward the dawn of the age of the Spirit Self, and we know in this way that something is again becoming objective to human beings—something that looks forward to the coming times that will be gained by what we have won through the time of the consciousness soul.

What, therefore, must be developed? It must unfold that, once again, as a matter of course, a "Sophia" becomes present. But we must learn to relate this Sophia to the consciousness soul, bring her down directly to human beings. This is happening during the age of the consciousness soul. And thereby Sophia becomes the being who directly enlightens human beings. After Sophia has entered human beings, she must take their being with her and present it to them outwardly, objectively. Thus, Sophia will be drawn into the human soul and arrive at the point of being so inwardly connected with it that a love poem as beautiful as the one Dante wrote may be written about her.

Sophia will become objective again, but she will take with her what humanity is, and objectively present herself in this form. Thus, she will present herself not only as Sophia, but as *Anthroposophia*—as the Sophia who, after passing through the human soul, through the very being of the human being, henceforth bears that being within her. And in this form she will confront enlightened human beings as the objective being Sophia who once stood before the Greeks.

Such is the progression of human evolutionary history in relation to the spiritual questions we have been considering. Here I must leave the matter to all those who wish to examine in even greater detail, following the destiny of Sophia, Philosophia, and Anthroposophia, how we may show how humanity develops progressively through those parts of the soul we call the intellectual soul, the consciousness soul, and the Spirit Self. People will learn how profoundly what Anthroposophy gives us is based in our whole being. What we receive through Anthroposophy is our *very own being*. This once floated toward us in the form of a celestial goddess with whom we were able to enter into relationship. This divine being lived on as

Sophia and Philosophia, and now we can once again bring her out of ourselves and place her before us as the fruit of true anthroposophical self-knowledge. We can wait patiently until the world is willing to test the depth of the foundations of what we have to say, right down to the smallest details. It is the essence of Anthroposophy that its own being consists of the being of the human being, and its effectiveness, its reality, consists in that we receive from Anthroposophy what we ourselves are and what we must place before ourselves, because we must practice self-knowledge.

7

THE GIFTS OF ISIS

Berlin, February 5, 1913

THOSE WHO GO THROUGH OCCULT TRAINING enter thereby into the spiritual worlds. They experience certain facts there. They meet with beings. The expression "to see the Sun at Midnight" is really only an expression for such a spiritual fact—for meeting spiritual beings who are related to the level of the Sun or solar existence.

When we ascend into higher worlds, we undergo certain experiences. When we do so, we experience much that is meaningful, but we also feel forsaken and alone. One could sum up these experiences as follows: You see a great deal, but what you most long for—precisely that you cannot experience.

After such an ascent, you would like to question all the beings you have met about the secrets you yearn for. That is the feeling you have. But all the beings who unveil so much that is immense and powerful remain dumb and silent at the very moment when you want to learn from them about the mysteries which you feel afterward are the most important of all.

Hence, today those who have risen to the higher worlds feel it to be the most painful thing that—despite the splendor, despite meeting with glorious beings—they still have an immense *emptiness* in their inner being. If nothing else were to happen, a protracted experience of this loneliness, this forlorn condition in the higher worlds, would finally bring about something like despair in one's soul.

But then something may take place—and usually does if the ascent has been undertaken according to the laws of initiation—

which may be a protection from this despair, at least in the first instance, though not permanently. What may occur is something like a remembrance, a memory entering the soul, or one might say a retrospect of the far-off times of the past, a kind of reading in the Akashic records about things long since past. One can characterize these things only by trying to clothe them in words that approximately cover the experiences. Clothed in such words, what a person experiences may be described as follows: When you as a modern human being ascend into higher worlds you are met by forlornness and despair. But images present you with certain events long past, showing you that in past times others ascended into the worlds into which you now desire to rise. In what you now behold as in a memory, you can recognize that your own soul in earlier incarnations participated in what people in ancient times experienced when they rose into the higher worlds.

It might even seem that what the soul today sees in far distant times is its own experiences in those past ages—in which case that soul would have been an initiate then. If this does not happen, such a soul would know that it was related to those who had risen into the higher worlds as initiates in ancient times. But now it feels lonely and forsaken, whereas those souls once initiated did not feel lonely and forsaken in the same worlds, but experienced innermost bliss. One can recognize that this was so because in those ancient times souls were differently constituted. Owing to these different predispositions, they experienced what they beheld in the higher worlds differently.

What does one actually experience? Beings of higher worlds, working upon the sense world from the supersensible worlds, are brought before the soul. One perceives the beings that stand behind our sense world. If one were to try to summarize what one sees one could characterize it as follows.

You feel yourself to be in the higher worlds. You are gazing down, as it were, into the sense world. You feel yourself somehow united with those spirits who have passed through the gate of death.

With them you gaze downward and see how they will use their forces to enter physical existence. You look down and see how forces are sent out of the supersensible worlds to bring about the processes of the different kingdoms of nature in the sense world. You see the whole current of events prepared for our world out of the higher worlds. Because when you are in the spiritual world you are outside your physical and etheric bodies, you look down upon them and see the forces in the cosmos, in the whole spiritual universe, that are working there on human physical and etheric bodies. Through the activity of the beings whose company you have entered, you learn to understand how the physical and etheric bodies come into existence in the physical world. You learn to understand this. You learn to understand how certain beings associated with the Sun send their activity into the Earth and work on the production of the physical and etheric bodies. You learn, too, to know certain beings associated with the Moon who work down out of the cosmos to cooperate on the production of human physical and etheric bodies.

Then, however, a great longing arises, a yearning that for a person of the present time becomes frightful. This is the longing to know something of the way the astral body and the "I" are born out of the cosmos, how they come into existence. Whereas one can see exactly how the physical body and the etheric body arise out of the forces of the cosmos, everything that could in any way guide us to understand how the astral body and the human "I" are produced is hidden. Everything that has to do with the astral body and "I" is veiled in the deepest darkness and secrecy. Thus the feeling grows that what you are in your innermost nature, what you yourself really are, is veiled from your spiritual sight, while what you are enveloped in when you are in the physical world is disclosed to you in full.

Human beings today experience all this when they rise to higher worlds. Those who undertook the ascent in ancient times also experienced it, but today we feel that great longing just described, which the souls of the past eras did not feel because they had no necessity for beholding their innermost being. They were so constituted that they felt inner satisfaction when they saw the beings engaged in the construction of the physical and etheric bodies. Souls initiated in past times experienced the highest satisfaction when they saw how spiritual beings worked down from the Sun to produce the physical and etheric bodies. However, in those ancient times this work performed by those beings presented itself in a different aspect. This explains the satisfaction. Today this work appears in such a way that one has to ask, Why all this preparation of the physical and etheric bodies if one cannot understand what these sheaths conceal? This is the difference between people today and those of old.

The period I am talking about with regard to these experiences is the time when Zoroaster initiated his disciples and guided them into the higher worlds. If students today were to be led into the higher worlds in the same way Zoroaster's were, they would feel that emptiness and loneliness referred to above. In Zoroaster's time those who were to be initiated experienced the working of Ahura Mazda on the physical body and the etheric body. As this wonderful mystery was unveiled they felt bliss and satisfaction, because they were constituted in such a way that they felt stirred inwardly when they saw how the sheaths we need if we are to accomplish our earthly mission come into existence. They found satisfaction in this.

Such was the Zoroastrian initiation. In this initiation, one could "see the Sun at Midnight." That is, those who were initiated did not look upon the physical form of the Sun, but upon the beings that are linked with the Sun. They saw the emanation of the forces that play into the physical body from the Sun. They saw how the forces that the Sun can send forth mold the human head and form the different parts of the human brain—for it would be folly for anyone to think that a marvelous construction like the human brain could come into existence merely through earthly forces. On the contrary, solar forces must work into them. These forces assembled the distinct lobular formation of the brain, which extends over the human face. Indeed, not only one but quite a number of beings work on the construction of the human brain. Zoroaster called these beings

"Amshaspands." They furnish the stimulus for the cosmic forces by which the human brain (including the upper nerves of the spinal cord, except the lower twenty-eight pairs of nerves) is constructed. Zoroaster also pointed out how other currents flow from beings linked with the life of the Moon. He showed how, in a truly wonderful way, the structure of the cosmos is adapted, and how from twenty-eight groups of entities—"Izeds" as they are called—currents are produced that build up the spinal cord with its twenty-eight lower pairs of nerve fibers. Thus the physical and etheric bodies are formed out of currents that stream forth from cosmic beings. Such were the mighty impressions that the initiates of Zoroaster received.

They received these impressions as the expression of the work of Ahura Mazda and felt inner bliss about what takes place in the world. If human beings today were to raise themselves in the same way into the higher worlds they would, of course, be capable of wonder. They, too, would be able to begin to experience bliss. But they would gradually pass on to the feeling that can only be clothed in words like these: "What is the purpose of it all? I know nothing about the being that passes from incarnation to incarnation! I know solely about those beings who in each new incarnation build up the sheaths out of the cosmos, but only the sheaths." Precisely that was the essence of the Zoroastrian initiation. It was the revelation of the connection between the earthly part of a human being and the life of the Sun. It was a characteristic of Zoroaster's time that people were able to absorb into their occult science the mysteries we have just described.

Souls in ancient Egypt—souls, for example, who went through the Hermes initiation—entered the higher worlds in a different way. When the Hermes initiation raised souls in ancient Egypt into the higher worlds, they felt themselves outside their physical and etheric bodies, and knew they were now in a world of spiritual facts and spiritual beings. The circuit of vision through which these souls were then led was wide. They were shown the individual beings and facts in detail, as might also happen to souls today. We must not imagine this as though they walked on physical feet. Their vision was guided, they wrestled with everything, and their sight was led into a region as wide as the universe. Then came a moment of experience. They felt as though they had to come to the end—as though they had been traveling in a country bounded by the sea and they had reached the shore. They knew they had come to the farthest point attainable. They experienced what can only be clothed in these words: "While you have been led in vision through cosmic spaces in regions of the wide universe, you have come to know the beings and forces that can be said to work on your physical and etheric bodies. Now you are entering the most holy places. Now you are entering a region where you really feel united with the being who works on that in you which goes from one incarnation to another— your astral body." A significant experience takes place at this point, for all things become to a certain extent different after it.

Immediately following this experience, one thing is no longer possible for those initiated. In the world they now enter on the shores of cosmic existence, they can no longer make use of their former standards of thought and powers of judgment. If they cannot divest themselves of all physical, earthly powers of judgment, if they cannot ignore what has led them so far, they cannot have this experience on the borderland of existence. They will not be able to feel united with the being who is active when the spiritual-psychic human being approaches birth into a new incarnation and seeks a nation, family, and parents to clothe itself in. All the beings the initiates have already come to know, who explain how the etheric and physical sheaths arise and are formed out of the cosmos, cannot explain what kind of forces are working in that being with whom they now feel united. Those other beings cannot explain the being building and weaving in the innermost astral being of the person. It becomes apparent to the seer, as it was apparent to the Egyptian soul going through Hermes initiation, that after the soul is outside its sheaths and has passed through the "cosmic existence," it feels itself united with a being. The soul can sense the qualities of this being only it feels itself as if within those qualities and not outside the being. The soul can know this being is really there, but at the same time it can know that it is within the being.

The first impression the candidate for initiation receives of this being is expressed in words as follows: The forces that bring the soul from one incarnation to another, as well as those that illuminate the soul between death and a new birth, lie within this being. But then a force like cosmic warmth surges toward you that conveys the soul from death to a new birth, and spiritual light surges toward you that illumines souls between death and a new birth. Then you feel how this warmth and this light stream from the being with which you are united. Now you are in a quite peculiar situation. You had to drink the cup of Lethe. You had to forget the art of understanding that formerly guided you through the physical world. You had to lay aside your former power of judgment, your intellectuality. For these would only lead you astray. But you have as yet gained nothing of a new kind. In the experience of the cosmic warmth that brings the soul to a new birth, you are within the sea of forces that illuminates the soul between death and a new birth. You experience the force and the light that issue from this being. You behold the being in such a way that you can only ask of it, "Who are you? For you alone can tell me who you are, and only then can I know what takes the essential part of me as a human being from death to a new birth. Only when you tell me can I know what my innermost nature is as a human being!"

But the being—with whom you know you are united—remains mute. You feel in the deepest part that you are united with the deepest part of the being. The urge for self-knowledge, to know what a human being is, rises—and yet the being remains silent. One must first stand for a while before this silent being, and feel deeply the longing to have the riddle of the universe solved in a new way, as it can never be done on the physical Earth. One must bring into this world, to this being, as a force out of oneself, the deep longing to have the riddle of the universe solved in this way, a way alien to physical existence. The soul must live entirely in the longing to have the enigma of the cosmos solved in this manner. Thus when one has felt oneself united with the mute spiritual being, and has lived in him longing for the solution we have described, then one feels that the force of one's own longing streams forth into this spiritual being with whom one is united. As this force of one's own longing for the solution of the riddle streams out into the spiritual being, it gives birth after a time to something like another being projected from it. What is born is not born like an earthly birth. One knows this at once by one's own vision. An earthly birth arises "in time," is accomplished in the course of time. But in this case, with regard to this being, one knows that the projection is born from him, but has been born from him since primordial times. It has always been born from him, and this birth has always been ongoing from primordial ages right up to the present. But until now this birth process of one being from another has not been visible to humanity. Until now it has been withheld from its sight. The birth process consists in this: it is really continuous, but now, because they have prepared themselves through their yearning to solve the riddle, human beings see it. It is now to be perceived in the spiritual world. One knows this is so. Therefore, witnessing this, one does not say to oneself, "Now a being is born." Rather, one thinks: "From the being with whom I am united, a being has always been born since primordial times; but now the process of the being's birth, and the being itself who is born, are perceptible to me."

What I have now pictured for you as far as it is possible in the words of our language is that to which the Hermes initiator led his pupils. And the feelings that I have just described (with halting words I might say, for the things contain so much that the words of our tongue can express them only in a halting way) were the experiences of the so-called Egyptian Isis initiation. The candidates undergoing Isis initiation reached the shore of universal existence. They gazed upon the beings that build up the physical body and the etheric body. They stood before the silent Goddess from whom warmth and light comes forth for the creation of the innermost part of the human soul. Then the candidates thought as follows: "That is Isis. That is the mute, silent Goddess whose countenance cannot be unveiled to one who sees only with mortal eyes. The countenance of Isis can be unveiled only to those who have worked themselves through to the shores of universal existence. Then they can see with eyes that endure from incarnation to incarnation and are no longer mortal. *For an impenetrable veil hides the form of Isis from mortal eyes.*"

When candidates had thus gazed on Isis and had experienced this feeling in their soul, they understood what has been described as the "birth." What was this birth? Candidates understood it as what may be called the resounding of the Music of the Spheres through all space. We may also describe it as the merging of the tones of this music with what is called the creative cosmic Word. This is the Word that permeates space and pours into beings all that has to be poured into them, as the soul has to be poured into the physical and etheric bodies after passing through the life between death and a new birth. Everything that has to be thus poured out from the spiritual world into the physical world, so that it may partake of a psychic, inner character, is poured in from the Harmony of the Spheres resounding through space. The Harmony of the Spheres gradually assumes such a form that it can be understood in its inner significance as the cosmic Word. This Word ensouls the beings who are vitalized by the forces of warmth and light that pour themselves into those arising from the divine forces and beings perceived with the vision already attained.

Thus did candidates of the Isis initiation look into the world of the Harmony of the Spheres, the world of the cosmic Word. Thus did they look into the world that is the true home of the human soul while it is living between death and a new birth. What is hidden deep in physical earthly human existence, veiling itself in the physical world as the world of the Harmony of the Spheres and the cosmic Word, lives between death and a new birth in the splendor of the light and warmth. In the Hermes initiation, it is experienced as the birth from Isis. There Isis stands before one, Isis herself on the one side, and on the other side the other being she has borne, whom one must address as cosmic tones and the cosmic Word. One feels oneself in the companionship of Isis and of the cosmic Word born of her. And this "cosmic Word" is, in the first place, the appearing of Osiris. "Isis in association with Osiris"—thus do they appear before direct vision. In the most ancient Egyptian initiation it was said that Osiris was both the spouse and son of Isis. And in that initiation the essential thing was that through it the candidate experienced the mysteries of psychic existence, which remains united with us when we pass between death and a new birth. Through the union with Osiris it was possible to recognize oneself in one's deeper significance as a human being.

What has been described brought it to pass that the Egyptian initiates met the cosmic Word and the cosmic tones as the elucidators of their own being in the spiritual world. That happened up to a certain point of time in the old Egyptian period—and only until then. Then it ceased. And as is evidenced also when one looks back today into ancient times by investigations into the Akashic records, there is a great difference between the experiences of the Egyptian initiate in the ancient Egyptian temples and what humans experienced later.

Let us bring before our souls what initiates experienced in those later stages. Then they could also be led through the vast spaces of the universe to the confines of existence. There they could meet with all the beings that construct the human physical and etheric bodies. They could approach the shores of being and could have the vision of the mute, silent Isis. They could apprehend in her the warmth being that contains the forces that lead human beings from death to a new birth. They could also come to know the light that illumines the soul between death and a new birth. For them, too, the longing arose to hear the cosmic Word and the cosmic harmony. This longing lived in their souls when they united themselves with the mute, silent Isis. But the Goddess remained dumb and silent!

In the later ages, no Osiris could be born. No cosmic harmony resounded. No cosmic Word expounded what now merely showed itself as cosmic warmth and cosmic light. In those later times, the souls of candidates for initiation could have expressed their experiences only by saying something like the following: "Thus, O Goddess, do I look up in grief to you. I am tormented by the thirst for knowledge, the yearning for knowledge. But you remain silent and speechless to the tormented and sorrow-laden soul that, because it cannot understand itself, seems to itself as if it were extinguished— obliterated to such a degree that it must lose its existence."

Sad was the Goddess's countenance, expressing thereby that she had become powerless to bring forth the cosmic Word and the cosmic harmony. One saw in her that she had been deprived of the power to bring forth and to have at her side Osiris as her son and spouse. One felt that Osiris had been torn from Isis.

Those who went through this initiation and came back into the physical world had a serious but resigned worldview. They knew her, Holy Isis, but they felt themselves to be "Sons of the Widow," and the world outlook of the "Sons of the Widow" was serious and resigned.

What occurred between the old initiation in which one was able to experience the birth of Osiris in the ancient Egyptian Mysteries and that later time when one met only the mute, silent mourning Isis and became a "Son of the Widow" in the Egyptian Mysteries? What happened during the time that separates the two phases of the Egyptian initiation? It was the time when Moses lived. For the karma of Egypt was fulfilled in such a way that Moses was not only initiated into the Mysteries of Egypt, but also took them with him. When he led his people out of Egypt, he took with him the part of the Egyptian initiation that added the Osiris initiation to the mourning Isis as she later became. Such was the transition from the Egyptian civilization to that of the Old Testament. Truly, Moses carried away the secret of Osiris, the secret of the cosmic Word! And if he had not left behind the impotent Isis, that which had to resound for him could not have resounded in the way necessary for him to understand it for the sake of his people: that great significant Word of the "I AM THE I AM. Thus the Egyptian Mystery was carried over into the ancient Hebrew Mystery.

I have tried to portray in words suited to such matters what the experiences were like in the Mysteries of Zoroaster and of Egypt. These things do not lend themselves to intellectual presentation. The essential thing is that the soul goes through experiences corresponding to what I have endeavored to describe. And it is important to enter into what took place in the soul of the candidates in later Egyptian initiation. It is important to enter into the experience of how they raised their souls into the higher worlds and met Isis with her sad mien and sorrow-stricken countenance. She showed this because she had to look upon the human soul, which was capable of feeling yearning and thirst for knowledge of the spiritual worlds, but could not be satisfied.

Thus also certain Greek initiates experienced the same being the Egyptians spoke of as the later Isis. Hence the seriousness of the Greek initiation where it appears in its solemnity. For what was it that was perceived by those about to be initiated? What had been experienced in earlier times in the supersensible worlds—what gave meaning to those supersensible worlds in that they resounded to the cosmic Word and cosmic tone—was now no longer there. The supersensible worlds were as though desolate and forsaken by the cosmic Word. The cosmic Word had forsaken those worlds humans had been able to enter in earlier initiation. The Zoroastrian initiates were able to feel satisfied when confronted in these worlds by those beings I have spoken of. They still felt satisfied by the cosmic light that they perceived as Ahura Mazda. They perceived it as masculine, of solar nature; the Egyptians perceived it as feminine, or lunar. Those who ascended higher in the Zoroastrian initiation also perceived the cosmic Word. They did not experience it so concretely as if born from such a being as Isis but they experienced it and knew the sphere of harmony and the cosmic Word.

In the later Egyptian time—and also in other lands during this late Egyptian time—when humans raised themselves into the higher worlds, they felt what a person today feels. People today rise up into the higher worlds. They become acquainted with all the beings that have to cooperate on the production of the physical and etheric bodies. And they feel forsaken and alone if nothing else appears than what has been said, because they have something in themselves that yearns for the cosmic Word and the cosmic harmony, and the cosmic Word and the cosmic harmony cannot resound today. Today we feel lonely and forsaken. In later Egyptian times people did not feel merely forsaken and desolate. If they were true "Sons of the Widow," that is to say if they were out of the physical and etheric bodies and in the spiritual worlds, they felt in a way that can only be described as follows: "The God prepared himself to leave the worlds you have always trodden when you felt the cosmic Word. The God has ceased to be active there." More and more this feeling condensed into what one may call the supersensible equivalent of what one encounters in the sense world as a person dies, when one knows he or she is passing out of the physical world. When the initiates of later Egyptian times rose up into the higher worlds they were partakers in the God's gradual dying. As one feels with a person who is passing into the spiritual world, so the initiates of the later Egyptian period felt how the God took leave of the spiritual world in order to pass over into another world.

The significant, remarkable part of later Egyptian initiation was that people really raised their life into the spiritual worlds, not into rapture and bliss, but in order to take part in the gradual decrease of a God who was present in these higher worlds as cosmic Word and cosmic sound.

Out of this frame of mind, the myth of "Osiris," who was torn away from Isis and conveyed to Asia, and for whom Isis lamented, gradually condensed. . . .

8

From the Fifth Gospel

I

OSLO, OCTOBER 6, 1913

YESTERDAY WE TURNED OUR ATTENTION to the period in the life of Jesus of Nazareth from about his twelfth year to his late twenties. You will certainly have realized from what I was able to tell you that this period brought much that was of profound significance, not only for the soul of Jesus of Nazareth but for the whole of human evolution. Your study of spiritual science will have shown that everything in the evolution of humanity is interconnected, and that an event of such importance in the life of a human soul so deeply bound up with the destiny of the human race is also important for the whole of evolution. Our studies are helping us to see the significance of the Golgotha event for human evolution from many different points of view. This particular course of lectures is intended to present the aspect we can gain by looking at the life of Jesus Christ. And so, having turned our minds yesterday to the period between his twelfth year and his baptism by John, we will turn once again to the soul of Jesus of Nazareth and consider what lived in this soul after the significant events that led up to his twenty-eighth or twenty-ninth year.

We may perhaps begin to get a feeling for this from the description of a scene that took place when Jesus of Nazareth was in his late twenties. It concerns a talk between Jesus of Nazareth and his mother—the woman who had been his mother for many years since the two families had become one. A deep and intimate understanding had developed between Jesus and this mother, far closer than his relationship to the other members of the family who lived in the Nazareth house. Jesus himself would have understood them, but they did not quite know what to make of him. Even in earlier years he and his mother had discussed many of the impressions that had gradually taken shape in him.

At the period in his life of which we are speaking, a memorable talk took place that lets us see very deeply into his soul. The experiences we spoke of yesterday had changed Jesus of Nazareth; infinite wisdom was now expressed in his very countenance. But as is always the case, though generally to a lesser degree, it had brought him inner sadness. The first fruit of his wisdom, the penetrating insight he was able to have into people around him, brought him deep sorrow. And whenever he had a quiet hour his thoughts turned more and more to something quite specific—to the great inner change, the revolution, that came in his twelfth year when the Zoroaster "I" passed into his own soul. He realized that in the early years following that event he had been aware only of the immense riches of this Zoroaster soul within him. In his late twenties he did not yet know that he was the reincarnated Zoroaster, but he did know there had been a tremendous change in his inner life. Now he often felt how different his life had been before that change.

Thinking back to those times he remembered the infinite warmth of heart that had been his. As a boy he had been inwardly quite detached from the world. He had been keenly sensitive to everything that speaks to human beings from the world of nature, aware of the whole greatness and splendor of nature. But he took little interest in anything taught in school! It would be quite wrong to think that up to his twelfth year, before Zoroaster entered his soul, this Jesus child had been particularly gifted or clever in the conventional sense. But he was uncommonly gentle and mild, capable of infinite love, with a deep, sensitive inwardness. He had real understanding for all that is human but no interest at all in the knowledge amassed through the centuries.

It seemed as if at that moment in the temple at Jerusalem all this had rushed out of his soul and all wisdom had streamed in to replace it. Now he was often mindful of how, before his twelfth year, his connection with the deeper spirit of the universe had been very different, as if his soul had been open to the depths of infinite space. His thoughts would go back to what his life had been like since his twelfth year, when he found himself able, in a way, to assimilate Hebrew learning, though this seemed to well up quite spontaneously in his soul. He would recall how he had been deeply shaken to discover that the Bath Kol could no longer inspire people the way it did before. Then, in his travels, all the different nuances of pagan knowledge and religious life had become known to him. He remembered how between his eighteenth and twenty-fourth years he had been in contact with the external achievements of humanity and how in his twenty-fourth year he had joined the Essene community and studied their secret doctrine and the people who dedicated their lives to it. His thoughts would often turn to those years.

But he also knew that it was only the store of knowledge people had accumulated from ancient times that had arisen in his soul— treasures of human wisdom, human culture, and moral achievements. He felt that from his twelfth year he had lived in all that was human on Earth. Now, however, he often recalled the time before he reached his twelfth year when he felt as if united with the divine grounds of existence, when everything in him was pristine, spontaneous, welling up from a warm and loving heart that united him closely with others. Now he felt lonely and isolated and had fallen into silence.

All these feelings led to a particular conversation between Jesus of Nazareth and the individual who was a mother to him. She loved him deeply and she had often spoken to him of the beauty and greatness of all the gifts that had shown themselves in him from his twelfth year. The relationship between him and his stepmother had become progressively closer, more noble and beautiful, but even to her he had never spoken of his inner conflict, and she had seen only what was great and beautiful. She had seen him grow wiser and wiser as he penetrated more and more deeply into the whole of human evolution. Much was new to her, therefore, in this talk, which was a kind of general confession, but she received it with a warm and tender heart. She had a kind of immediate understanding of his sadness, the mood in which he yearned for everything he had been before his twelfth year. And so she tried to comfort him by speaking of all the noble and splendid gifts of which he had given evidence since then. She reminded him of everything she had learned from him about the renewal of the great Jewish doctrines, judgments, and treasures of the law. She spoke of all that had revealed itself through him. But his heart grew heavy as his mother was speaking in this way, prizing so highly what he himself felt he had inwardly grown beyond. Finally he said to her, "Be that as it may, but if I or someone else were able to renew all the spiritual treasures of ancient Hebrew wisdom, what would this signify for humanity? All this is, in reality, meaningless today. If there were still people with ears to hear the wisdom of the ancient prophets, then it would be of value to them if that wisdom could be revived. Yet if Elijah himself were to come today"—so said Jesus of Nazareth— "and proclaim to present-day humanity the best of what he learned in the realms of heaven, there would be no one with ears to hear the wisdom of Elijah, nor of the older prophets, of Moses or anyone else, as far back as Abraham. Everything these prophets would have to proclaim would fall on deaf ears today. Their words would be preached to the winds. Everything I have and hold in my soul has therefore become valueless."

This was the sense in which Jesus of Nazareth spoke. He also spoke of someone who only recently had been a great teacher, yet his words had made no real impact. For, Jesus said, although the old sage Hillel [c. 60 B.C.E–10 C.E.] could not equal the ancient prophets, he was nevertheless a great and profound teacher. Jesus knew well what Hillel had meant to many of the Jewish people, having gained considerable authority as a teacher even in the difficult times of Herod. His soul had been full of great wisdom. And Jesus knew how little heed had been paid to the heartfelt words Hillel had spoken. Nevertheless it was said that Hillel had restored the Torah, the oldest codex of Hebrew law, which had been lost to the people. He brought the original Hebrew wisdom back to life. He would also walk through the land like a true teacher of wisdom. Mildness was his main character trait and he was like a kind of Messiah. All this is narrated in the Talmud and can be confirmed in the ordinary way. People were full of praise for Hillel and had much good to say of him. I can only mention a few things to indicate the mood and vein in which Jesus of Nazareth spoke of Hillel to his mother. Hillel is described as a man of mild and gentle character who achieved tremendous things through this very gentleness and loving kindness.

One story that has been preserved about him shows him to have been preeminently a kind and patient man, ready to meet anyone who came to him. Two men once had a wager on the possibility of rousing Hillel to anger, for it was known that no one could ever make him angry. One of the two men said, "I will go to any lengths to make Hillel angry." If he achieved this, he would win the bet. At a time when Hillel was particularly busy, much involved in his preparations for the Sabbath, a time when someone like him really should not be disturbed, the man knocked on his door, and without any politeness or using the proper form of address—Hillel was the president of the highest ecclesiastical court and used to being treated with respect—shouted, "Hillel, come to the door, come to the door quickly!" Hillel put on his coat and came to the door. The man said brusquely, "Hillel, I have a question." Hillel replied, "My son, what is your question?" "I want to know why the Babylonians have such narrow heads." Hillel said in the mildest of tones, "The Babylonians have narrow heads because their midwives lack in skill." The man went away, thinking to himself that this time Hillel had remained unruffled. A few minutes later he came back again and called out gruffly, "Hillel, come to the door. I have an important question!" Hillel put on his coat again, came to the door and said, "Well, my son, what is your question?" "I want to know why the Arabs have such small eyes." Hillel answered mildly, "The vastness of the desert makes their eyes small; they get small from looking out on the great desert." Again Hillel had remained unruffled, and the man was getting concerned about winning his bet. He therefore returned a third time, calling out in a gruff voice, "Hillel, come to the door. I have an important question to ask you." Hillel put on his coat, came to the door, and asked as mildly as before, "My son, what do you wish to know?" "I want to know why the Egyptians have such flat feet." "Because the ground there is so swampy," answered Hillel, and calmly returned to his work. Some minutes later the man returned and said to Hillel that he did not have a question to ask this time, but he had laid a bet that he would make him angry and he did not know how to achieve this. Hillel answered mildly, "My son, it is better for you to lose your bet than for Hillel to lose his temper."

The legend is told to show how kind and gentle Hillel was with everyone who importuned him. Such a man, said Jesus of Nazareth to his mother, is in many respects like the prophets of old; many of his utterances sound like a revival of the ancient wisdom of the prophets. Jesus cited some beautiful things Hillel had said and then continued: "People say Hillel is like an ancient prophet who has come again. I take a special interest in him because it is dawning on me that there is a special connection between him and me; it seems to me that the knowledge I have, and everything that lives in me as a great spiritual revelation, does not come from Judaism alone." And that was also true in Hillel's case. He was born a Babylonian and only came to Judaism later. He, too, was of the House of David, connected with it from ancient times, just as Jesus of Nazareth and his kinsmen were. And Jesus went on to say: "If I, also a son of the House of David, were to do as Hillel did and utter the sublime revelations that have brought enlightenment to my soul and are the same sublime revelations as were given to the Hebrews of old, none would have the ears to hear today."

Pain had entered deeply into Jesus' heart because he knew that in times past the Hebrew people had been told the greatest truths in the world, and their bodies had been such that they could understand those revelations. Now times had changed and so had the bodies of the Hebrew people, so that they could no longer understand the revelations of the Fathers.

As if to sum up everything he had to say on the subject, Jesus told his mother: "The revelation of ancient Judaism is no longer suitable for the Earth, for the old Jews have passed away; the ancient revelation must be considered worthless on Earth today."

Strangely enough, his mother listened calmly to what he had to say about the worthlessness of what she held most sacred. But she loved him tenderly, and in her inmost heart she was able to understand something of what he had to tell her. He then went on to tell her how he had wandered into pagan places of worship and what he had experienced there. He remembered how he had fallen to the ground when standing at the pagan altar, and how he had heard the Bath Kol in its altered form. And then something like a memory of the ancient Zoroastrian teachings came back to him. He did not yet know with certainty that he bore the Zoroaster soul in him, but the old Zoroastrian wisdom, the old Zoroaster impulse rose up within him during the talk. Together with his mother he experienced the reality of this mighty impulse. All the beauty and glory of the ancient Sun wisdom rose up in him. And he remembered that when he had lain by the pagan altar he had heard something like a revelation. The words of the altered Bath Kol had come to him—I spoke them for you yesterday—and he repeated them to his mother:

Amen.
Evils reign,
Bearing witness both to I-ness
Separating itself
And to selfhood's guilt—
Incurred through others
Experienced in the daily bread,
Wherein the will of the heavens
Does not reign,
Because humanity has separated itself
From Your kingdom,
And forgot Your names,
You Fathers in the heavens.

All the greatness of the Mithras worship came before his soul with these words, rising as though from an inner genius. He spoke at length to his mother about the grandeur and glory of the old paganism, about how the separate ancient Mysteries of Asia Minor and southern Europe had merged in the Mithras cult. Yet he also had a dreadful inner feeling of how that ancient religion had gradually changed and fallen prey to the demonic powers he himself had experienced in his twenty-fourth year. Everything he had experienced at the time came back to him. It appeared that the ancient Zoroaster wisdom, too, was something to which people of his own time were no longer receptive. For the second time he said significant words to his mother: "Even if all the old Mysteries were revived and with them everything that had once been so great in the pagan Mysteries, the people no longer exist who could hear it. All those things are of no avail. If I were to go and proclaim to people the changed message of the Bath Kol which I heard, if I were to make known the secret of why people are no longer able to live in communion with the Mysteries when in physical life, or if I were to proclaim the ancient Sun wisdom of Zoroaster, the people no longer exist who would be able to understand. Today all this would turn into demonic nature in people, for it would resound in them but they would not have the ears to hear. People are no longer able to hear what was once proclaimed and heard."

Jesus of Nazareth now knew that the changed voice of the Bath Kol he had heard call out to him the words "Amen, the Evils hold sway" was ancient sacred teaching. One all-powerful prayer had been said in all the Mystery places, but it had since been forgotten. He now knew that something of the ancient Mystery wisdom had been given to him when he had been out of his body at the pagan altar. Yet he also realized, and said so to his mother, that it was not possible for people of his time to gain understanding of those Mysteries.

Continuing the talk with his mother, he spoke of the things he had learned among the Essenes. He spoke of the beauty, greatness, and glory of their doctrine, and remembered their gentleness and sweet temper. For the third time he spoke significant words, which had come to him when he conversed with the Buddha in his vision: "It is not possible for all people to be Essenes. Hillel was right when he said, 'Do not cut yourself off from the community but work and be active in the community, with love for your fellow human beings; for what indeed are you all on your own?' That is what the Essenes do, however; they cut themselves off, withdrawing from the world to live a life of holiness, and this brings misfortune on others. For the rest of humanity must suffer if they go apart."

He then told his mother the event he had witnessed—I spoke of this yesterday: "Once I left the Essenes after an important, personal conversation, and when I reached the main gate I saw Lucifer and Ahriman running away. Since then, dear mother, I know that the Essenes protect themselves from them with their lifestyle and their secret doctrine, and Lucifer and Ahriman have to flee from their gates. But by sending Lucifer and Ahriman away the Essenes are making them go to other people. They gain blessedness by saving themselves from Lucifer and Ahriman." Having lived among the Essenes, Jesus knew that there was a way of reaching the heights where we unite with the divine and spiritual, but it could only be done by individuals and at the cost of others. He knew now that the connection with the world of the divine and the spirit could not be established in the Hebrew, the pagan, or the Essene way.

These words entered his mother's loving heart with tremendous power. Throughout the talk he had been at one with her, as though they were one. The whole soul and the whole "I" of Jesus of Nazareth lay in those words. Let me speak of a secret connected with the talk Jesus had with his mother before the baptism by John. Something passed from Jesus to his mother. Not only did he wrest all these things from his soul in words, but having been so close to her from his twelfth year, his whole essential nature passed to her with his words, and he was now in a condition as if beyond himself, as if his "I" had been lost to him. His mother, on the other hand, had a new "I," which had descended into her, as it were: she had become a different person. If we study this and try to find out what happened, a strange fact emerges.

The dreadful pain and suffering that was wrested from the soul of Jesus poured into his mother's soul, and she felt at one with him. Jesus himself felt that everything that had lived in him from his twelfth year had gone from him in the course of this talk. The more he spoke of it, the more was his mother filled with all the wisdom that lived in him. All the events that had lived in him from his twelfth year now came to life in his mother's loving heart. For him, however, they seemed to have vanished; he had put into his mother's soul, into her heart, everything he had been living with from his twelfth year. This caused his mother's soul to change. . . .

II

BERLIN, NOVEMBER 18, 1913

I have spoken of events occurring in the life of Jesus of Nazareth from his twelfth year to his baptism in the Jordan as they appear in the Fifth Gospel. I spoke of the significant experience Jesus of Nazareth had in a pagan place of worship and was able to show that by reading the Akashic record we are able to see that he had an impression of demons surrounding the altar in that place of worship. Let me briefly remind you how he fell down as if dead, as if removed to another world where he was able to perceive the divine and spiritual secrets of the ancient doctrines taught in the pagan Mysteries. This enabled him to gain a living idea of what paganism had once been and what it had become in his day.

I mentioned that during that time—when he was in an altered state of consciousness at a pagan altar—he heard words proclaimed as though from the world of the spirit. These told a secret from the most ancient sacred doctrine of pagan peoples, the secret of how the human being got caught up in the material, physical world of the senses. He heard a voice coming from the worlds of spirit, the voice that had spoken to the pagan prophets of old. What he heard was a kind of cosmic Our Father, which says what the inner destiny of humanity must inevitably be, because from birth to death humankind is bound up with earthly matter. It was later reversed to become the earthly Our Father. I was able to say the words of the cosmic Our Father for the first time when we laid the foundation stone [for the first Goetheanum] in Dornach. I am going to read them again, for these words truly hold the original teachings of pagan humanity.

Amen.
Evils reign,
Bearing witness both to I-ness
Separating itself
And to selfhood's guilt—
Incurred through others
Experienced in the daily bread,
Wherein the will of the heavens
Does not reign,
Because humanity has separated itself
From Your kingdom,
And forgot Your names,
You Fathers in the heavens.

Those were approximately the words Jesus of Nazareth heard in pagan lands—the secret of the earthly human being as it was presented in ancient sacred teachings. They hold deep secrets of human evolution. Jesus was able to hear them and they entered deeply into his soul when he was nearing his twenty-fourth year. From then on he knew words that had once, in early times of human evolution, sounded from the world of the spirit. They seemed so great and powerful to him that he felt, especially in the light of impressions gained at the derelict pagan center of worship, that there was no longer anyone on Earth who could understand them.

We have seen that in three successive periods of his young life he gained profound insight into Judaism, paganism, and the Essene Order. We have seen that each in turn proved a source of deep suffering, for each time Jesus came to the understanding that they might still exist if human conditions were such that they could be received, but that those conditions could no longer be created.

That was the fruit of this period in Jesus' life. The Fifth Gospel shows that before he received the Christ into himself Jesus realized that in the course of evolution human beings had developed faculties that obscure the faculties of earlier times. Because of this, people were no longer able to receive the messages from the world of the spirit that the ancient Hebrews and pagans had been able to receive.

Jesus' connection with the Essenes had forced him to think that the way the Essenes were able to reunite with the world of the spirit was open only to a small band of people and not to the whole of humanity. Their road thus seemed equally impossible. Poor, poor humanity, he thought, you would not be able to understand the pagan prophets of old if they were to speak again; you would not be able to understand the Hebrew prophets of old if they were to speak again, and not all of you will be able to aim for the goal the Essenes are seeking to attain; only a small band can do this, seeking perfection at the cost of the rest of humanity.

I am putting this in a few dry words. To him it was life, a painful inner reality. With infinite compassion he shared the suffering of all humanity, compassion he had to feel in order to mature to the point where he would be able to take the Christ Spirit into himself.

Before this, however, Jesus of Nazareth had an important talk with the individual known to us as his foster mother or stepmother. We know that the true biological mother of the Nathan [Luke] Jesus, the child who in his twelfth year had received the Zoroaster spirit into himself, had died soon after that time, and that her soul had long since been in the world of the spirit. You also know from lectures I have given in earlier years that the father of the Solomon [Matthew] Jesus child had died and that the two families of the two children had become a single family in Nazareth, bringing Jesus and the other children together with the Zoroaster mother. We know that Jesus of Nazareth's father died when Jesus returned from a relatively long journey in about his twenty-fourth year, and that Jesus of Nazareth was now living alone with his foster mother. Generally speaking, this mother had needed some time to gain deep inner understanding of all the profound experiences Jesus of Nazareth had gone through. As the years went on, the souls of Jesus and his foster mother progressively merged one into the other, as it were.

In the time immediately after his twelfth year, Jesus had to cope with his deep, painful inner experiences on his own. The other members of the family really only saw a form of dementia developing. His mother, however, found a way of gaining increasing understanding. And so it came about that in his twenty-ninth or thirtieth year Jesus of Nazareth was able to have that important talk with his mother. This had a profound effect, as we shall see.

Essentially the talk was a kind of review of everything that Jesus of Nazareth had experienced from his twelfth year onward. The Akashic record shows how the talk went. Jesus of Nazareth first of all spoke of experiences gained between his twelfth and sixteenth or eighteenth years, when he had gradually experienced inwardly the ancient Hebrew teachings. He had not been able to gain such experience through anyone in his social environment, which was also true of the words he had spoken among the scholars in the temple, much to their surprise. But inspirations would always rise up in him, and he knew that they came from the world of the spirit. Hebrew teachings arose in him in such a way that he knew he was the possessor of those ancient teachings, though at the time none had ears to hear them. He was on his own with those teachings and it caused him great pain to be thus alone.

His mother had much to say when he told her that even if the voices of the Hebrew prophets were to be heard again at that time, there would be no one to understand them. She said that Hillel, for example, had been a great teacher of the law. Jesus of Nazareth appreciated Hillel for what he had been and had meant for Judaism. I need not tell you of Hillel's significance; you will find it fully recognized in Judaic literature. Hillel had renewed the best virtues and teachings of ancient Judaism. He had also brought renewal to Judaism by the fact of his own personal nature, not because he was a scholar but because everything he did, and above all his feelings, will, and desires, and his way of dealing with people, clearly showed the transformation all forms of true wisdom bring about in the human soul. Hillel was rightly acclaimed for patience in dealing with others, a much-praised virtue in Judaism though people no longer really understood it. The way he had come to work among the Hebrews had been unusual. He was originally from Babylon but from a family descended from the David family itself who had been transplanted there by the Jews at the time of exile. Hillel thus combined elements he had taken up in Babylon with the Hebrew nature that pulsed in his blood. A well-known legend tells of the way this influenced his inner life.

The story goes that one day Hillel was just arriving in Jerusalem where the most renowned Hebrew scholars had met for various discussions, with arguments going to and fro concerning the secrets of Hebrew teachings. Hillel did not have any money, being a poor man. It was very cold, but he nevertheless climbed a small hill in front of the house where the discussions were held so that he might follow them through the window. He did not have the entrance money. The night was so cold that he was frozen stiff, and when people found him there in the morning they had to thaw him out first. However, by going though this he had been able to participate in the discussion in his etheric body. And while the others only heard abstract words flying to and fro, Hillel had perceived a world of wonderful visions that transformed his soul. . . .

Jesus of Nazareth also knew the influence this man had had. Not only did he know what Hillel had done, but his own inner ear had heard the great Bath Kol, a voice from heaven, when the secrets once made known to the prophets had arisen within his own soul. And he therefore knew that even Hillel had perceived only a faint echo of something their Hebrew ancestors had once been able to hear. Now their descendants were no longer able to hear even the faint echo that sounded in Hillel's voice, let alone the great Bath Kol.

All this lay heavy on his heart, and he spoke of it to his mother. He told her what he had suffered, how week after week he recognized more and more clearly the nature of the ancient sacred teachings of the Hebrews and that their descendants no longer had the ears to hear what once had been the words of the great prophets.

And now his mother understood, and was able to receive his words with deep feeling and a heart full of understanding.

He then spoke of the experience he had had after his eighteenth year when he had traveled in Jewish and pagan regions. It was only now that he told his mother of how he had come to a pagan place of worship that had been abandoned by its priests. A deadly, highly infectious disease had afflicted the local people. When they saw Jesus, the news spread like wildfire that a very special individual was coming. For it was a characteristic of Jesus of Nazareth that he made an impression wherever he went, simply by the way he bore himself. The greatest sorrow of those people was that their priests had abandoned them and their altar stood unused. Now they thought Jesus of Nazareth was coming as a priest to perform the offering service. Soon a large crowd had gathered around the derelict altar. Jesus of Nazareth was not willing to perform the offering rite, but he saw the deeper reasons for the people's suffering. He saw something that may be put as follows.

In the past, proper offering services had been performed at those altars, an outer ritual to reflect the ancient Mystery revelations of those pagan countries. In ancient and most holy times those rites had been performed in the right mood by the priests, and the divine spirits with whom those pagan peoples were connected would take part in the rite. Jesus knew this from direct perception. But the offering rites had gradually fallen into decadence and been corrupted. The priests no longer had the right attitude, and the result was that instead of the good divine spirits of old, demons now reigned in those places of worship. And these demons were responsible for the people's sufferings. Jesus of Nazareth saw the demons gathered in the place. They challenged his clairvoyant eye, as it were, and he fell down as one dead. As he fell, the people realized that he had not come to perform the offering at their altar. They took to their heels, and at that moment he saw how the world of the old pagan gods had changed into a world of demons and realized that these were the reason for the people's sufferings.

Inwardly he was then taken back to ancient pagan times when the true revelations of ancient sacred teachings had come down to the people. And it was on this occasion that he heard the cosmic Our Father that I read to you. Then he knew how far removed the humanity of his time, both pagans and Hebrews, had become from the ancient teachings and revelations. He himself had gained his knowledge of Judaism through the voice of the great Bath Kol. Paganism had come to him in a terrible vision that was very different from any abstract communication, for it changed his soul. And so he knew that people no longer had ears to understand what in Judaism had once sounded in the voices of the prophets, or what had once come down to the pagans of old. He told all this to his mother in moving words.

Then he spoke of being in the Essene community, especially of something that would have been difficult to understand if his mother had not already developed such deep understanding. He told her how on one occasion, as he left an Essene gathering, he had seen Lucifer and Ahriman flee from the gates. He knew that Essene methods could not be used by the masses. They enabled people to unite with the world of the divine spirit, but only by rejecting Lucifer and Ahriman. And if this was done, Lucifer and Ahriman were given even greater opportunity to go to others and enmesh them more deeply in Earth existence, which meant that those other people could not share in the union with the world of the spirit. In the light of this experience Jesus of Nazareth knew that the Essene way, too, could not serve the whole of humanity, being possible only for a small band of people. This was the third painful realization that came to him.

His way of telling these things was unusual. His words did not merely go across to his mother but they were like living beings that entered her heart. As the profound meaning of these words—a meaning full of suffering but also filled with profound love for humanity—entered her soul, she felt inwardly strengthened by a power that came from him, and she felt that her soul was changing.

It was as though everything that lived in Jesus' soul had gone over into his mother's soul in the course of this talk. And it was the same also for him.

Here the Akashic record reveals something strange. *Jesus of Nazareth spoke in such a way that the words wrested from his soul that entered the heart and soul of his mother always carried a piece of his own "I" with them.* We might say that his own "I" seemed to go across, as it were, to his mother on the wings of his words, though it did not in fact go across; it was merely that his mother felt she was given new life by those words. The strange effect of this talk was that the soul of the woman who had been the physical mother of the Nathan child came down from the world of the spirit and united with the soul of the foster mother. After that talk, the soul of the Nathan child's true mother had been received into the stepmother's soul. Virginity was reborn, as it were. The transformation of the mother's soul as another soul entered it from worlds of the spirit is deeply moving to the spiritual observer who perceives that from then on the stepmother had become the vessel holding the mother who had been in the world of the spirit from Jesus' twelfth to thirtieth years.

For Jesus himself it was as if he had given his "I" to his mother, and now only physical body, etheric body, and astral body lived in him, as though governed by cosmic laws. The urge arose in this threefold body to go to the individual he had met in the Essene community, who had been no more an Essene than himself but had also been accepted by the community. The urge arose to go to John the Baptist. During the baptism the Christ Spirit entered the body of Jesus of Nazareth, as we know from the other four Gospels, a body that had put its "I"—which was bound up with that body's essential nature and all the suffering experienced in it—into the words that had gone out to his mother's soul. The threefold body received the Christ Spirit into it, which then took the place of the other "I" in those three bodies. . . .

III

Particular importance clearly attaches to everything that happened after the talk Jesus of Nazareth had with his mother. I have shown you how this presents itself in the Fifth Gospel, as I would like to call it. Now, to begin with I would like to draw attention to what happened immediately after the talk, that is, between it and the baptism by John in the Jordan. I am going to present the facts as they come to direct intuitive perception. They will be given without further explanation, so that everyone can have their own thoughts on the subject.

We have seen that after the period from Jesus of Nazareth's twelfth to twenty-ninth or thirtieth year (some details of this have been given) Jesus had a talk with the woman who was his stepmother or foster mother, the physical mother of the Solomon child. The fruits of his experiences during those years entered with such energy into the words Jesus spoke that a tremendous power went over into his mother's soul with them. The power was such that the soul of the natural mother of the Nathan child was able to descend from the world of the spirit where she had been from about the twelfth year of that child, enter into the soul of the foster mother, and fill it with her spirit. And for Jesus of Nazareth himself the outcome was that the Zoroaster "I" left him, as it were, with those words. The being who now set out on the road to the baptism by John in the Jordan was essentially the Nathan Jesus with the three outer bodies constituted in the way we have discussed, without the Zoroaster "I" but with the effects of that "I," so that everything the Zoroaster "I" had been able to pour into those three outer bodies was indeed present within them.

The being who then was Jesus of Nazareth followed a vague cosmic urge, as it were—vague to him but quite specific as far as the cosmos was concerned—and went to the Jordan to be baptized by John. You will understand why he cannot be called a human being in the ordinary way. For the Zoroaster "I" that had filled this being from his twelfth year had now gone. It merely lived on in its effects.

When this Jesus of Nazareth being set out to go to John the Baptist, the Fifth Gospel tells us that he first of all met two Essenes. He had often talked to them on the occasions I have described to you. He did not recognize them immediately, because the Zoroaster "I" was no longer in him. They recognized him, however, for the physiognomy which had developed when the bodies were holding the Zoroaster "I" had not changed, at least to outward appearance. The two Essenes addressed him, saying, "Where are you going?" Jesus of Nazareth replied, "To a place souls like yours do not wish to see, where humanity's pain can feel rays of the forgotten light!"

The two Essenes did not understand those words. Realizing that he failed to recognize them they said, "Jesus of Nazareth, don't you recognize us?" His answer was, "You are like stray lambs, and I shall have to be the shepherd from whom you have gone astray. If you truly know me you will soon run away from me again. It was a long time ago that you ran away from me!" The Essenes did not know what to make of him, for it seemed impossible to them that such words could come from a human soul. They looked at him in uncertainty. He went on to say, "Why do you clothe yourself in forms that deceive? Why is there a fire burning within you that has not been kindled in my Father's house? You bear the mark of the tempter; he has made your wool glitter and shine with his fire. The hairs of that wool pierce my eyes. You lost lambs, the tempter has filled your souls with arrogance; you met him in your flight."

When he had said those words, one of the Essenes asked, "Did we not show the tempter the door? He no longer has any part in us." Jesus of Nazareth replied, "You did show him the door, but he went away to other people. Now he is grinning at you from the souls of those other people all around you! Did you think to elevate yourselves by bringing down others? You consider yourselves to be at a high level; yet this is not because you have reached a high level but because you have reduced others to a low level. That is why they are lower. You have remained where you were, and you only see yourselves higher than they are." The Essenes were taken aback. At that moment, however, Jesus of Nazareth vanished from view. They were no longer able to see him.

Their eyes were as if blinded for a while; then they felt the urge to look into the far distance. There they saw something like a mirage: the countenance of the one who had just stood before them had become enlarged to giant proportions. And from this countenance came words that entered deeply into their souls: "Vain are your efforts, for your hearts are empty because you have allowed the spirit who deceptively hides pride within the mantle of humility to enter into you!" They stood for a while as if numbed by the countenance before them and the words it had spoken. Then the mirage vanished, and Jesus of Nazareth was no longer with them. They looked around. He had walked on and they saw him a long way off. The two Essenes went home and never told anyone what they had seen. They kept silence until they died.

I am giving these facts just as the Akashic record shows them, and everyone can have their own thoughts about them. This is important at the present moment, for the Fifth Gospel may well emerge in greater detail as time goes on, and any theoretical interpretation would merely interfere with what is to come.

Jesus of Nazareth continued on his way to the River Jordan for a while. He met someone who may be said to have been in deepest inner despair. Jesus of Nazareth said, "To what pass has your soul brought you? I saw you eons ago, and you were different then." The desperate man said, "I was a high dignitary; I had come far in life. I went from holding one office to the next in the human order of affairs, and it went fast. Seeing others lag behind in their attainment to dignity while I myself was rising higher and higher, I often said to myself: 'You must be a rare individual; your great virtues are raising you above all others!' I was enjoying good fortune and fully appreciated this." Those were the words of the desperate man. He then went on to say, "Then something appeared to me as if in a dream as I was asleep. It was as if a question was put to me in my dream, and I immediately knew that I felt shame before this question. For the question put to me was 'Who made you so great?' And in my dream a spirit stood before me who said, 'I have raised you high, but this means that you are mine!' And I felt ashamed; for I had thought I owed my advancement entirely to my own merits and talents. And then another spirit came—I could feel the shame I experienced in my dream—and this spirit said that my rise was not due to any merit of my own. And I felt so ashamed in my dream that I had to flee. I left all my offices and titles behind and am now wandering aimlessly, seeking but not knowing what it is I seek." Those were the words of the desperate man. And as he spoke that spirit appeared again, standing between him and Jesus of Nazareth, and the figure of the spirit blocked out the figure of Jesus. The desperate man felt that this spirit had something to do with the Luciferic element. And Jesus of Nazareth vanished while the spirit still stood between them, and then the spirit also vanished. The desperate man then saw that Jesus of Nazareth had gone past him and was some distance away. He resumed his aimless wanderings.

Jesus of Nazareth then met a leper. Jesus of Nazareth asked, "To what pass has your soul brought you? I saw you eons ago, and you were different then." The man said, "People cast me out because of my disease! No one wanted to have anything to do with me, and I did not know how to provide myself with the essentials of life. I wandered about aimlessly in my pain and came to a wood. Something like a luminous tree stood in the distance and drew me to itself. I could do nothing but go to that tree, as if driven. It then appeared as if something like a skeleton emerged from the luminosity of the tree. And I knew: death itself stood before me. Death said, 'I am you! I feed on you.' And I was afraid. But death said, 'Why are you afraid? Did you not always love me?' But I knew I had never loved death. And as death said the words 'Why are you afraid? Did you not always love me?' it changed into a beautiful archangel. He then vanished and I fell into a deep sleep. I did not wake until morning and found myself sleeping by the tree. From then on my leprosy has grown worse and worse." When he had told his story, the spirit he had seen by the tree stood between him and Jesus of Nazareth and changed into an entity he knew to be Ahriman or something Ahrimanic. As he was still looking, the entity disappeared, and so did Jesus of Nazareth. Jesus had in fact been walking on for some while. And the leper had to go on his way.

After these three encounters, Jesus of Nazareth came to the River Jordan. Let me mention again that the baptism by John was followed by the event known as the temptation, which is also described in the other Gospels. The form the temptation took was that Jesus Christ did not face one spiritual entity but that the whole went in three stages, as it were.

First Jesus Christ faced an entity that was close to him because he had seen it when the desperate man had come to him. Because of that encounter he was able to sense that it was Lucifer. This is a highly significant combination of circumstances. And then the temptation by Lucifer happened, which is put in words as "I shall give you all the realms of the world and their glory if you recognize me as your lord." The Lucifer temptation was repulsed.

For the second attack, Lucifer returned but also the spirit who had stood between Jesus of Nazareth and the leper, the spirit he had felt to be Ahriman. There followed the temptation given in the other Gospels in the words "Cast yourself down; nothing shall happen to you if you are the Son of God." This temptation, in which Lucifer could be cancelled out by opposing him with Ahriman and vice versa, was also repulsed.

The third temptation came from Ahriman only. Jesus Christ was asked to make stones into bread, and this temptation was not completely repulsed at the time. Because Ahriman was not completely vanquished, later events then took the course they did, as we shall hear. Because of this, Ahriman was able to work through Judas.

You see, an Akashic intuition has arisen concerning a moment we have to consider to have been tremendously important in the whole Jesus Christ evolution and therefore in Earth evolution. It was as if the way in which Earth evolution is connected with the Luciferic and Ahrimanic element had to be gone through once again. Those were the events that took place between the talk Jesus of Nazareth had with his foster mother and the baptism by John in the Jordan. The Nathan Jesus, in whom the Zoroaster "I" had been active for eighteen years, had been prepared by the events I have described to take the Christ Spirit into him. It is extraordinarily important that the point thus reached present itself to us in the right way if we are to understand this aspect of human evolution on Earth. This is why I have tried to bring in a number of insights gained through occult research, so that you may understand this aspect of our human evolution on Earth.

Perhaps it will be possible at some later date to speak here also about the things I have spoken of in Leipzig, where I attempted to make a connection between the Christ event and the Parzival event. Today I will merely touch on this in connection with the facts given in the Fifth Gospel, hoping to discuss it further the next time we meet. Let me point out that the meaning and the whole course of human evolution come to expression in all kinds of ways within that evolution. They are imprinted on it, as it were, so that evolving humanity can gain some insight into the course of events, providing they are seen in the right light. I am not going to discuss the connection between the Parzival idea and the Christ evolution here, but rather something that was inherent in everything I said in Leipzig.

In the first place we have to consider how Parzival, who was several centuries after the Mystery of Golgotha, presents himself to us. He marks an important step in the working of the Christ event in a human soul. Parzival was the son of a knight-errant and the lady Herzeleide. The knight went away even before Parzival was born.

His mother suffered pain and was in torment even before he was born. She wanted to protect her son from everything connected with knightly virtues and from developing one's powers by being a knight. She brought him up in such a way that he knew nothing of the outside world and of what it had to offer. Parzival was to grow up in the solitude of nature, knowing only what nature could teach. He was to know nothing of what normally goes on among knights and among other people. The story even says that he knew nothing of the religious ideas that existed in the world. His mother only told him that there is a God who is behind everything. He wanted to serve God. But he knew no more than this: that he might serve God. Everything else was withheld from him.

However, the urge to be a knight was so powerful that he was driven to leave his mother one day and go out into the world, to find what the urge demanded. After many wanderings he came to the Grail Castle. The best description of what happened there—best in relation to what we can gather from the spiritual record—was given by Chrétien de Troyes, who was also a source for Wolfram von Eschenbach's *Parzival.* We learn that in his wanderings Parzival once came to a wooded region by the seashore where two men were fishing. At his request they showed him the way to the castle of the Fisher King. He reached the castle, entered, and saw a weak, sick man lying on a couch. The man gave him a sword. It was his niece's sword. Parzival also saw a squire enter with a lance from which blood was dripping onto the squire's hands. Then a maiden carrying a golden chalice entered, and the light that shone from the chalice was stronger than all other lights in the hall. A meal was served. Each time another course was served, the chalice would be carried past Parzival into the next room where the Fisher King's father would be given nourishment from it.

All this had seemed to Parzival to be something to marvel at, but at an earlier stage in his wanderings a knight had advised him not to ask many questions. So he did not ask about the things he saw, intending to ask only the next morning. But when he woke the next morning the castle was empty. He called out but no one came. He thought the knights had gone hunting and wanted to follow them. In the castle yard he found his horse, saddled and ready. He rode away and had to be quick to get across the drawbridge; his horse actually had to take a leap, for the drawbridge was pulled up right behind them. He saw no sign of the knights, however.

We know, of course, what this was about: Parzival had not asked the question. The most wondrous thing appeared before him and he did not ask. He had to be told again and again that it was part of his mission to ask about the wondrous things he encountered. He did not ask, and he was made to realize that by not asking he had caused a kind of ill fate.

We see an individual brought up away from the culture of the outside world, not meant to know anything of that culture, who was intended to ask about the mysteries of the Grail when these came before him, but to ask in a virginal way, as a soul not influenced by the usual culture. Why was he to ask in that way? I have suggested on a number of occasions that the Christ impulse brought about a deed but that humanity was not immediately able to understand what had happened. On the one hand, therefore, the fact that the Christ had flowed into the Earth's aura had had a continuous influence, independent of what people might think and dispute in all kinds of theological dogmas. For the Christ impulse continued to work! And the Western world took shape under the influence of this Christ impulse, which may be said to have worked on human souls at a deep-down level and behind the whole of historical evolution. If it had only been able to take effect insofar as people had understood it and fought over it in their disputes, it could not have contributed much to human evolution. But at the time of Parzival an important moment came when the Christ impulse had to be taken one step further.

Parzival was therefore not meant to learn of the sacrifice made on Golgotha and what the apostles, the Church Fathers, and others later taught in different theological streams. He was not meant to know how knights put themselves and their virtues at the service of the Christ. He was only meant to be in touch with the Christ impulse deep down in his soul to the extent that was possible in his time. That relationship would have been clouded if he had learned what was being taught about the Christ. The Christ impulse worked not in what people did or said, but in the soul's experience when it is wholly given up to its supersensible influence. That was to have been the case with Parzival. External teachings always belong to the world of the senses. The Christ impulse worked at a level that was beyond the senses and was meant to influence Parzival's soul at that level. The one and only thing he was meant to do was to ask his question in the place where the significance of the Christ impulse could be revealed—at the Grail. His question was to be induced not by any of the reverence the knights believed they owed to Christ, nor by any of the reverence the theologians believed they owed to Christ, but simply by the fact that his soul was virginal, though in accord with the time in which he lived. He was to ask what the Grail might reveal, and indeed what the Christ event could mean to humanity. He was meant to ask! Let us hold on to this.

Someone else was not meant to ask. The story is well known [from Schiller's poem]. It was the undoing of the young man at Sais [in Egypt]. He wanted to see the image of Isis unveiled and felt compelled to ask, doing what he was not supposed to do, He was the "Parzival" of the time before the Mystery of Golgotha. At that time, however, the young man was told, "Take care lest your soul is unprepared when what lies behind the veil is revealed!" Parzival is "the young man of Sais" after the Mystery of Golgotha. He was not to receive any special preparation but was to be guided to the Grail with his soul still virginal. He failed to do the most important thing, for he did not ask, he did not seek to have the mystery unveiled to his soul. That is how times change in human evolution.

We know—to begin with these things have to be referred to in an abstract way, but we shall be able to go into more detail later—that this concerns the unveiling of the Isis Mystery. Let us recall the image the ancients had of Isis and the Horus child, the mystery of the connection between Isis and Horus, the son of Isis and Osiris. That is putting it in an abstract way, however. The young man at Sais was not sufficiently mature to have the mystery revealed. When Parzival rode away from the castle, having failed to ask about the mysteries of the Grail, among the first people he met was a woman, a bride mourning her newly dead bridegroom, who was lying across her knees. That is the image of the mother mourning her son, the pietà theme so often seen. It provides a first hint of what Parzival would have learned if he had asked his question. He would have known the connection between Isis and Horus in its new form, the connection between the mother and the Son of Man. And he should have asked the question!

Here we see a profound indication of progress made in the course of human evolution. Something that must not happen in the time before the Mystery of Golgotha ought to happen after that Mystery, for humanity had progressed in the meantime. The soul of humanity had changed, as it were.

As I said, we shall discuss all these things more fully later on. Here I am merely giving a brief indication. But they are only of real value to us if we make them truly fruitful. The fruit to be gained from the Parzival mystery, to which the image of the young man at Sais has been added, is that we learn to ask questions in a way that is in accord with our own time. Learning to ask questions is to follow the upward stream in human evolution.

After the Mystery of Golgotha we have essentially two streams in human evolution, one that holds the Christ impulse and gradually takes us to the heights of the spirit, and one that represents a continuation of the descent, as it were, taking us into materialism. At the present time the two streams are confused to the extent that by far the greater part of our civilization is tainted by the materialistic stream. We must therefore look without bias or prejudice at everything the science of the spirit is able to tell us of the Christ impulse and everything connected with it so that we may realize that the soul needs inner development in the spirit in order to balance an outer world that is inevitably getting more and more materialistic. We must learn from elements such as those presented that we have to learn to ask questions.

We must learn to ask questions in the spiritual stream. In the materialistic stream everything is designed to stop people from asking questions. Let us consider the two side by side to get a clear picture of their nature. On the one hand we have people who are materialists, which does not mean they may not follow various spiritual dogmas, recognizing the world of the spirit in words and in theory. But that is not what matters. What matters is that our souls enter wholly into the spiritual stream. Those who are in the materialistic stream may be said to be people who do not ask questions, for they know it all. It is the characteristic feature of materialism that such people know everything and do not wish to ask questions. Even the very young know everything today and do not ask questions. It is felt that people are free, with their value as individuals enhanced, if they can always form their own opinions. The problem is, how does this personal opinion develop? We grow into being part of the world. With the first words we hear as children we take something in. We continue to grow, taking in more and more, and do not realize how we take things in. Our karma has made us such as we are, and because of this we like some things more and others less. We grow up, forming our opinions, and reach the age of twenty-five, which as far as forming opinions goes is already quite respectable in the eyes of some critics. We feel our judgment to be mature, believing it to be our own. Yet anyone who is able to see into souls knows that it is based on nothing more than the outside life in which we find ourselves, which has become concentrated in our own soul. We may even get into conflict by believing our own judgment to indicate one thing or another for us. Believing ourselves to be independent we become all the more slavishly dependent on our own inner life. We form opinions but are completely unable to ask questions.

We only learn to ask questions when we are able to develop the inner balance that allows reverence and devotion to be retained when it comes to the sacred spheres of life, and when we are able to have an element in us that always seeks to remain independent of even our own judgment in relation to anything that comes to us from those spheres. We only learn to ask questions by being able to develop an expectant mood, enabling life to reveal something to us; by being able to wait; by feeling some hesitation in applying our own judgment, especially in relation to anything that should flow in a sacred way from the sacred spheres of existence; by not judging but asking questions, not only of people who may be able to tell us, but above all of the world of the spirit. We should face that world not with our opinions but with our questions, indeed in a questioning mood and attitude.

Try to get a really clear understanding through meditation on the difference between meeting the spiritual aspects of life with opinions and meeting them with questions. You have to experience the radical difference between the two. This difference is connected with an element in our present time that needs to be given special attention. Our spiritual stream can grow and develop only if we learn to see the difference between questions and opinions. We do, of course, have to use our judgment in daily life, and I therefore did not say that we have to be cautious about using our judgment in all situations. No, it is in relation to the deeper secrets of the world that we must learn to develop an expectant, questioning mood. Our spiritual movement will progress through anything that recognizes and encourages that mood in a relatively large part of the human race. It will be inhibited by anything that goes against the spiritual stream by way of unconsidered opinions. If at truly solemn moments in life we seek to reflect what we may gain from a story such as the legend of Parzival, who was meant to ask questions when he went to the Grail Castle, that story can become an example to us in our movement. And many other things will become clear in connection with this.

Looking back once more to human evolution before the Mystery of Golgotha, we have to say that at that time the human soul had a heritage that came from the time when it descended from heights of spirit to its incarnations on Earth. It preserved this heritage from one incarnation to the next. People thus had an ancient clairvoyance in those days that gradually died away. As incarnation followed incarnation, the old clairvoyance was getting weaker and weaker. That ancient clairvoyance was connected with the nature of the human being in the external world; our external perceptions made with eyes and ears are also connected with this. Before the Mystery of Golgotha, people were like children: they learned to walk and to talk, and while the elementary powers of ancient clairvoyance still existed they also learned to see clairvoyantly. They learned this like something that came to them as they entered into relationship with other people, just as they learned to speak because of the way the larynx is organized. They did not stop at learning to speak, however, but progressed to elementary clairvoyance. This was bound to the human organization as it then was in the physical world, with clairvoyance inevitably assuming the character of the human organization. Debauchees could not bring a pure nature into their clairvoyance; pure individuals were able to bring purity to their clairvoyance. That is only natural, for clairvoyance was connected with the immediate human organization.

Because of this it was important that the secret of the connection between the world of the spirit and the physical Earth world that had existed before Jesus Christ came to Earth should not be revealed to human beings who had the ordinary human organization of that time. That organization first had to be transformed and become mature. It would have been wrong for the young man at Sais to see the image of Isis in his unprepared state.

The ancient clairvoyance had vanished by the fourth post-Atlantean age, which is when the Mystery of Golgotha took place. The human soul was then organized differently, so that the world of the spirit had to remain closed to it unless it felt the urge to ask questions. The powers that were harmful to the human soul in the old times cannot touch it now if the question is put about the secret of the Grail. This secret concerns the element that had flowed into the Earth's aura since the Mystery of Golgotha. What had not flowed into it before and now has flowed into the Earth's aura as the secret of the Grail would remain forever unknown unless we ask. We must ask questions, which means we must feel the urge to let an element that already exists in the soul truly develop.

Before the Mystery of Golgotha, that element was not in human souls because the Christ was not present in the Earth's aura. At that time those who beheld the image of Isis in the right spirit and fathomed its secret could have done so because of such ancient clairvoyant powers as remained, making use of all that was in them as their human nature.

Since the Mystery of Golgotha those who begin to ask questions will be able to find the right way of doing so, and will also get the right feeling for the new Isis Mystery. What matters today, then, is to ask the right questions, that is, to develop the right attitude to the spiritual view of the world that can now be presented. Those who merely want to judge may read all the books and lecture courses without learning anything apart from mere words. Those who approach in a questing mood will learn far more than can be found in the words. They will find that those words bear fruit in the powers of growth that lie in their own souls. Anything we are told out of the spirit must become real inner experience. This is what matters.

We are especially reminded of this when we are presented with the significant events that occurred between the talk Jesus of Nazareth had with his mother and the baptism by John in the Jordan. These things can only have meaning for us if we meet them with a questioning mind and are alive with the need to know what was happening at the important watershed moment that separates the time before the Mystery of Golgotha from the time after the Mystery of Golgotha. It would be best to let these things live in your soul. Essentially everything they are meant to tell us is to be found in the narrative itself. We do not need to add a great deal of interpretation.

I wanted to make this general remark especially in connection with this part of the Fifth Gospel, indicating that in our present time it is once again important to understand the Parzival mood. Richard Wagner has tried to embody it in music and drama. I do not wish to enter the great dispute in the world at large concerning his *Parsifal.* The science of the spirit does not enter into partisanship. Far be it from us, therefore, to become embroiled in the dispute between those who wish to keep Wagner's *Parsifal,* the most significant document of the new Parzival mood that exists today, in Bayreuth, where it will have a certain protection, and those who want to hand it over to Klingsor's realm. Basically, the latter is already happening. I have been concerned to show that the Parzival mood has to be present as the Christ impulse continues to work at a time when human powers of judgment, our higher consciousness, do not yet enter into this, but when the spiritual approach to life should show the need for this mood more and more clearly and the need for many other things of which we shall speak in the winter months that lie ahead.

IV

COLOGNE, DECEMBER 17, 1913

. . . I said that his stepmother gained increasing understanding for what lived in him. Something now took place that was to be a significant step in preparation for the Mystery of Golgotha—a talk between Jesus of Nazareth and his stepmother. The Akashic record shows this. Her understanding had grown to a point where he could speak to her of the threefold pain he had experienced at the decline of humanity as he had seen it in Judaism, paganism, and in connection with the Essenes. And as he spoke to her of all the pain he had suffered in loneliness, he could see that this moved her.

One of the most magnificent impressions to be gained in the occult field is to perceive the nature of this talk. Nothing like this is to be found in the whole of Earth evolution. I am not saying "nothing greater," for the Mystery of Golgotha was, of course, greater, but "nothing like it." He was not saying mere words as he spoke to his mother. His words were like living entities that passed from him to his stepmother, and his soul lent them wings, endowing them with special powers. All the tremendous suffering he had gone through passed into his stepmother's soul on the wings of his words. His own "I" went with every word, and this was no mere sharing of words or thoughts; it was a living soul moving from him to his stepmother's soul in the words of his infinite love and infinite pain. And he was able to present the three experiences he had known as a great panorama. The whole process was further enhanced because Jesus of Nazareth gradually let the conversation turn into something that had come to him out of the threefold pain he had experienced over the decline of humanity.

It is truly difficult to put into words what he said to his stepmother, summing up his experiences, as it were. We are prepared through the science of the spirit, however, and so an attempt may be made to convey the meaning of the final part of this talk, using formulations and expressions from that science to help us. What I am going to say now was not said exactly like this, of course, but you can get an approximate idea of what Jesus intended to evoke in his stepmother's heart. Looking back, the whole evolution and life of humanity on Earth can be seen to be like an individual human life, though it would change in later generations, even if people were not conscious of this.

We might express it by saying that post-Atlantean life presented itself to his mind's eye. First, after the great natural event, an ancient

Indian civilization evolved, with the Holy Rishis presenting their tremendous wisdom to humanity. In other words, this was a highly spiritual civilization. Jesus of Nazareth went on to say that the spiritual forces that were active in the ancient Indian period were very different from those in later times, just as in an individual life the forces active in childhood, between birth and the seventh year, are different from those in later life. In those days these forces extended over the whole of life, not only up to the seventh year, and human evolution was therefore different from what it became later. People would know all their lives what today's children know and experience up to their seventh year. Today we think the way we do between our seventh and fourteenth and our fourteenth and twenty-first years because we have lost the powers we had in childhood, powers that are turned off in the seventh year. In the first post-Atlantean age these powers poured out over the whole of a human life and people were therefore clairvoyant. They were able to rise to greater heights with those powers. That was the golden age in human evolution.

There followed an age when the powers that are otherwise only active between the seventh and fourteenth years extended to the whole of life. In the third era the powers that today are active between the fourteenth and twenty-first years were active, and after this humanity lived in an age when the powers that are otherwise active between the twenty-first and twenty-eighth years were poured out over the whole of human life. With this, Jesus of Nazareth said, we are coming close to the middle of human life, which is in the thirties. Then the powers of youth cease to grow and we begin the descent. We are now living in an age, he said, which corresponds to the period from the twenty-eighth to the thirty-fifth years in an individual life, and these are the years when the life of humanity begins to go into decline. Individuals still have other powers that enable them to live on, but humanity as a whole has nothing left. This is the painful truth. Humanity is about to enter the ageing process; its youth has passed and it is between its twenty-eighth and thirty-fifth years. From where can new powers come, now that the powers of youth are exhausted?

This is how Jesus of Nazareth spoke to his stepmother about the decline that was coming for the whole life of evolving humanity. His words were full of unutterable pain, and it was clear that the prospect for humanity was quite hopeless. He knew that individuals would continue to live beyond their thirty-fifth year because some residual powers remained in them. Humanity as a whole had no such powers left; something new had to come, something an individual human life needed between the twenty-eighth and thirty-fifth years. The power that must illumine individual human beings when they advance from their twenty-eighth year to their thirty-fourth year had to come from the macrocosm and illumine the Earth.

Reading those words of Jesus of Nazareth in the Akashic record, one realizes that humanity as such was then growing old. As he spoke to his mother of these things, putting the meaning and significance of human evolution into words, he knew, at a moment when his very self entered into his words, that something of his own true nature went away with them. His words had become his very self. This was also the moment when the soul entity that until then had lived in his natural mother, who had died after the event in which the Zoroaster soul had come to him from the other Jesus boy, and who from Jesus' twelfth year had been in realms of spirit, entered the stepmother's soul. From then on his own mother's spirit lived in the soul of the Nathan Jesus boy's stepmother.

Jesus of Nazareth had united himself intensely with the words in which he expressed all the pain he felt at the suffering of humanity. And it was as if his self had vanished from the shell provided by the physical, etheric, and astral bodies, with the shell being again as it had been when he was a little boy, only that it was now also filled with everything he had suffered from his twelfth year on. The Zoroaster "I" had gone, and all that remained in the shell was what survived of those powerful experiences. Now an impulse arose in the threefold shell. It drove him to take the road that would lead him to

John the Baptist by the River Jordan. He went on his way as though in a dream, yet it was not a dream but a higher state of consciousness, and only the threefold shell was there, filled with the spirit and impulses of the experiences gained after his twelfth year. The Zoroaster "I" had departed. The threefold shell guided him, and he was scarcely conscious of anything around him. With the "I" departed, he was wholly given up to his direct vision of human destiny and of human needs. . . .

9

SOPHIA AND ACHAMOTH

Leipzig, December 28, 1913

MANY PEOPLE TODAY who may be naturally inclined to understand anthroposophically oriented spiritual science will need to clear up various contradictions that can arise in their minds. In particular, souls can be led to experience a certain contradiction when they wish to take seriously the memories of a festival season like that around Christmas and New Year. When we take these memories seriously, it becomes clear to us that as we try to gain knowledge we must penetrate into human spiritual history if we are to understand our own spiritual evolution correctly. . . .

Among the varied forms of knowledge we try to reach through our anthroposophical studies, we must of course include knowledge of Christ, that fundamentally important impulse—we have called it the Christ impulse—which came at the beginning of our era. If we wish to understand the Christ impulse we must ask ourselves how deepened anthroposophical knowledge could allow us to penetrate more effectively into the course of human evolution than those who lived at the time of the Mystery of Golgotha. Was it not much easier for them to penetrate this mystery, whose secret is specially bound up with the evolution of humanity, than it is for us at this great distance in time? That might be a troublesome question for people who want to seek an understanding of Christ in the light of Anthroposophy. It might become one of those contradictions that have a depressing effect just when we want to take seriously the deeper principles of our anthroposophical knowledge. This contradiction can be cleared away only when we call up before our souls the whole spiritual situation of humanity at the beginning of our era.

If we try—at first without religious or similar feeling—to enter into the psychic disposition of humanity at that time, we make a most peculiar discovery. We can say to ourselves that we will rely on what cannot be denied even by minds most given over to externals; we will draw on ancient tradition as found in history, but we will try to penetrate that part of it which embraces the purest spiritual life. In this way we may hope to lay hold of essential elements in the evolution of humanity. Let us therefore try to enter quite historically into the endeavors that were made by, say, people two hundred years before the Mystery of Golgotha and a hundred and fifty years after it to deepen their thinking in order to understand the secrets, the riddles, of the world. If we do so, we realize that, during the centuries before and after the Mystery of Golgotha, a change of far-reaching significance occurred in human souls with regard to the life of thought. We find that a large part of the civilized world received the influence of what Greek culture and other deepened forms of thinking had achieved some centuries previously.

When we consider what humanity accomplished by its own efforts, not in response to any impulse from without, and how much was attained by so-called sages in the Stoic sense (which includes a good many people in Roman history), then we are bound to acknowledge that these conquests in the realm of thought and ideas were made at the beginning of our era, and that Western life has not added very much to them. We have gained an endless amount of knowledge concerning the facts of nature. We have been through revolutions in our ways of thinking about the external world. But the thoughts, the ideas themselves, through which these advances have been made, and with which people tried to discern the secrets of existence in external, spatial terms, have really developed very little since the beginning of our era. All these ideas were present in the souls of that period—even those the modern world is so proud of, including the idea of evolution. What might be called an intellectual laying hold of the world, a life of ideas, had reached a certain summit, and not only among particular individuals such as the pupils of Socrates a little earlier. This world of ideas had become popular in a limited sense and had spread widely over southern Europe and other regions. Truly, this deepening of thought is astonishing.

An impartial history of philosophy would have to pay special attention to the triumph of human thinking at that time.

But if we now take these highly significant advances in the realm of ideas, and on the other hand the secrets bound up with the Mystery of Golgotha, we become aware of something different. We realize that as the story of the event on Golgotha became known in that age, an immense wrestling of thought with that mystery took place. We see how the philosophies of the period, especially the Gnostic philosophy in its profounder form, struggled to bring all the ideas it had gained to bear on this one purpose. It is most important to let this struggle work upon us, for then we come to recognize that it was in vain. The Mystery of Golgotha appeared to human understanding as though dispersed through far-distant spiritual worlds. It would not unveil itself.

When I speak of the Mystery of Golgotha I do not wish to invest this term with any coloring drawn from religious traditions or convictions. I shall be concerned only with objective facts that are fundamental to human evolution, and with what physical and spiritual observation can bring to light. I shall leave aside everything that individual religious creeds have to say about the Mystery of Golgotha and look only at what happened in the course of human evolution. I shall have to say many things that will be substantiated and made clear only later on.

In setting the Mystery of Golgotha beside the deepest thought of that time, the first thing that strikes one is, as I just said, that the nature of this mystery lies far, far beyond what can be reached by the development of thinking. The more one studies this contrast, the more one is brought to recognize the following. You can enter deeply into the thought world that belongs to the beginning of our

era. You can try to bring alive before your soul what thinking meant
for Greece and Rome. You can call up before your soul the ideas
that sprang from that thinking. And you come to the feeling that,
yes, that was the time when thought underwent an unprecedented
deepening. Something happened with thought; it approached the
human soul in a quite new way. But if, after living back into the
thought world of that time and recreating it in your soul, you bring
clairvoyant perception to bear on this experience, then suddenly
something surprising emerges. One feels that something is happening far, far away in the spiritual worlds and that the deepening of
thought is a consequence of it.

We have already called attention to the fact that behind our
world lie other worlds. Let us call them, as we usually do, the astral,
the Devachanic, and the higher Devachanic worlds. We must first
remember that these worlds lie behind our own. Now, if you raise
the clairvoyant state of your soul to full activity within you, you will
receive the impression that a complete explanation of the deepening
of thought at that time is to be found neither in the astral world nor
in the lower Devachanic world. Only if you place your soul in the
higher Devachanic world—this is the clairvoyant insight—will you
experience what streams through the other two worlds and penetrates right down into our physical world where it is recognizable as
the radical transformation of human thought taking place over the
centuries.

As far as the physical plane is concerned, there is no need to be
aware, when steeping oneself in that past world of ideas, of anything
being communicated having to do with the Mystery of Golgotha.
One can leave it out and simply acknowledge that, no matter what
happened over there in Palestine, external history indicates that in
Greece and Rome an infinite deepening of thought took place. Let
us draw a circle around this Greek and Roman thought world and
make it an enclosed island, as it were, in our soul life, an island shut
off from everything outside. Let us imagine that no report of the
Mystery of Golgotha reached it. When we inwardly contemplate

this world, we certainly find there nothing known today about the Mystery of Golgotha. What we find is an infinite deepening of thought, indicating that something happened in human evolution that took hold of the innermost being of the soul on the physical plane. We are persuaded that in no previous age and among no other people had thinking ever been like that. However skeptical we may be, however little we may care to know about the Mystery of Golgotha, we must admit one thing—that in this island world we have enclosed there was a deepening of thought that was never previously known.

If one places oneself in this thought world, and has a clairvoyant faculty in the background, then one feels truly immersed in the individual character of this thought. And then one realizes that, yes, as this thinking flowers into idea with Plato and others, as it passes over into the world we tried to enclose, it has a quality that sets the soul free. It has a quality that lays hold of the soul and brings it to a loftier view of itself. Whatever else you may apprehend in the external world or in the spiritual world makes you dependent on those worlds. But in thinking you take hold of something that lives in you and that you can experience completely. You may draw back from the physical world, you may disbelieve in a spiritual world, you may refuse to know anything about clairvoyant impressions, you may shut out all physical impressions—but with thoughts you can live in yourself. In your thinking you lay hold, as it were, of your own being.

But then—and it cannot be otherwise if one enters with clairvoyant perception into this sea of thought, as I might call it—a feeling of the isolation of thought comes over one. This is the feeling that thought is still only thought. It lives only in the soul. One cannot draw from it the power to go out into a world where the ground of the rest of our being—the ground of what else we are—is to be found. In the moment one discerns the grandeur of thought, one discerns its unreality. Then one can see also how there is fundamentally nothing to sustain thought in the surrounding world one has come to know through clairvoyance.

Then why should thought be there at all? The physical world can do nothing but falsify it. Those who wish to be pure materialists, who refuse to ascribe to thought any primal reality of its own, would really prefer to prohibit it, for if the natural world is the only real world, thought can only falsify it. It is only because materialists are illogical that they do not embrace the only theory of cognition that goes with monistic materialism—the refrain-from-thinking, no-more-thinking theory. But this disquieting awareness of the isolation of thought comes to us if we clairvoyantly immerse ourselves in the world of thought. It is as though we were standing quite alone with it. Only one thing remains, but it does remain. Something comes toward us, even though it is from a spiritual distance, separated from us by two worlds. It becomes apparent—this is what the clairvoyant soul understands—that the true origin and fountainhead of what is in the life of thought lies in the third world. It is a powerful experience for clairvoyant souls to immerse themselves, alone with their thinking, in the time when thinking underwent its deepening. It is a powerful experience to shut out everything, including knowledge of the Mystery of Golgotha, and to reflect how the thought content on which we still nourish ourselves came forth in the Greco-Roman world. Those who do so should then turn their gaze to other worlds and feel a star that belongs to a higher spiritual world rising over the Devachanic world. The power that makes itself felt in the thought world of Greco-Roman antiquity rays out from this star. Having recognized this, one should then feel oneself here on Earth, carried away from the world of today and plunged into the Greco-Roman world, with its influence spreading out over other regions at that time, before the Mystery of Golgotha. However, as soon as one lets the spiritual world make its impression, the star or spiritual being appears again, shining over Devachan. One recognizes then that the experience of the isolation of thought and of the possibility of thought having undergone such a deepening at the beginning of our era is a consequence of the rays shining out from this star in the higher spiritual world. Then a feeling arises that at first knows nothing of the historical tradition of the Mystery of Golgotha. This feeling is that, yes, you are there, you feel yourself living in the Greco-Roman world of ideas, with all that Plato and others were able to give to the general education of humankind, with what they have imparted to human souls. Then you wait, and, as though deep in the background of spiritual life, the star appears that sends forth its rays of power, and you know that what you have experienced is a result of that power.

This experience, when one goes through it, does not rely on any kind of tradition, but impartially seeks the origin of what took place in the Greco-Roman world. At the same time, however, one experiences being separated by three worlds from understanding the root causes of that Greco-Roman world. And then, perhaps, one turns to the people of the time who tried in their own way to understand the change. Even contemporary outer scholarship has come to recognize that in this period of transition at the beginning of our era some religious and philosophical geniuses lived. They can best be encountered by looking at Gnosticism. Gnosis is known in the most varied ways. Externally, remarkably little is really known about it, but from the available documents one can still get an impression of its endless depth. We will speak of it only insofar as it bears on our present considerations.

Above all we can say that the Gnostics had a feeling for what I have just described: that for the causes of what happened one must look to worlds lying infinitely far away in the background. This awareness was passed on to others, and if we are not superficial we can, if we will, see it glimmering through what we may call the theology of St. Paul, and in many other manifestations also.

Those who now steep themselves in the Gnosis of that period will have great difficulty in understanding it. Our souls are too much affected and infected by the fruits of the materialistic developments of the last few centuries. In tracing back the evolution of the world we are too readily inclined to think in terms of the Kant-Laplace theory of a cosmic nebula, of something quite material.

Even those who seek a more spiritual conception of the world think of this cosmic nebula or something similar when they look back to the beginning of time. Modern people, even the most spiritual, feel happiest when they are spared the trouble of discerning the spiritual in the beginnings of cosmic evolution. They find it a great relief when they can say to themselves that this or that rarefied form of material substance was there to start with, and that out of it everything spiritual developed side by side with everything physical. And so we often find souls who are greatly comforted when they can apply the most materialistic methods of inquiry to the beginning of the cosmos and arrive at the most abstract conception of some kind of gaseous body.

That is why it is so difficult to enter into the way Gnosis thinks. For what Gnosis places at the beginning of the world carries no suggestion of anything at all material. Those who are thoroughly attuned to modern education will perhaps be unable to restrain a slight smile if invited to think, as Gnosis proposes, that the world in which they find themselves, so beautifully explained by their Darwinism, bears no relation to a true picture of how the world began. Indeed, such people will hardly be able to help smiling when they are asked to think that the origin of the world resides in that cosmic being who is beyond all concepts, not to be reached by any of the means that are applied nowadays to explaining the world. In the primal Divine Father—says Gnosis—lies the ground of the world, and only in what proceeds from him do we find what the soul can struggle through to if it turns away from all material conceptions and searches a little for its own innermost depth. And this is Silence: the eternal Silence in which there is neither space nor time, but silence only.

It was to this duality of the primal Father and the Silence preceding time and space that the Gnostics looked. Then, from the union of the primal Father with the Silence, as it were, the Gnostics conceived other existences—one can equally well call them worlds or beings—proceeding, and from these others, and again others, and

again others, and so on through thirty stages. Thirty of these existences, which can be called worlds or beings—Aeon is the name generally given to them—precede our own world. Only at the thirtieth
stage or, more strictly speaking, at the thirty-first stage did the
Gnostics posit a condition prior to our present mentality—a condition so delightfully exemplified by Darwinism.

One can get a clear idea of what is meant by this Aeon world
only by thinking that the thirty-first stage encompasses not only
what your senses perceive as the external world, but also the way that
your thinking as a physical human being tries to explain it. It is easy
enough to come to terms with a spiritual conception of the world if
we say yes, the external world is certainly maya, but with thinking
we can penetrate into a spiritual world—and hope that with this
thinking we really can reach the spiritual world. But for the Gnostics
this is not so. For them, this thinking belongs to the thirty-first
Aeon, to the physical world. So not only sense perception, but also
human thinking lie outside the thirty Aeons who may be beheld
through the stages of spiritual evolution, revealing themselves in ever
mounting perfection.

One can easily imagine the smile that comes to materialist
monists, standing at the summit of their time, if they are asked to
believe in thirty preceding worlds—thirty worlds with a content
entirely different from anything their thinking can conceive—but
such was the view of the Gnostics.

The Gnostics, too, of course, asked themselves, "How is it with
this world?"

We will disregard for a while what we have ourselves said about
the world in the sense of the early twentieth century. What I am
now telling you must not be taken as offering a convincing world
picture. In the Anthroposophy of the twentieth century we have naturally to get beyond Gnosticism, but just now we want to immerse
ourselves in it.

Why is this surrounding world, including the human faculty of
thinking about it, shut off from the thirty Aeons? We must look,

said the Gnostic, to the lowest but still purely spiritual Aeon. There we find the Divine Sophia, the Divine Wisdom. She had evolved in a spiritual way through the twenty-nine stages, and in the spiritual world she looked up to the highest Aeon through the ranks of spiritual beings or worlds. But one cosmic day, it became evident to her that if she was to maintain a free vision into the spiritual world of the Aeons, she had to separate something from herself.

She separated from herself that which existed in her as *desire*. This desire, no longer present in the Divine Sophia, the Divine Wisdom, now wanders through the realms of space and permeates everything that comes into being there. Desire does not live only in sense perception, but also in human thinking, and in the longing that looks back to the spiritual world. But it always exists as something cast out into the souls of human beings. As an image of the Divine Sophia cast out from her, this desire, *Achamoth*, lives thrown out into the world and permeating it.

If you look into yourself without raising yourself into spiritual worlds, you look into the desire-filled world of Achamoth. Because this world is filled with desire, it cannot disclose within itself what is revealed by looking out into the world of the Aeons. Far away in the world of the Aeons—according to the Gnostics—the Aeons' pure spirituality engenders what they called the Son of the Father-God and the pure Holy Spirit. Here we have another generation, as it were, another evolutionary line, different from that which led to the Divine Sophia. As in the propagation of physical life the sexes are separate, so in the progression of the Aeons another stream originated from a very high level in the spiritual world. This was the stream of the Son and the Holy Spirit stemming from the Father. In the world of Aeons one stream led to the Divine Sophia and another to the Son and the Holy Spirit. If one rises through the Aeons, one comes eventually to an Aeon from whom arose both the lineage leading to the Divine Sophia and that leading to the Son and the Holy Spirit. From there we ascend to the Father God and the Divine Silence.

Because the human soul is shut off with Achamoth in the material world, according to the Gnostics, it has a longing for the spiritual world—above all for the Divine Sophia, from whom it is separated through being filled with Achamoth. This feeling of being separated from the Divine, of not being within the Divine, is actually experienced, according to the Gnostics, as the material world. The Gnostics see what one might call (borrowing a Greek word) the *Demiurgos*, the cosmic architect who originates in the divine-spiritual world, but is bound up with Achamoth.

This Demiurgos is the real arch-creator and sustainer of what is permeated with Achamoth and matter. Human souls are woven into his world. But they are also imbued with a longing for the Divine Sophia. The Son and the Holy Spirit in their pure divine spirituality appear as though in the far distance of the Aeon world, but they appear only to those who have, according to Gnosis, raised themselves above everything in which Achamoth, the desire that pervades space, is embodied.

Why this longing in souls that have been drawn into the world of Achamoth? Why, after their separation from the divine-spiritual world, do they feel longing for it? The Gnostics asked themselves these questions. They said that Achamoth had been cast out from Divine Wisdom, Divine Sophia, but before Achamoth had completely become this material world, where we now live, something like a brief raying out of light from the Son of God came to her. But then the light immediately vanished again. This was an important concept for the Gnostics. In the remote past, Achamoth—the same Achamoth who lives in human souls—had been granted a glimpse, which had immediately disappeared, of divine light. However, this glimpse lives on in the memory of human souls, no matter how deeply enmeshed in the material world these souls may be. "I live in the world of Achamoth, the material world," a Gnostic soul might say. "I am surrounded with a sheath drawn from the material world, but when I sink into my inner being, a memory comes to life within me. The element that holds me bound to the material world longs after the Divine Sophia, the Divine Wisdom—because the being of Achamoth, which lives in me, was once illuminated by a ray from the Son of God, who dwells in the world of the Aeons."

We should try to picture clearly to ourselves a soul such as this, a disciple of Gnosis. There were such souls; they are not a hypothetical invention. Anyone who studies history with understanding will come to realize through the external documents that many such souls lived in that period.

We need to see clearly why there are such strong objections nowadays to what I have been saying. What will a levelheaded contemporary have to say about Gnosis? We have already had to listen to the view that the theology of Paul gives an impression of rabbinical subtleties far too intricate for a sensible monist to be concerned with. Such a materialist monist looks out proudly over the world and draws it all together with the simple concept of evolution or with the still simpler concept of energy. Such a monist says, "Now at last we have grown up. We have acquired ideas that give us a picture of the world based on energy. But when we look back at those children, those poor dear children, who centuries ago built up their Gnosis out of their childishness, we find they imagined all sorts of spirits, thirty Aeons! That is what the human soul does in its nursery play. The mature soul today, with its far-reaching monism, has left such fancies far behind. We must look back at this Gnostic infantilism with indulgence—they are really charming!"

Such is the mood prevailing today. It is not easily teachable. If a Gnostic, with a soul born of Gnosis, were to stand before you, he (or she) might also take the liberty of expressing his outlook somewhat as follows: "I understand very well how you have become so proud and arrogant, with your ideas of evolution and energy, but this is because your thinking has become so crude and simple and primitive that you are satisfied with your nebulae and your entirely abstract concepts. You say the words 'evolution' and 'energy' and think that you have got something, but you are blind to the finer spiritual life that seeks its way up into what rises through thirty stages above anything you have."

But for us the antithesis mentioned at the beginning of this lecture becomes all the sharper. We see on the one hand our own time, with its quite crude and primitive concepts, and on the other Gnosis. And we have seen how Gnosis employs endlessly complicated concepts—thirty Aeons—in order to find in the course of evolution the Son of God and the Holy Spirit, and to find in the soul the longing for the Divine Sophia and the Holy Spirit.

Let us ask ourselves, Is it not from the deepening of thought in the Greco-Roman world that we have gained what we have carried so splendidly far in our thoughts about energy and evolution? And in this Gnosis, with its complicated ideas, so unsympathetic to our contemporary mentality, are we not looking at something quite strange? Are these not a colossal contrast? Indeed they are. And the contradiction, lying like a weight on the soul, becomes even greater if we reflect on what we said about clairvoyant souls. They can transpose themselves into the thought world of the Greeks and Romans, and then see the world with the star, of which we have spoken. And mingled everywhere with this deepening of Greek thought we find that other deepening which Gnosis exemplifies. Yet when we look at this with the aid of Anthroposophy and do not yet have the power to understand what the star means, separated as we are from it by three worlds, we cannot take the Gnostics' understanding of what happened at that time in the historical evolution of humanity, for it could never satisfy us. It would throw no light on what is shown to the clairvoyant soul.

It is not my wish that you should treat our considerations today as offering an explanation of anything. The more you feel that what I have told you is not an explanation, the more you feel that I have put before you contradiction after contradiction and have shown you only *one* occult experience, the perception of the star, the better will you have understood me, for today. I would wish you to see clearly that at the beginning of our era something appeared in the world that influenced human understanding and was yet far, far from being understood. I would like you to feel that the period at the beginning of our era was a great riddle. I want you to feel that something happened in human evolution that seemed at first like a deepening of thought, or a discovery of thought, and that the root causes of this are a profound enigma. You must seek what appeared in the maya of the physical sense world as a deepening of Greco-Roman thought. You must seek it in hidden worlds.

10

THE LEGEND OF THE NEW ISIS

Dornach, January 6, 1918

To UNDERSTAND THE OSIRIS-ISIS MYTH in the present day, we must view it with the sensations and feelings that were in the soul, in the heart, of the Egyptian. We have done so by selecting a few characteristic features. And these characteristic features should bring before our soul's gaze the resonances that once sounded over from ancient times into newer times. While their meaning was lost through the Mystery of Golgotha, they must be clarified again today—precisely for the better understanding of the Mystery of Golgotha. Before our soul's gaze must stand all the mystery that at first could be divined only when the Egyptian felt the words that described Isis: "I am the All, I am the Past, the Present, and the Future; no mortal has yet lifted my veil." We will now contrast this Osiris-Isis myth with another Osiris-Isis myth, quite another one. And in the relation of this other Osiris-Isis myth I must count upon your freedom from prejudice, your impartiality in the highest degree, in order that you not misunderstand it. This other Osiris-Isis myth is in no way born out of foolish arrogance; it is born in humility. It is also of such a nature that perhaps it can only be related today in a most imperfect way. But I will try to characterize its features in a few words.

First of all, it is up to each person—though that can be only provisionally—to decide when to relate this Osiris-Isis myth. I can relate it today only approximately, superficially, even banally. But, as I said, I will try to relate it, disregarding as much as possible any prejudices and calling upon your unbiased understanding. This other Osiris-Isis myth then has somewhat—I say "somewhat"—the following contents.

It was in the age of scientific profundity, in the midst of the land of the Philistines. Upon a hill in spiritual seclusion a building was erected which was considered to be very remarkable in the land of Philisterium.

(I should just like to say that the later commentator adds a note here that "the land of Philisterium" means not merely the very nearest environment.)

If one wanted to use Goethe's language, one could say that the building represented an "open secret." For the building was closed to none, it was open to all, and in fact everyone could see it at convenient times. By far the greater number of people saw nothing at all. Far the greater number of people saw neither what was built nor what it represented. Far the greater number stood before an open secret, a completely open secret.

A statue was intended to be the central point of the building. This statue represented a group of beings: the Representative of the Human Being, and a Luciferic and an Ahrimanic figure. People looked at the statue and, this being the age of scientific profundity in the land of the Philistines, did not know that the statue was in fact only the veil for an invisible statue. But the invisible statue itself remained unnoticed, for it was the new Isis, the Isis of a new age.

Some few persons of the land of scientific profundity had once heard of this remarkable connection between what was visible and what, in the shape of Isis, was concealed behind the visible thing. And then, in their profound allegorical-symbolic manner of speech, they asserted that this combination of the human figure with Lucifer and Ahriman signified Isis. With this word "signified," however, they not only ruined the artistic intention from which the whole thing was supposed to proceed—for an artistic creation does not merely signify something, but is something—but they completely misunderstood all that underlay it. For the point was not in the least that the figures signified something, but that they already were what they appeared to be. And behind the figures was not an abstraction of the new Isis, but an actual, real new Isis. The figures "signified" nothing at all, but they were in fact, in themselves, what they made themselves out to be. But they possessed the peculiarity that behind them was the real being, the new Isis.

Some few who in special circumstances, in special moments, had nevertheless seen this new Isis, found that she was asleep. And so one can say that the real underlying statue concealed behind the external statue is the sleeping new Isis, a sleeping figure—visible, but seen only by a few. Some of them, at very special moments, turned to the inscription, which is in plain view, but which also has been read by only a few people at the spot where the statue stands in readiness. And yet the inscription stands clearly there, just as clearly as the inscription once stood on the veiled form at Sais. And indeed this is what the inscription says: "I am the Human Being, I am the Past, the Present, and the Future. Every mortal should lift my veil."

One day, another figure approached the sleeping figure of the new Isis, and then came back, again and again, somewhat like a visitor. And the sleeping Isis considered this visitor her special benefactor and loved him. And one day she believed in a particular illusion, just as the visitor believed one day in a particular illusion: the new Isis had an offspring, and she considered the visitor whom she looked on as her benefactor to be the father. He regarded himself as the father, but he was not. The visiting spirit, who was none other than the new Typhon, believed that he could acquire a special increase of his power in the world if he took possession of this new Isis. So the new Isis had an offspring, but she did not know its nature; she knew nothing of the being of this new offspring. And she moved it about, she dragged it far off into other lands, because she believed that she must do so. She trailed the new offspring about, and after she had trailed and dragged it through various regions of the world it fell to pieces, into fourteen parts, through the very power of the world.

Thus the new Isis had carried her offspring into the world and the world had dismembered it into fourteen pieces. When the visitor, the new Typhon, became aware of the fact, he gathered together the fourteen pieces, and with all the knowledge of natural scientific profundity, he made a being again, a single whole, out of the fourteen pieces. But this being obeyed only mechanical laws, the law of the machine. Thus a being had arisen with all the appearance of life, but obeying the laws of the machine. And since this being had arisen out of fourteen pieces, it could reproduce itself again, fourteenfold. And Typhon could give a reflection of his own being to each piece, so that each of the fourteen offspring of the new Isis had a countenance that resembled the new Typhon.

And Isis had to follow all this strange affair, half divining it; half divining she could see the whole miraculous change that had come over her offspring. She knew that she herself had dragged it about, that she herself had brought all this to pass. But there came a day when she could receive it again in its true, its genuine form from a group of spirits that were elemental spirits of nature; she could receive it back from nature elementals.

As she received her true offspring, which had been stamped into the offspring of Typhon only through an illusion, a remarkable clairvoyant vision dawned upon her: she suddenly noticed that she was still wearing the cow's horns of ancient Egypt, in spite of having become a new Isis.

And lo and behold, when she had thus become clairvoyant, the power of her clairvoyance summoned—some say Typhon himself, some say Mercury. And through the power of the clairvoyance of the new Isis he was obliged to set a crown on her head in the place where once the old crown, which Horus had seized from her, had been, that is to say, on the spot where she developed the cow horns. But this crown was merely of paper—covered with all sorts of writings of a profound scientific nature, still it was of paper. And she now had two crowns on her head, the cow horns and the paper crown embellished with all the wisdom of scientific profundity.

One day through the strength of her clairvoyance the deep meaning arose in her, as far as the age could reach, of what is described in St. John's Gospel as the Logos. The Johannine significance of the Mystery of Golgotha arose in her. Through the power of the mystery, the power of the cow horns took hold of the paper crown and changed it into the actual gold crown of genuine wisdom.

These then are the main features that can be given of the new Osiris-Isis legend. I will not, of course, make myself the commentator who explains this legend. It is the other Osiris-Isis legend. But it must set one thing definitely before our souls. Even though the power of action bound up with the new Isis statue is at first weak, exploring, and tentative, it is to be the starting point of something that is deeply justified in the impulses of the modern age, deeply justified in what this age is meant to become and must become.

In recent days, we have spoken of the withdrawal of the Word, as it were, from the direct soul experience from which it originally gushed forth as from a spring. We have seen how we live in the age of abstractions, when human words and concepts have only an abstract meaning, when human beings stand far away from reality. The power of the Word, the power of the Logos, however, must be recaptured. The cow's horns of the ancient Isis must take on quite a different form.

It is difficult to speak of these things using modern abstract words. It is better for these things if you try to bring them before the eye of your soul in such imaginations as have been brought before you, and to work over these imaginations (allowing them to remain imaginations). It is very important for the new Isis to transform the cow horns through the power of the Word which is to be regained through spiritual science, so that even the paper crown covered with writing in the new, deeply profound scientific vein will become a genuine golden crown.

Now, one day someone came before the provisional form of the new Isis statue, and up above on the left a humorous figure had been placed whose mood was a cross between seriousness, a serious idea of the world, and, yes, what seemed like a chuckle about the world. And lo and behold, this person was standing in front of the figure at a particularly opportune moment, and the figure became alive and said quite facetiously: Humanity has forgotten it, but already centuries ago something was proffered to the new humanity, something about the nature of the new humanity, insofar as this new humanity still masters only the abstract word, the abstract concept, the abstract idea and is far removed from the reality. This new humanity is limited by words, and is always asking, Is it a pumpkin or is it a flask?—when it just so happens that a flask has been made from a pumpkin. The new humanity always clings to definitions, always stops short at words! In the fifteenth, sixteenth, and seventeenth centuries—said the chuckling being—humanity still had some self-knowledge about this peculiar propensity for taking words in a false sense, not relating them to their true reality, but taking them in their most superficial sense. Today, however, humans have forgotten what in those centuries had been put at their disposal in the service of their self-knowledge.

Still chuckling, the being then said: What modern humanity should take as the true remedy for its abstract spirit is depicted on a tombstone in Moelln in the Lauenburg district. On this tombstone is drawn an owl *(Eule)* holding a mirror *(Spiegel)*. And people say that Till Eulenspiegel, after he had wandered, performing all sorts of buffoonery and pranks, was buried there. It is said that this Till Eulenspiegel really existed, that he was born in the year 1300, went to Poland, even reached Rome. In Rome he had a wager with the court jesters over all sorts of odds and ends of wisdom and committed all the other Till Eulenspiegelisms, which indeed can be read in the literature about Till Eulenspiegel himself.

Scholars—and scholars are indeed very learned today and take everything with extraordinary gravity and significance—have naturally discovered . . . well, they have discovered various things, for example, that Homer didn't really exist. The scholars have naturally also discovered that there never was a Till Eulenspiegel. One of the chief reasons why the actual bones of the actual Till Eulenspiegel (who supposedly was merely the representative of his age) are not supposed to lie beneath the tombstone in Lauenburg on which is depicted the owl with the looking glass, was that another tombstone had been found in Belgium upon which there was likewise an owl with a mirror. Now these learned ones naturally have said, for it is logical, isn't it (and if they are anything it is logical)—how does it go again in Shakespeare?: For they are all honorable men, all, all, all! Logical they all are! Anyway, they said that if the same sign is found in Lauenburg and in Belgium, then naturally Eulenspiegel never existed at all.

Generally in life if one finds a second time what one has found a first time, this is taken as a reinforcement. But it is logical, is it not, in these things to take matters so. Well, we say, if I have one franc, then I have one franc. I believe it. So long as I know that I have only a franc, I believe it. But then I get another and I now have two. Now I believe that I don't have any at all! That is the same logic. This in fact is the logic that is to be found in our science . . . If I were to recount to you where you find this logic, and how very frequently!

But what is the essential point of Eulenspiegel's buffoonery? You can look it up in the book: the main thing in Till Eulenspiegel's buffoonery always consists in the fact that Eulenspiegel is given some sort of commission, and that he performs it purely literally and, naturally, carries it out in the wrong way. For obviously if, for instance, to exaggerate somewhat, one were to say to Eulenspiegel (whom I now take as a representative figure), "Bring me a doctor," he would take the word literally and would bring a person who had graduated as doctor from a university. But he might quite possibly bring a person who was, excuse the strong language, a total idiot, going only by the sound of the word. All the fooleries of Till Eulenspiegel are like this; he goes only by the word taken literally. But this makes Till Eulenspiegel the perfect representative of the present age. Eulenspiegelism is a keynote of our modern times. Words today are far removed from their original source, ideas are often still farther removed, and people do not notice it, but behave in an Eulenspiegel way to what civilization happens to serve up. Which is what made it possible for Fritz Mauthner, in a philosophical dictionary, to argue that all philosophical concepts are actually merely words, that they no longer have any connection with any kind of reality. People now-adays have no notion how far what they call ideas, and even ideals, are removed from reality. In other words, humanity doesn't know at all that it has made Eulenspiegel into its patron saint, that Eulen-spiegel is still wandering through the lands.

One of the fundamental evils of our time rests in the fact that modern humanity flees from Pallas Athene, that is, from the god-dess of Wisdom, and clings to her symbol, the *owl*. And humanity no longer has the least idea of it, but it is true, as I have often shown, that the foundation of external knowledge is merely a re-flection—but in a mirror, it is ourselves that we see!

And so the owl. I mean that the modern scientific profundity, looking into the mirror, into the maya of the world, sees simply its own owlish face.

These are the things the being at the left above the modern Isis statue chuckles and snickers over, and many other matters which, out of a certain human courtesy, shall not be mentioned at the moment. But I hope to call forth a feeling that this peculiar repre-sentation of human mysteries through the real presence of the Luciferic and the Ahrimanic spirits, together with the Representa-tive of Humanity itself, will arouse a state of consciousness among humans that wakes those very impulses in the soul necessary for the coming age.

"In the primordial beginning was the Word, and the Word was with God, and the Word was a God." But the word has become phrase, it has withdrawn from its origin. The word sounds and resounds, but its connection with reality is not sought; people don't endeavor to investigate the primary forces of what goes on around them. And one can investigate these fundamental forces, in the sense of the present age, only if one realizes that the essences we call Luciferic and Ahrimanic are really bound up with the microcosmic forces of humanity. And one can understand reality today for the human being living between birth and death only if one can form a few ideas of the other reality, which indeed we have often studied, that lies between death and a new birth. For one reality is only the pole of the other reality, the inverted pole of the other reality.

We have mentioned how, in ancient times, when human beings reached maturity they not only experienced a change such as still occurs today in the change of voice or some other part of the bodily organism, but also underwent an alteration of the soul. We have indicated how the ancient Osiris-Isis myth was in fact connected with the disappearance of this alteration of the soul. What used to arise in humanity through those essences and forces we spoke of yesterday must come again differently, inasmuch as human beings experience the force of the word, the force of the thought, the force of the idea in a new form. It must not now be something that arises through the forces of nature from the depths of the bodily organization, like the change of voice in the boy, something that embellishes the human being with the power of the animal organization and functions invisibly upon the head as cow horns. No, there must be a conscious grasping by people of the meaning of the Mystery of Golgotha, of the true power of the Word. A new element must be drawn into uman consciousness, radically different from the elements people still enjoy describing today. This new element, however, will be relevant to the social life, to the pedagogy of humanity, when pedagogy, or the theory of education, comes out of the tragic state in which it exists today.

What does the deeply profound Eulenspiegelism—I should say "natural, scientific profundity"—speak of principally when it speaks of the human being? Of what does even a great part of modern poetry speak? It speaks of the physical origin of the human being in connection with physical beings in the line of descent. Fundamentally the so-called modern, the much-renowned modern, theory of evolution is nothing but a conception placing the doctrine of physical descent in the center. For the idea of heredity plays far the greatest role in the theory of evolution. It is a one-sided idea. People are thoroughly satisfied with such one-sidedness, for nowadays they think that in this way one can be very learned. So one can indeed, with quite arbitrary explanations of things, drawn apparently from deep logic, but in reality from misty allusions to the real thing.

Yesterday we saw an example of whole literatures being written because people have lost the connection of a concept with the original experience from which the concept proceeded: the symbol of the cross. A whole literature has been written about it, the cross has been related to everything imaginable. We saw yesterday what it is really about. The same has been done in regard to many other things, and people think themselves very profound when they do it.

I will remind you of one case. Just think how infinitely important many people think themselves to be these days when they believe that they are speaking as we have spoken here today! A fair number of people say, in fact very frequently (you can read it any moment in the papers) and always with great solemnity—"The letter kills, but the spirit gives life." And with this, one thinks one has said something most profound. But one should inquire about the origin of such a saying. It goes back to the times when one had living concepts that indeed still had a connection with what had been undergone and experienced. When one talks today there is little connection, especially between the word and its place of origin. If you want to have a right connection between words and sentences and their origins, then I advise you to read the little book in which Swiss-German proverbs have now been collected. One still finds in these popular proverbs an original harmonizing of what is said with the direct experience. By the letter is meant, as you know, the alphabetical script in contradistinction to the ancient kind which the imaginative life drew out of the spirit, as we described yesterday. This ancient spirit gave life, and the liveliness of that epoch of human evolution produced imaginative atavistic clairvoyance. But there was a consciousness that this epoch must in turn be succeeded by another, that the letter must come which would kill the ancient liveliness.

And now relate that with all I have said about the actual nature of consciousness in connection with death. For the letter kills, but it also brings the consciousness that must be overcome again through another consciousness. The sort of disdainful rejection that modern journalistic folly attaches to the proverb "The letter kills but the spirit gives life" is not what is meant; instead, the sentence is connected with impulses of human evolution. It implies approximately: In ancient times, imaginative times, Osiris times, the spirit kept the human soul in a state of dulled liveliness; in later times the letter called forth consciousness. That is the interpretation of the sentence, that is what it originally meant. And in many instances, just as in this one, people today are very ready with opinions, with arbitrary explanations, because they do not connect anything with them.

This does not prove that what the modern profound scientific method has to say about the idea of heredity is false, only that the other pole must be added when one speaks of heredity. If people point to their childhood, and back from childhood to birth, if they ask themselves, "What do I carry within me?" then the answer is: what parents and ancestors have carried within them and transmitted to me! There is, however, another way of looking at the human being, which we do not as yet practice, which people in the future must practice, and which must be put in the center of pedagogy, the art of education. This is not a looking back at having been younger, but the proper consideration of the fact that with every day in life one becomes older. As a matter of fact, modern humanity understands only that one has been young once. It does not understand how to grasp realistically that one gets older with every day. For humans do not know the word that must be added to the word "heredity" when one sets becoming older against having been young. If one looks to one's childhood, one speaks of what one has inherited; in the same way, when one looks toward getting older, one can

speak of the other pole. Just as one speaks of the gate of birth, so
one can speak of the gate of death. One question arises: What have
we gained from our forefathers by entering this life through the gate
of birth? The other question arises: What perhaps do we lose, what
becomes different in us through the fact that we are approaching the
coming times, that we get older with every day? What is it like when
we consciously experience becoming older with every day?

That, however, is the demand placed on our age. Humanity must
learn to become older consciously with every day. For if humans
learn to become older consciously with every day, then this really
means a meeting with spiritual beings, just as being born and possessing inherited qualities means a descent from physical beings.

I will speak next of the way these things are connected: of the
important inner impulse that must draw near the human soul if the
soul is to find what is so necessary for the future, what alone can
round out and complete the one-sided teachings of natural science.

Then you will see why the new Isis myth can stand beside the old
Osiris-Isis myth, why both together are necessary for the humanity
of today, why other words must be combined with the words that
resound from the statue of Isis at Sais in ancient Egypt: "I am the
All, I am the Past, the Present, and the Future; no mortal has lifted
my veil." Other words must sound into these so that they may no
longer echo one-sidedly into the human soul today. In addition
there must resound the words "I am the Human Being, I am the
Past, the Present, and the Future. Every mortal should lift my veil."

11

THE SEARCH FOR THE NEW ISIS (1)

Dornach, December 24, 1920

IN THE FEAST OF CHRISTMAS the Christian world receives something that leads all Christians directly to contemplation of the highest questions concerning human development on Earth.

Consider the historical process from whatever perspective you wish. Try to relate historical events to insights into humanity's development on Earth. Try however you will to establish a meaning for this earthly becoming. You will find no explanation of this mystery in so "popular," so widely understandable a form, as the idea of the Mystery of Golgotha contained in the Feast of Christmas.

Look back to the beginning of human unfolding on the Earth. Follow it through the millennia to the Mystery of Golgotha. You will find that, however great the accomplishments were among ancient communities of peoples, those accomplishments were only a kind of preparation or preparatory stage for what happened for humanity through the Mystery of Golgotha.

Again, if you follow what happened since then, you will find you can understand it *only* when you remember that the Christ who went through the Mystery of Golgotha has been active in human evolution ever since.

Many things in human evolution may at first appear incomprehensible. But let us investigate them without small-mindedness or prejudice—for instance, prejudices such as the belief that unknown divinities come to our help just where *we* consider that help to be needed, without our having to lift a finger. If we leave aside such views, we shall find that we can recognize even in the most painful events in world history what significance and meaning earthly evolution acquired through the fact that Christ passed through the Mystery of Golgotha. It is right, therefore, for us to study precisely the Mystery of Golgotha—of which the Christmas Mystery is a part—from those points of view that can reveal, as it were, the meaning of the whole of human evolution.

We know what an intimate connection there is between what takes place in the moral-spiritual sphere of human evolution and what takes place in nature. A certain understanding of this bridge between natural existence and the cosmic moral order enables us also to approach another relationship that we have been contemplating for many years—the relationship of the Christ to that being whose outer reflection appears in the Sun. The followers and representatives of the Christian impulse were not always so hostile toward acknowledging this relationship between the Sun Mystery and the Christ Mystery as they often are today when Christianity has fallen into decadence. Dionysius the Areopagite, who has often been mentioned here, calls the Sun "God's monument." In Augustine, too, we continually find allusions—we find such allusions too even in Scholasticism—referring to the fact that the outwardly visible stars and their movements are images of a divine-spiritual existence in the world.

If we want to grasp what is most important from the point of view of the tasks of the present age, however, we must understand the Christmas Mystery in a much greater context than is usually done. Therefore I would like to remind you of something I have referred to repeatedly over the years. I have told how, when we consider human evolution, we can look back upon a sequence of ages. We can look back upon the first post-Atlantean age, filled with the deeds and experiences of the ancient Indian nation. Next, we can look back upon the ancient Persian epoch of post-Atlantean humanity, then upon the Egyptian-Chaldean, and upon the Greco-Latin, until we come finally to the fifth epoch of post-Atlantean humanity, our own. The sixth and the seventh epochs will follow this one.

Now, I have drawn your attention to the fact that the Greco-Latin or fourth epoch of post-Atlantean humanity stands, as it were, in the middle, and that a certain relationship exists between the third and the fifth epochs—that is, between the Egyptian-Chaldean epoch and our own. There is similarly a certain relationship between the ancient Persian and the sixth epoch (which will follow our own fifth epoch)), and between the ancient Indian and the seventh epoch. In each of these epochs certain things repeat themselves in a special way. You can read about this in my little book *The Spiritual Guidance of the Individual and Humanity.*

I once pointed out that the great astronomer Johannes Kepler, successor to Copernicus, felt that his solar-planetary system repeated in a certain senses—in a way appropriate to the fifth post-Atlantean age—what had lived as the world picture in the Egyptian priestly Mysteries. Kepler himself expressed this most radically when he claimed to have borrowed the vessels of the ancient Egyptian teachers of wisdom and carried them into modern times. Today, however, I want us to think about something that stood more or less at the center of the religious rites performed by the priests of the Egyptian Mysteries. I want us to consider the Mysteries of Isis.

To call up before our minds the spiritual connection that exists between the Isis Mystery and what lives in Christianity, we need only recall Raphael's famous painting the *Sistine Madonna.* The Virgin holds the child Jesus in her arms. Behind her are clouds, which are really the faces of pure children. Thus we can imagine that the child Jesus came down to the Virgin from the clouds, through a condensation, as it were, of the subtler cloud substance. But Raphael's painting, which was created wholly out of a Christian spirit, is nothing other than a kind of repetition of what was revered in the Egyptian Isis Mysteries, which portrayed Isis holding the child Horus. This image is entirely consonant with Raphael's picture. Naturally, however, we must not be tempted to interpret this superficially, as many people have done from the eighteenth century through the nineteenth up to our own time. In other words, we should not consider the story of Jesus Christ and all that belongs to it merely as a metamorphosis or transformation of ancient pagan Mysteries. You know from *Christianity as Mystical Fact* how these things must be considered. Nevertheless, as I explained in that book, there is a sense in which we can point to a certain spiritual congruence between what arose in Christianity and in the ancient pagan Mysteries.

The center of the Isis Mystery is the death of Osiris and Isis's search for his dead body. We know that Osiris—the representative of the Solar Being, or Spiritual Sun—was killed by Typhon (Set), who is none other than the Egyptian Ahriman. We know therefore that Ahriman kills Osiris, throws him into the Nile, and the Nile carries the body away. Isis, Osiris's wife, sets out on her quest and finds him in Asia. She returns him to Egypt, where Ahriman, the enemy, cuts his body into fourteen parts. Isis buries these in various places, so that from then on they belong to the Earth.

Contemplating this story, we can see how profoundly Egyptian wisdom conceived the connection between the heavenly and the earthly powers. Osiris is, on the one hand, the representative of the solar powers. At the same time, in that he passed through death he is, in various places simultaneously, the force that brings all that grows out of the Earth to fruition. Filled with spirit, the ancient Egyptian sages see how the powers that shine down to us from the Sun communicate themselves to the Earth and become part of it. They see how, buried in the Earth, these powers return what comes to fruition from the Earth to humanity. This story lies at the basis of the Egyptian view of the world.

One of the pyramids depicts the whole event most meaningfully. Not only did the Egyptians write down their solution to the great cosmic mysteries in hieroglyphs, but they also expressed this solution in their architectural constructions. One of the pyramids was built so precisely that its shadow, because of the Sun's position, disappeared into the base of the pyramid at the spring equinox and only reappeared at the autumnal equinox. Thereby the Egyptians showed that the forces that shone down from the Sun are now buried in the Earth and stimulate the forces of the Earth so that it may produce the fruit humanity needs.

This, then, is the idea we find present in the minds and hearts of the ancient Egyptians. On the one hand, they looked up to the Sun, the lofty Sun Being, and honored him. At the same time, they related how this Sun Being was lost in Osiris, sought by Isis, found again, and thereafter able to continue his activity in a new and transformed way.

Today, in our fifth post-Atlantean age, we are called to repeat much that appeared in Egyptian wisdom but in a different form. Therefore we must learn to spread abroad again among human beings an understanding of the Mysteries of the Egyptian priests. But we must do so out in the light of Christ—out of spiritual science and in a form suited to our own age. For the Egyptians, Osiris was in a certain way a kind of representative of the Christ who had not yet come. They looked upon Osiris as the Sun Being, but they imagined that this Sun Being had somehow disappeared and must be found again. We cannot imagine that our Sun Being, the Christ, who has now passed through the Mystery of Golgotha, could be lost for human beings, for he once came down from spiritual heights, united himself with the human being Jesus of Nazareth, and now remains forever with the Earth. He is present. He exists. As the Christmas carol proclaims each year anew, "Unto us a Savior is born." This expresses the eternal, not the transitory nature of this event. Jesus was born at Bethlehem not only once, then, but essentially is born continuously. He remains with Earth existence. What Christ is for us cannot be lost.

The Isis legend, however, is to be fulfilled in another way in our time. We cannot lose what Osiris gives us in a higher form through Christ. But we can lose, and have lost, what we see portrayed for Christian understanding as standing beside Osiris. We have lost Isis, the Mother of the Savior, the Divine Wisdom, Sophia. And if there is to be a renewal of the Isis legend, it must truly be renewed. It cannot mean for us that Osiris is killed by Typhon-Ahriman and carried away by the waters of the Nile and found again by Isis, so that his body, cut into pieces by Typhon-Ahriman, may be buried in the Earth. No, my dear friends, we must somehow rediscover the Isis legend—the Isis Mystery—but we must form it out of Imagination for our own times. An understanding for the eternal cosmic truths will return when we learn to compose imaginatively, as the Egyptians did. For this, we must first find the true myth of Isis.

The ancient Egyptians, like all human beings living before the Mystery of Golgotha, were still permeated by Luciferic powers. Now, if Luciferic powers are within us—and live, move, and weave in our inner lives—the result is that the Ahrimanic powers will show themselves in all their effectiveness to our outer vision. Thus the Egyptians who were permeated by Lucifer rightly saw a world picture where Ahriman-Typhon is active. Now, we must realize that Ahriman permeates modern humanity. Ahriman moves and surges in contemporary human beings, just as Lucifer moved and surged in the Egyptian world. And when Ahriman works through Lucifer, we see a picture of the world in a Luciferic form. How and where can we see it? This picture of the world made in Lucifer's image has become increasingly popular and has been adopted in all circles of thought that consider themselves progressive and enlightened.

To understand the Christmas Mystery, we must always remember that Lucifer is that power which tries to retain the world picture at an earlier stage. Lucifer is the power that tries to bring into the present worldview what existed at earlier stages of evolution. Lucifer wants to retain what existed in earlier periods. All that was moral in earlier periods also exists of course today. Morality always has a great importance for the present: moral deeds work as future seeds for later cosmic creations But Lucifer is only interested in removing the moral forces from our worldview. He wants to allow only the laws of nature to appear in this world picture. Thus the impoverished human being of modern times possesses a wisdom of the

world in which the stars move according to purely mechanical necessity, devoid of morality; so that the moral meaning of the world's
order cannot be found in their movements.

This is a purely Luciferic world picture. The ancient Egyptians
looked out into the world and saw in it Ahriman-Typhon who takes
Osiris away from them. In the same way, we must look at our world
picture which has become Luciferic, at the mathematical-mechanical
world picture of modern astronomy and other branches of natural
science, and realize that the Luciferic element rules in *this* world picture, just as the Typhonic-Ahrimanic element ruled the Egyptian
world picture. Just as Egyptians saw their outer world picture in an
Ahrimanic-Typhonic light, so modern humanity, because it is Ahrimanic, sees it with Luciferic traits. Lucifer is there: Lucifer is active
there. The Egyptians imagined that Ahriman-Typhon was active in
wind and weather, in the snowstorms of winter. Likewise, if we wish
to understand things, we must imagine that Lucifer appears in the
sunshine and the light of the stars, in the movements of the planets
and of the Moon. The worldview of Copernicus, Galileo, and
Kepler is Luciferic. Just because it is in keeping with our Ahrimanic
forces of knowledge, its content—please note the distinction—its
content is Luciferic.

At the time of the Mystery of Golgotha, the being that enables
humans to behold the world cognitively, worked in a twofold way as
the Divine Sophia, the wisdom that sees through the world. Divine
Sophia, Heavenly Wisdom, was present in the double revelation: to
the poor shepherds in the fields and to the wise men from the East.
This wisdom was still to be found in its later form among the
Gnostics. The early Christian Fathers and teachers of the Church
learned from them and used what they learned to enable them to
understand the Mystery of Golgotha. But this wisdom could not be
transplanted into more recent times. It was overwhelmed and killed
by Lucifer, just as Osiris was once killed by Ahriman-Typhon. We
have not lost Christ, our Osiris. We have lost the one who for us
takes the place of Isis. Lucifer killed her. But the Isis Being killed by

Lucifer was not sunk in the Earth, as Typhon sank Osiris into the Nile. Lucifer bore this Isis Being, the Divine Wisdom whom he killed, out into cosmic spaces. He sank her in the cosmic ocean. Today, when we look out into this cosmic ocean and see stars connected only by mathematical lines, then we see what spiritually permeates the world—the Divine Sophia, the successor of Isis—dead and buried there.

We must give form to this myth, for it sets forth the truth of our times. We must speak of the dead and lost Isis, the Divine Sophia, in the same sense as the ancient Egyptians spoke of the dead and lost Osiris. With a power that, although we cannot yet rightly understand it, is nevertheless in us—the power of the Christ, the new Osiris power—we must set out in search of the corpse of the new Isis, the Divine Sophia. We must approach Luciferic natural science and seek the coffin of Isis there. In other words, we must find in what natural science gives us something that stimulates us inwardly toward Imagination, Inspiration, and Intuition.

To do this will bring us the help of the Christ in us—who remains obscure and hidden in darkness if we do not illuminate him with Divine Wisdom. Armed with this force of the Christ, the new Osiris, we must set out in search of Isis, the new Isis. Lucifer does not cut Isis in pieces, as Ahriman-Typhon did with Osiris. On the contrary, Isis in her true form is spread out in the beauty of the whole universe. Isis shines out of the cosmos in an aura of many shining colors. We will learn to understand this Isis when we look out into the cosmos and see it in its aura of shining colors.

But just as Ahriman-Typhon once came to cut Osiris into pieces, so Lucifer now comes to dissolve the multiplicity of colors. He blends and merges, unites and crams together into a single whole, the parts that are so beautifully distributed over the heavens, the limbs of the new Isis which go to make the great firmament of the heavens. Even as Typhon cut Osiris in pieces, so Lucifer blends the manifold colors that stream down to us from the whole aura of the cosmos into a uniform white light that then streams through the universe. This is the light that Goethe combated in his *Theory of Colors*, repudiating the statement that it contains all the colors, which in truth are spread out over the marvelous and manifold and secret deeds of the whole cosmos.

We must persevere in our quest to find Isis again! And once we have found her, we must learn how to put out into the universe what we are able to penetrate. We must be able to place before ourselves in a living way all that we have acquired through the newly found Isis, so that the whole cosmic heavens become spiritual for us again. We must understand Saturn, Sun, Moon, Earth, Jupiter, Venus, and Vulcan from within. We must transpose what Lucifer has made of Isis into the heavenly spaces, just as Isis buried parts of the body of Osiris, cut into pieces by Typhon-Ahriman, in the Earth. We must realize that through the force of the Christ we must find an inner astronomy that will show us again the cosmos moving and working by the power of the spirit. When we have this insight into the cosmos that is awakened through the newfound Isis power of the Christ—which is now the power of the Divine Sophia—then Christ, united with the Earth since the Mystery of Golgotha, will become active within us, because then we shall know him. It is not the Christ that we lack, but the knowledge and wisdom of Isis, the Sophia of the Christ.

This is what we should inscribe in our souls as a content of the Christmas Mystery. We must realize that in the nineteenth century even theology came to look on Christ merely as the human being of Nazareth. This means theology is completely permeated by Lucifer. It no longer sees into the spiritual foundations of existence. External natural science is Luciferic. Theology is Luciferic. Naturally, speaking of the inner aspect of the human being, we could just as well say Ahrimanic, as I have just explained. In the same way we could say of the ancient Egyptians that they were inwardly Luciferic, while outwardly their perception of the world was Ahrimanic.

Human beings today must grasp the Christmas Mystery in a new way. They must realize that, for Christ to appear to them, they must seek Isis first. The cause of the misfortunes and troubles in modern civilization is not that we have lost Christ, who stands before us in a far greater glory than Osiris did in the eyes of the Egyptians. We have not lost Christ and do not need to set out to find him, armed with the force of Isis—what we have lost is the *cognition*, the *intuition*, of Jesus Christ. This is what we must find again, with the help of the force of Jesus Christ in us.

This is how we must look upon the content of the Christmas festival. For many modern people Christmas is nothing but an occasion for giving and receiving presents, something they celebrate every year by habit. The Christmas festival has become an empty phrase like so many other things in modern life. And it is just because so many things have become empty phrases that modern life is so full of calamities and chaos. This is the deeper cause of the chaos in modern life.

If we could develop the right feelings for what have become empty words, empty phrases, in modern life, and if these feelings could enable us to find the impulses needed for renewal, then this community that calls itself the anthroposophical community would be worthy of its existence. We should understand how terrible it is that events such as the Christmas festival should be maintained as mere phrases. We should be able to understand that in future this must not happen, and that many things must be given a new content, so that instead of acting out of old habits, we might act out of new and fresh insight. If we cannot find the inner courage necessary to do this, then we share in the lie that maintains the yearly Christmas festival as an empty phrase. We celebrate it without true feeling. Do we really rise to the highest concerns of humanity when we give and receive presents every year at Christmas out of habit? Do we lift ourselves to the highest concerns of humanity when we listen to the words—which have also become empty—spoken by the representatives of this or that religious community? We should forbid ourselves to continue in this inner hollowness of our Christmas celebrations. We should make the inner decision to give true and worthy content to such a festival, which should raise humanity to the under-standing of the meaning of its existence.

When you stand before the Christmas tree and open the presents given out of habit and the Christmas cards containing the usual phrases, ask yourselves whether the feelings in your hearts and souls could raise humanity to an understanding of the sense and meaning of its earthly evolution! All the trouble and sorrow of our time is due to this: we cannot find the courage to lift ourselves above the phrases of our age. But a new content must be found. This must happen! A content must come that can give us new feelings to stir us, even as those who were true Christians were stirred in the first Christian centuries, those who experienced the Mystery of Golgotha and the appearance of Christ upon the Earth as the highest that humans could experience. We must remember that and create some-thing similar in our souls.

Our souls will attain matchless feelings when, as modern human beings, we feel the duty to experience the new myth of Isis. This myth tells how Lucifer kills Isis and transfers her body into the cos-mic spaces that have become a mathematical abstraction. This abstraction is the grave of Isis. The search for Isis follows, and then her rediscovery through inner cognitive spiritual powers. These put what the stars and planets can reveal through inner life into the place of the lifeless sky. The planets and stars therefore appear as monuments of the spiritual powers surging through space. We con-template the manger in the right spirit if we let the powers that surge through space kindle our feeling and then look at the being who was drawn into the world through the child. We know that we bear this being within us, but we must bring understanding to him. As the Egyptians looked from Isis to Osiris, we must learn to look again to the new Isis, the holy Sophia.

Christ will appear in spiritual form during the twentieth century not simply because something happens outwardly, but to the extent that we find the power represented by holy Sophia. Our time tends to lose this Isis-power, this power of the Mary. It was killed by all that arose with the modern consciousness of humankind. New forms of religion have, in part, killed just this view of the Mary.

This is the mystery of modern humanity. Mary-Isis has been killed, and she must be sought, just as Isis sought Osiris. But she must be sought in the wide space of heaven, with the power that Christ can awaken in us, if we give ourselves to him aright.

Let us imagine this correctly. Let us immerse ourselves in the new myth of Isis that is to be experienced. Let us fill our souls with it. Only then shall we experience in a true sense this Holy Eve of Christmas, leading us into Christmas Day, Christ's Day.

Our anthroposophical community could be a community of human beings bound together in love through their common search. Let us realize this most intimate and dear task. Let us go to the manger in spirit and bring our sacrifices and our gifts to the child. Let us do so in the knowledge that something priceless must enter our souls so that, as modern human beings, we may rise to the tasks that could lead humanity out of barbarism into a truly new civilization. . . .

> Isis-Sophia
> Wisdom of God
> Lucifer has slain her,
> And on wings of cosmic forces
> Carried her away into the depths of space.
> Christ-Will
> Working in us
> Shall tear her from Lucifer
> And on grounds of spiritual knowledge
> Call to new life in human souls
> Isis-Sophia
> Wisdom of God.

12

THE SEARCH FOR THE NEW ISIS (2)

Dornach, December 25, 1920

IF WE WANT TO UNDERSTAND THE EVENT OF GOLGOTHA in the light of the Christmas Mystery, we can look in two directions. We can look toward the starry heavens with all their secrets, or we can look toward our own inner being with all its secrets. In other lectures I have spoken of how the wise men from the East recognized *from the starry heavens* Jesus Christ's arrival on the Earth and how simple shepherds in the field received the proclamation of the Savior of humankind from visions arising *from the inner human being*.

Today, we will turn our attention again to these two directions from which, in reality, all knowledge comes—from which therefore the highest knowledge of all, the knowledge of the very meaning of the Earth, also had to come.

When we look back before the Mystery of Golgotha, we find that the human soul has a quite different relationship to the universe and itself than it does after the Mystery of Golgotha. This is not immediately evident when one observes history outwardly. The ancient form of knowledge belongs largely to the millennia extending long before the Mystery of Golgotha. By the time the Mystery of Golgotha was drawing near, this form of knowledge had already grown weaker. In fact, it was only exceptional individuals like the three Magi from the East who possessed the far-reaching knowledge they manifested. On the other hand, only those particularly sensitive to inner things like the shepherds—common folk—could bring such visions out of sleep as the shepherds did. Both the Magi and the shepherds, however, manifested the same legacy of ancient knowledge through which humanity had once been related to the universe.

It could not be said, especially of the actual present, that humanity clearly expresses the way of knowing that entered human evolution with the Mystery of Golgotha. Speaking generally, however, what we are going to speak about this evening holds true. The pre-Christian attitude to the starry heavens was such that people did not see the stars in the prosaic, abstract way they are seen today. That people of old spoke of the stars as if they were living beings is not attributable, as our imperfect science believes, to fantasy, but to a spiritual—although instinctive and atavistic—perception of the heavens. Looking at the starry heavens in ancient times, people did not see merely points or surfaces of light. They also saw something spiritual, something that made them able to describe the constellations as they did, for to them the several planets of our system were ensouled by living beings. They saw the spiritual in the heavens. They also saw the mineral and plant kingdoms in their spiritual reality. In fact, they saw these three regions of existence with the *same* cognitive capacity. They spoke of the stars, minerals, and plants as ensouled beings.

We must not think that the cognitive capacities of the ancients were similar to ours. A little while ago I spoke to you about a stage of knowledge which, although it was not so very different from our own, is nevertheless difficult for many people to imagine today. I said that the Greeks, in the earliest period of their culture, did not see the color blue, that the sky was not blue above them. They perceived colors that lie more on the active red-yellow side. They paint with the shades of blue known to us. Blue came only later into human perception.

Imagine all shades of blue being absent from the world, and green looking different than it does today. You will realize that the world around the Greeks did not appear to them as the world appears to us today. For those of even earlier times the surrounding world was even more different. But the spiritual withdrew from the world that the ancients saw. The spiritual withdrew from stars, minerals, and plants. As it withdrew, the vivid active colors became duller. In contrast, what we experience as blue appeared out of the depths. As the faculty for the perception of blue and the darker colors increased, what ancients experienced in their astrology—which spoke a living, active, colorful language—changed into the gray, colorless geometry and mechanics we know today. We can no longer read the secrets of the starry worlds as we draw this geometry and mechanics from our inner being. Astrology changed into the world of celestial mechanics and mathematics that we picture today following Copernicus, Galileo, and Kepler.

That is one side. The other side is that in ancient times people had access to a deep, inner faculty for perceiving what streamed from the Earth around them as the Earth's auras. These auras—or qualities—announced themselves to inner faculties of perception as the counterpart of the starry heavens. In ancient times human beings were finely sensitive to the characteristics of the climate of their country, of the soil on which they lived. Chalk and granite soils were experienced as radiating different auras from the Earth. What they felt in this way was not an obscure feeling or dull experience. It arose like colors or clouds that they felt and experienced inwardly. And as they experienced the Earth's depths, they experienced the human soul of their fellows and the life of animals in the same way. The experiences were more living, more intense. They gazed into the spirituality of the starry heavens, of the minerals and plants, with atavistic, instinctive clairvoyance as if it were a faculty of outer knowing. They perceived what was living spiritually in the Earth's depths with an instinctive inner vision. They spoke not merely of chalk soil but experienced specific elemental beings: one kind from chalk soil, other kinds from granite or gneiss. They felt what was living in other human beings as an aura but as an aura from the Earth in which they were clothed. They particularly felt the animals with their auras as beings of the Earth. They felt as if the ground, soil, and the inner warmth of the Earth continued on in the whole animal world. When they saw the butterflies over the plants they saw them drawing along with them what was rising from the Earth. They saw in an auric cloud what flitted from the Earth in animal life.

All this gradually withdrew, leaving behind for the human faculty of perception of an exteriorized, prosaic world. Humanity now began to see the colored world as we see it—without perceiving the spiritual. What human beings had once seen through inner perception was transformed into our modern knowledge of nature; what had been seen spiritually through outer perception was transformed into modern mathematics and mechanics.

So we have on the one hand the qualities that the simple shepherds in the field brought to their inner vision, from which we have developed the modern view of nature. And on the other hand we have what the Magi from the East brought to their faculty of perceiving the star, from which we have developed our dry mathematics and mechanics. The faculties of outer and inner perception were still so rich in certain individuals at that time that the mystery of the birth of Jesus could announce itself from these two sides.

What underlay this faculty of perception? During the period between death and a new birth, during the time through which we live before entering through birth into earthly existence, we pass through the actual cosmic expanses. Our individuality is not then bound to the space enclosed by the skin; our existence is spread over cosmic expanses. The faculty of magical vision still demonstrated by the wise men from the East was essentially a faculty which entered strongly into human beings from the period between death and birth—it was a "prenatal" faculty. In those who were pupils of the Magi, what the soul had lived through before birth in the world of stars awakened to become a special faculty. When these pupils developed this particular faculty they were able to say: "Before I came down to this Earth I had definite experiences with Mercury, the Sun, the Moon, Saturn, and Jupiter." And when this cosmic memory arose in them they used it to behold the spiritual in the whole external world and the destiny of human beings on Earth. They saw it out of their memory of existence before birth in the world of stars.

The faculties by which they perceived the Earth's depths, the mysteries of the souls of men and of the nature of the animals, were faculties that developed in seed form in incarnate human beings and first manifested after death. They were postmortem faculties. They became creative after death. But they were youthful, seminal faculties. However, although these faculties become particularly creative after death, in earthly life they arise as potentially germinal forces during the first period of that life, in the child. The forces of growth in a child that spring from the spiritual withdraw in later life. They withdraw and we are then filled rather with precisely those forces that were there before birth. After death, these forces reappear. It was only specially gifted people who retained them on into old age. I have mentioned in the past that such faculties of genius as we have in the later years of life are due to the fact that we have remained more childlike than those who do not have these faculties or have them less. Maintaining childlike faculties into later life equips us with inventive faculties and the like. The more we can retain childlike faculties, the more creative we are. But these creative forces appear again especially after death.

Among some pre-Christian cultures, the after-death faculties could be fructified by faculties remaining from before birth. Because such cultures cultivated the kind of knowledge possessed by the Magi from the East less, this knowledge withdrew and the after-death knowledge began to predominate. Because the prebirth faculties were able to fructify the after-death faculties, the gift of prophecy developed—the gift of foretelling the future prophetically with the after-death faculties. The so-called Hebrew Prophets were people in whom the after-death faculties were particularly developed. But these faculties did not remain merely instinctive as in the simple shepherds in the field to whom the annunciation was made. They were penetrated by the other faculties which had developed to greater intensity among such people as the wise men from the East, and which led to special knowledge relating to the secrets of the starry sky and the events in the heavens.

It will now be clear to you why the proclamation to the shepherds and the knowledge of the wise men had to agree. The knowledge possessed by the latter was such that they were able to behold deep secrets of the starry heavens. The vision came to them out of out of an enhancement of the knowledge of the worlds in which we live between death and a new birth. This knowledge enabled them to penetrate the starry heavens. They saw that from the world that does not primarily belong to life between birth and death but to life between death and a new birth, a being, the Christ, was coming down to the Earth. Thus the approach of Christ was revealed to them out of their knowledge of the stars.

And what was the revelation to the shepherds in the field whose special faculty was to experience the Earth's depths? The *Earth became something different* when the Christ was drawing near. The Earth felt this approach of Christ and bore in herself new forces because of Christ's approach. The pure-hearted shepherds in the field felt out of their depths what the Earth was reflecting. They felt the way in which the Earth was reacting to the approach of Christ. The Earth's depths proclaimed to the shepherds the same message that the cosmic expanses proclaimed to the Magi from the East.

This was a time when remnants of the old knowledge still existed. We are concerned here with those who were exceptional, even in those days, with people like the three Magi from the East and those special shepherds in the fields. Both retained in their own way what had more or less disappeared from humanity in general. This was why the Mystery of Golgotha, when its time was drawing near, could be proclaimed to them as it was.

We must study these things in such a way that we add the knowledge that comes from spiritual science to the ordinary, historical view. We must try, as it were, to fathom the expanses of space and the depths of the life of the soul. If we fathom the expanses of space in the right way and from a particular point of view, we learn to understand how the wise men experienced the approach of the Mystery of Golgotha. If we try to plumb the depths of the life of the soul, we learn to understand how the shepherds received the tidings of what was coming so near to the Earth that the Earth herself became aware of the approach of these forces. The faculties connected with existence before birth that were manifested in the Magi correspond to a more intellectual element, an element of knowledge or insight. Intellectual meant something different in those times than what it is today. What worked in the shepherds corresponds more to will. Will represents the forces of growth in the universe. The shepherds were united in their will with the Christ Being who was approaching the earth. We feel, too, how the stories of the wise men—so inadequately recorded in the modern Bible—express the kind of knowledge with which the wise men approached the Mystery of Golgotha. It came from their consciousness to the external universe. We feel that the story of the proclamation to the shepherds points to the will, to the heart, to the life of inner emotion. "Revelation of the God from the heavens and peace to those on Earth who are of good will." We feel the streaming of the will in the proclamation to the shepherds. The light-filled knowledge that the Magi possessed is of a quite different character.

We realize the profundity and significance of the knowledge in the Magi and the proclamation to the shepherds as narrated in the New Testament when we try to fathom the nature of human knowledge and of human will—faculties connected with existence before birth and after death.

I have said that what was a living world of spirit to the ancients— the stars, the minerals, and the plants—became mathematics and mechanics for us. What was once inner knowledge has drawn to the surface. If we picture to ourselves the knowledge in the shepherds as being inward and what manifested in the Magi as outward, it was the outer knowledge in the Magi that reached into space to perceive the spirit. The inner life of the shepherds, on the other hand, led to spiritual perception of the Earth's depths. During the further evolution of humanity, the inner kind of knowledge manifested in the shepherds grew increasingly outward to become outer perception, what we call empirical perception. What gave the Magi their knowledge of the world of the stars drew inward, backward toward the brain, and became our mathematical, mechanistic world. There was a *crossing*. What was inner knowledge—pictorial, naive, instinctive imagination—in pre-Christian times became external knowledge, sense perception. And what was once outer knowledge, which encompassed the world of stars, drew inward and became the dry, geometrical-mathematical, mechanistic world we now draw forth from within us.

Through their inner enlightenment people today perceive only what is mathematical, mechanical. Only outstanding spirits like Novalis are able to feel and express the poetry and deep imagination of this inner mathematical world. What Novalis hymns in such beautiful language is, for the ordinary person today, the dry world of triangles and squares, sums and differences, like the two forces in a parallelogram. Ordinary human beings are prosaic enough to feel this world to be barren, dry. They have no love for it. Novalis, an exceptional being, sings its praises because an echo of what this world was before it had drawn inward still lived in him. Then it was the world out of which the spirit of Jupiter, Saturn, Aries, Taurus, and Gemini was perceived. It was the ancient light-filled world of stars that has withdrawn and, in the first stage of its withdrawal, becomes the world that seems to us to be dry, mathematical, and mechanistic.

The faculty that in the shepherds intensified to hearing the voice of the angel in the heights has likewise become dry, barren, and feeble in us. It has become our perception of the outer sensory world. Today we perceive minerals and plants with it, while before, although it was scarcely expressed, we perceive the Earth's depths or the world of humans and animals.

What has faded into today's mathematical-mechanistic universe was once astrology and contained so great a cognitive power that Christ was revealed to the Magi as a heavenly being.

Knowledge of Christ's deep influence on the Earth, the whole power with which he would work in the Earth—what he would be for the Earth—came to the shepherds in the fields. Today's ordinary sensory knowledge—with which we see only the green surface of grass, the brown skins of animals, and the like—was still inward then and had not yet drawn outward to the eyes, the skin.

We must find the way back again. We must rediscover how the inner faculty that is now dry mathematics may intensify images to Imagination. We must learn to grasp the Imagination given us by initiation science. What do these imaginations contain? They continue the faculty with which the Magi from the East recognized Christ's approach. The imaginations are the sprouts that follow what the ancients saw in the starry constellations, in star imaginations, mineral imaginations, gold, silver, and copper. The ancients saw in imaginations. The mathematical faculties of today are their offspring, their continuation. They are the faculties that today understand the imaginations. By the development of these inner faculties we must to seek to understand the Christ Being today.

Outer perception must also be deepened. Outer perception itself descended from what were once inner experiences, our instinctive nature. The power that was still inward in the hearts of the shepherds in the field is only in eyes and ears today; it has shifted entirely to our outer part and hence perceives only the outer tapestry of the sense world. This power must go still further outward. To do so we must be able to leave the body and attain Inspiration. Then this Inspiration—a faculty of perception attainable today—will be able to give out of initiation science the same as was given in the annunciation to the shepherds' naive, inner knowing.

What astrology was to the Magi and heart vision was to the shepherds comes together in modern humanity in the knowledge that comes from initiation science through Imagination and Inspiration. Through it we can rise to the spiritual realization of the living Christ. We must learn to understand how Isis, the living, Divine Sophia, had to disappear when the time came for the development that drove astrology into mathematics, geometry, and the science of mechanics. Living Imagination must resurrect her from the dead field of mathematics, phoronomy, and geometry. This means we must find Isis again, a new Isis, who is the Divine Sophia. We must find if the power of Christ—ours since the Mystery of Golgotha—is to become truly living, that is to say, filled with light within us.

We are standing before this very point of time. The outer Earth will not provide us with those things we have become accustomed to desiring in modern times. The conflicts called into being by the terrible catastrophes of recent years have already changed a large part of the Earth into a field where culture lies in ruins. Further conflicts will follow. Human beings are preparing for the next great world war. Culture will be ruined in more ways. There will be nothing to be had from what seems to us to be of most value for knowledge and the will. Outward earthly life, insofar as it is a product of earlier times, will pass away. It is vain to believe that the old habits of thought and will can continue. A new kind of knowledge must arise, a new kind of willing in all domains. We must familiarize ourselves with the idea that our civilization will vanish. We must look into the human heart, into the spirit dwelling in us. We must have faith in the heart and the human spirit so that by all we are able to do in the ruins of the old civilization, truly new forms may arise.

These forms will not arise if we do not bear in mind with all seriousness what must happen to humanity. Read the book *How to Know Higher Worlds* and you will find it said that one who desires to attain higher knowledge must understand what is called "the meeting with the Guardian of the Threshold." This meeting means that willing, feeling, and thinking must separate in a certain way and that a trinity must arise out of the chaotic unity in us. This understanding must come to students of spiritual science as they become clear what the Guardian of the Threshold is. It must also come to the whole of modern humanity in regard to the course of civilization. In inner experience, though not in outer consciousness, humanity is passing through the region that can also be called a region of the Guardian of the Threshold.

Modern humanity is passing over a threshold at which a guardian, an important guardian, stands. The guardian says with great seriousness above all this: "Do not cling to what has come as a transplant from ancient times. Look into your hearts, your souls, so that you may be capable of creating new forms. You can create these new forms only when you have faith that the powers of knowledge and of will for this spiritual creation can come out of the spiritual world." What is an event of great intensity for individuals who enter the worlds of higher knowledge is happening unconsciously in present-day humanity as a whole. Those who have linked themselves together as the anthroposophical community must realize that it is one of the most needed of all things in our days to bring humanity to understand this region of passing through the threshold.

We must realize as knowers that our thinking, feeling, and willing separate and must be held together in a higher sense. In the same way, modern humanity must understand that spiritual life, the life of rights, and economic life must separate and create a form of union higher than the state has been up to now. No programs, ideas, ideologies can bring individuals to recognize the necessity of this threefoldness of the social organism. Only profound knowledge of the onward development of humankind reveals that this development has reached a threshold where a guardian stands. The guardian demands of those who are advancing to higher knowledge: "Submit to the separation in thinking, feeling, and willing." To humanity as a whole he says: "Separate what has up to now been interwoven in a chaotic unity in the idol of the state. Separate this unity into a spiritual life, an equity state, and an economic state." Without this, no progress is possible for humanity. The old chaos will break out again. If this happens it will not take a form that humanity needs. It will take an Ahrimanic or Luciferic form. Only spiritual scientific knowledge of the passing of the threshold in our day can give the true Christ form to this chaos.

If we understand Anthroposophy, we understand this is something the Christmas festival also speaks of. The child in the crib must represent humanity's spiritual development into the future. The shepherds in the field and the Magi from the East went to see how what was going to advance humanity appeared in the form of a little child. Modern humanity must likewise make its way to Initiation to perceive, in the form of a little child, what the threefold social organism based on spiritual science must do for the future. If the old form of the state is not "threefolded," it will break down. It will break down on the one side into a wholly chaotic, completely Ahrimanic and Luciferic spiritual life, and on the other side into a Luciferic-Ahrimanic economic life. These would drag the state in tatters after them. In the East more Ahrimanic-Luciferic spiritual states will occur; in the West an Ahrimanic-Luciferic economic life. This will happen if human beings do not realize how to avoid this by permeating their being with Christ and bringing about—out of their knowledge and will—the "threefolding" of what is trying to separate.

This will be human knowledge permeated by Christ. It will be human willing permeated by Christ. It will express itself in no other way than that the idol of the unitary state will become threefold. Those who stand properly in the spiritual life will recognize, as did the shepherds in the field, what it is that the Earth experiences through the Christ. And those who stand rightly within the economic life, within the economic associations, will unfold, in the true sense, a will that brings a Christ-filled social order.

13

SOPHIA AND PISTIS

Dornach, March 26, 1922

THERE IS MUCH TALK NOWADAYS about the difference between faith and knowledge. Among other things, it is often said that by what it has to say—by the very nature of its content—Anthroposophy should describe itself as a faith, not as a science. Basically, people make such distinctions because they have little insight into either what faith has meant in the course of human evolution or what knowledge or science really is.

All faith—everything associated with the word "faith"—goes back to very ancient times in human evolution. It goes back to times when the breathing process played a much greater role in human life than it does today. Today, with our present soul disposition, we pay little attention to breathing. We breathe in and out. But we do not experience consciously anything special as we do so.

The content of faith in ancient time always stressed the meaning of breath. We need only recall the Old Testament, where the creation of humanity is related to the inhalation of the breath. We need only remember, for example, what I have said about the striving of people in ancient India to achieve higher knowledge by regulation of the breathing process. This striving made sense at a time when, even in ordinary life, human beings were more aware of their breathing process. As I have said repeatedly, this was a period of evolution when humans saw around them not only dead nature as we do today; they also saw soul and spirit working in all natural things and events. Ancient humanity saw soul and spirit at work in every river, spring, and cloud, and in the wind itself. In those days, human beings strove to make breathing more and more conscious. They did so by regulating the breath—inhalation, holding the breath, and exhalation. Through such regulation, they gave birth to what we may call *self-consciousnes*—that is, to the experience of the "I" or the "I am." This was a time when, even in ordinary life, perception or conscious experience of breathing played a large role. With today's ordinary consciousness, we can have little idea of what this was like. Let me try to give you an idea.

The breathing process falls naturally into inhalation, holding of breath, and exhalation. The process is regulated by human nature. Practitioners of Yoga, however, regulated it differently. Just as a person who studies today develops a different way of thinking from everyday life, so, in times when breathing played a special role in life, Yogis evolved a different kind of breathing from everyday breathing. Today, however, we don't want to develop yogic breathing. We want to develop ordinary observation.

When people in ancient times inhaled, they felt that what was spiritual in the beings and events of the outer world entered them from the outer world with the air they breathed in. When they breathed in, they experienced, for instance, gnomes and nymphs. They experienced all that was soul and spirit in surrounding nature. And when they breathed out—sent the breath out again—these beings became invisible to them once more. They merged, as it were, with the surrounding nature, and were lost.

Thus, they breathed in and knew that soul and spirit lived in the world of outer nature. They felt united with this soul and spirit of external nature. The experience had a kind of intoxicating (I use the word only for comparison) effect. Breathing in, they entranced or intoxicated themselves with the soul and spirit of the surrounding world. Breathing out, they became cool and sober again. Thus they lived in a dual process—alternately intoxicating and sobering— whereby they entered into a mutual interplay with the soul and spirit of the surrounding world.

There was something else as well. In breathing in—intoxicating themselves with soul and spirit as it gently rose from the stream of living breath into their heads—they felt beings of soul and spirit filling them inwardly, uniting with their own bodily being. We can express what they felt somewhat as follows. They breathed in the soul and spirit of the surrounding world. It filled their heads. They were aware of it. They felt it. They held their breath and then, as they breathed out, they felt they were returning the feeling of soul and spirit to nature.

All this was intimately connected with daily life. Here's a simple example. Consider a piece of chalk. Nowadays, when you take hold of the chalk, you first look at it, then you grasp it and pick it up. It was different in that ancient epoch. Today, when we look at the chalk, we have a certain thought. Then we pick up the chalk. In ancient times, it was not like that. People looked at the chalk, breathed in what emanated from it spiritually, then breathed out again. Only then, in exhaling, did they take hold of the chalk. For them, breathing in was equivalent to contemplation, breathing out to action.

People then lived in a kind of rhythmic interplay with their surrounding world. In fact, this rhythmic interplay was preserved into far later times but without the living and seeing consciousness of ancient times. Think for instance how in the nineteenth century farmers would still thresh corn rhythmically by hand in country places. "Look, and thresh. Look, and thresh." The rhythm corresponded to a certain breathing process.

Later, the inner experience corresponding to inhalation vanished from human perception. Human beings only perceived—even today only perceive—the breath that goes into the head.

Earlier, human beings perceived how the inhaled air—which was like an intoxication—entered the head and united with sense impressions. Later, this was no longer the case. What goes on in our chest organization is lost to consciousness. We no longer perceive the breath pouring upward, because in effect our sense impressions have grown stronger and blot out what rises in the breath. Yet even today, whenever you see or hear, the breathing process is there in your process of seeing, and in your process of hearing, too. In ancient humanity breathing itself lived strongly in hearing and seeing. In human beings today, seeing and hearing live so intensely that breathing is eclipsed, toned down, overwhelmed. Imagine what the people of ancient times perceived, entrancing them, pouring throughout their heads, till they exclaimed, "Ah, the nymphs! Ah, the gnomes! How the nymphs whirl in my head, how the gnomes hammer, how the undine wave and surge through my head!" That no longer exists for us. Today the hammering, surging, and whirling are eclipsed and overwhelmed by what comes from actual seeing or hearing, which fills our head.

There was thus a time when human beings had a stronger perception of the breath streaming upward into the head. It continued into the epoch when they perceived all these things intermingled. They still had some perception of the after-echoes of the hammering of the gnomes, the waving of the undines, the whirling of the nymphs. They still perceived the connection of these after-echoes with their perceptions of sound and light and color.

In a still later time, what was still perceived of the breathing process was lost altogether. Then those who still had a vestige of that consciousness—and still knew that breathing had once brought the soul and spirit of the world into human beings—gave a name to what remained with them of sense perception in its connection with breathing. They called it *Sophia*.

But they no longer inwardly perceived breathing itself. The spiritual content of breathing was deadened or, rather, maimed and paralyzed by sense perception.

The ancient Greeks especially felt this. The Greeks did not have the idea of science that we have today. If you had told them of the kind of learning that is taught in our universities, it would have seemed them as though someone were constantly pricking their brain with tiny needles. It would have been unintelligible to them that people could derive any satisfaction from this "science." If they had been called upon to assimilate such a science, they would have said, "It makes the brain hurt, it wounds, it stings and pricks the brain." They still wanted to perceive something of that blissful pouring of the entrancing breath in which, as it streams inward, all that is heard and seen merges.

The ancient Greeks, in effect, still had a perception of an inner life in the head. They called this inner life *Sophia*. And those who loved to unfold this Sophia in themselves—who were especially inclined to devote themselves to Sophia—were the ones who called themselves philosophers. The word "philosophy" points undoubtedly to a living inner experience. The hideously pedantic way of learning philosophy, where you merely cram it, as the undergraduates say, was quite unknown in ancient Greece. Philosophy expressed the inner experience "*I love Sophia.*"

Just as the breathing process, passing into the body was received in the head in sense perception, so the rest of the body received the exhaled air. As the sense perceptions, all that was seen and heard, flowed into the entrancing experience of the inbreathed air as it poured into the head, so the bodily feelings—the inner experiences of the body—merged with the exhaled air. The exhaled air with its calming and sobering quality—extinguishing perception—merged with the bodily feelings kindled in walking and working. Action, activity, was connected with exhalation. Whenever people were active, whenever they did some work, they felt as though soul and spirit was going from them. Whenever people worked, they felt as though they were pouring soul and spirit into things. "I receive soul and spirit, it entrances my head, it unites with what I see and hear. But when I do something, I breathe out, and soul and spirit goes away. It goes into whatever I am hammering, or taking hold of. It goes into all the work I do. I let the soul and spirit go. I convey it to outer things—when I churn the milk for instance, or do any other kind of work externally. I let the soul and spirit flow into the things." Such was the feeling, the experience, in ancient times.

But this perception of exhalation—with its sobering influence—came to an end. Only a trace of it was left in ancient Greece. The Greeks were still able to feel, to some extent, that when they were working they were giving something spiritual to the things.

Later, however, bodily feeling—the feeling of effort and fatigue in the work—eclipsed everything in the breathing process. As the inhalation process was maimed in relation to the head, so exhalation was maimed in relation the rest of the body. Bodily feeling—the feeling of exertion, the feeling of becoming heated—paralyzed the process of spiritual exhalation. It was paralyzed by all that lived in human beings by which they felt their own strength as they applied it to their work. People no longer felt the outbreathing process as fatigue. They felt a force working within them—felt the body permeated with energy and strength.

This force was *Pistis*, or faith. It was the feeling of the divine, of the divine force and energy that enables a person to work.

Thus, wisdom and faith—Sophia and Pistis—flowed together in the human being. Wisdom moved toward the head, while faith lived in the whole person. Wisdom, in effect, was only the ideal *content*. Faith was this ideal content's inner *force*. The two belonged together—hence the name of a Gnostic text preserved from antiquity, the *Pistis Sophia*. In Sophia, there was a thinning out, a dilution, of the experience of inhalation; in faith, there was a condensation or thickening, of exhalation. Thereafter, wisdom grew thinner still and, as it continued to dilute, it became "science." Simultaneously, the inner force continued to "thicken," until finally people felt only their bodies. We lost the consciousness of what faith, or Pistis, truly is.

Thus it came about that humanity—no longer able to sense the real connection between faith and science—severed the two. The mere content of faith was now supposed to arise subjectively as it were, from within, while science was united with the outer sense perceptions. First, there was *Sophia*, then *scientia*—contemporary ordinary science—a thinned and diluted Sophia. Originally, Sophia had been a spiritual being whom humanity had felt inhabiting the head.

Today, we have only the specter of that being. This should become a sort of meditation for us—that science is only the ghost of wisdom.

The same is true of faith, or what is called faith today, only in this case the change has not been put into words. Faith today is not the inwardly experienced faith, the Pistis of antiquity. It is something subjective, deeply bound up with personal egoism. It is the "thickened" faith of ancient times. There was a time when, in this thickened faith, people still experienced the objectively divine within their being.

Nowadays, faith is only found rising out of the body like subjective smoke. Thus we might say that just as science is still the ghost of erstwhile wisdom, so faith today is still the "clod" of former faith—the old Faith, grown thick and heavy.

When these things are seen together, we shall no longer judge as superficially as many people do today, saying that Anthroposophy is a mere faith, something to be believed. Such people do not know what they are saying. They have never acquainted themselves, from true human history, with the former union of faith and wisdom, the inner experience of oneness between faith and wisdom. Where does one find an account of history as I have described it here today? Where do historians speak of the breathing process and what it was for human beings when it was an utterly different inner experience from what ours is today? If historians do become conscious of the facts, then how abstract on the one hand and how crudely material on the other does what once was a real entity of soul-and-spirit and soul-and-body become?

When the evolution of faith had reached a certain point, human beings had to receive something quite definite into the content of faith. In ancient times, humanity experienced the divine in the content of "faith." Ancient human beings experienced the divine in consciousness, in the exhalation process. But consciousness of the exhalation process was lost. Humanity lost consciousness of how the divine goes out in exhalation and is conveyed into the things we work upon. Consciousness of the divine needed to be recalled to life in human beings. In due time, humanity obtained this by receiving into itself an idea for which there is no outer earthly reality. That the dead rise up out of their grave has no earthly reality. Therefore the Mystery of Golgotha has no real content for anyone who merely describes the life of Jesus until his death. There is nothing much in that. To modern theology—to tell the truth—Jesus himself is no longer very much. There is nothing much in the way theology today describes the story of Jesus' life—a human being goes through different experiences and then dies. No, the mystery only begins with the Resurrection, with the living life of the Christ Being after the physical body had passed through death. This, after all, is also what St. Paul affirms: one who does not receive into consciousness the idea of the Resurrection has received nothing at all of Christianity. Hence, modern theology is only a "Jesusology." It is no real Christianity. Christianity requires an idea that points to a reality that does *not* take place on Earth as a direct sense perception. It needs an idea that, as idea, raises us into the supersensible. An inner experience in consciousness raised ancient humanity into the supersensible. I have told you how yogic students were led to the conscious inner experience of their infancy. They experienced the impressions of earliest infancy—of what works plastically, forming and molding the human being in earliest childhood. What we know nothing of in ordinary life was made conscious by yogic exercises. The whole of the prenatal life, even before conception, when the human soul in the spiritual world before descending to take on a physical corporeality, was made conscious.

Afterward, no more remained of this experience than an idea. The idea is in the Gospels: "If you do not become as little children, you cannot penetrate into the realms of the heavens." This saying truly refers to the very same experience—only at that point it was no longer an immediate living reality. It was like a memory of how, long ago, human beings had been able to transplant themselves far back into the time of earliest childhood and had been able to experience the realms of the heavens from which they had descended through birth into physical existence. It is scarcely to be supposed that human beings today have any clear idea of what is meant when they hear from the Gospels or from other ancient texts about "the realms of the heavens." They think, well, yes, certainly, I have seen that on Earth there are the realms of France, England, and so forth; the Earth is divided into realms and dominions. Such realms as there are here on Earth are up there too: the realms of the heavens. People today can have no concrete idea of the realms of the heavens if they cannot conceive what is familiar down here transplanted there. I think in English they even say "the *kingdoms* of the heavens." But you get no real idea of what lies behind this expression, "the realms, or kingdoms, of the heavens." In fact, the Gospel generally puts it in such a way that you are even less able to see what it really means. For the Gospel speaks of the realms (or kingdoms) of God, of which people today cannot think at all but are content merely to let the words resound.

The truth is that the heavens of old were precisely what is spread out all around us as the great sphere of the universe. And what was the "realm," the "kingdom"? Philology aside, let us here have recourse to an observation given by pure anthroposophical method. The realm is what *reaches*, far and all around us. It is what reaches far and away, sounding forth and speaking. We must rise to this conception. Throughout the heavens, for one who learns to hear, soul and spirit sound forth. We see only the heavens, but we hear the cosmic Word, sounding and reaching with its sound throughout the heavens.

Those who cannot become like little children cannot perceive the Word of the heavens—the Word that speaks out of the heavens on all sides. And if we call the earthly realms "realms," and earthly rulers, "rulers of these realms," we ought to have the hidden notion that these rulers can speak or sing so loud that their voice sound forth throughout their several realms. This used to be expressed symbolically in the giving of laws, which were proclaimed with trumpet calls to the four quarters of the heavens. This made the "realm" a reality. The realm was not the mere surface on which so many human beings dwelt; the realm was what the trumpeting angels carried forth into the far reaches of space, as the content of the laws that were given.

Yet this was only a memory. Another concept had to come, related to the will. (The former concept was related to the idea, to thought.) A will-related concept must be related to what accompanies human beings when they pass through the gate of death. After death, the will remains, as the energy that a human being unfolds. It accompanies the human being through the gate of death with the content of cosmic thoughts. The human will, filled with world thoughts, accompanies us into the spiritual worlds when we die. The new concept appealed to this will. This was the concept of the risen Christ—of he who lives on even when dead for the Earth. This was the strong and mighty, force-filled concept—not merely a recalling of childhood but a pointing-forward to death, appealing to that in us which passes with us through the gate of death.

Thus we find, founded in the evolution of history, the bursting-in of the Christ concept and of the whole Christ impulse.

It must of course be admitted that even today there are many on Earth who know nothing of the Christ. And the knowledge of those who do know of him is generally poor. Nevertheless, they learn something of the Christ, even though, because of modern materialism, the concept and feeling of Christ that they bear within them is not the right one. And then there are also many human beings upon Earth who live in more ancient forms of religion. Here a great question arises.

The Mystery of Golgotha, I said, is a fact. Christ died for all humanity. The Christ impulse has become a force for all the Earth. In this objective sense—apart from consciousness—Christ is there for Jews and pagans, Christians, Hindus, Buddhists, and all other religions. Christ is there. Since the Mystery of Golgotha Christ lives in the evolutionary forces of all earthly humankind. Yet it still makes a difference whether a human being lives within a Christian or a non-Christian region. However, we can study *what* the difference is only when we perceive the connection between a person's earthly life and the life he or she unfolds between death and a new birth. Let us consider those who, in earthly life were Buddhist or Hindus and so received in life no idea or feeling about Christ at all. When they pass through the gate of death, they take with them into the cosmos after death what a human being can learn and discover about nature, the outer world environment, on Earth. There would be no knowledge of nature in Heaven if people, when they enter the realms of the heavens through death, did not carry with them knowledge of Earth. When we pass through the gate of death, we carry with us into the supersensible realms what we receive and absorb here on Earth. It is only through us that the supersensible worlds have any knowledge of mineral, plant, and animal nature on Earth. But it is different with one who knows something of Christ— especially with those who can conceive that Christ lives in them, according to the words of St. Paul, "Not I, but Christ in me." They carry not merely knowledge of Earth into the supersensible world, but the knowledge of earthly humanity. Thus, even today, both are carried over. Christians carry knowledge of earthly humanity—of the bodily, earthly formation of human beings. The Hindus, Buddhists, and so on carry the knowledge of what surrounds us. Human beings, even today, complement one another in the contributions they give to the supersensible worlds when they pass through the gate of death.

It is of course becoming more and more necessary that all the secrets we can experience—in and through us *as human beings*—be borne into the heavens. Humankind must become increasingly "Christened," through and through. This, above all, is important— that what we experience only here on Earth, *as human beings with other human beings,* be carried through the gate of death by means of Christianity. This is a most essential truth.

Take for example the Hindus or the Buddhists. They bear into the spiritual world through the gate of death all that they experience in contemplating the world, in sensing and feeling the world—all the thoughts about minerals, all the sensations about plants, the feelings about animals. With all they experience they enrich the knowledge of the gods in the supersensible world.

What, then, of Christians? They take through the gate of death what they experiences in social relationships with their fellows— things that one can experience only as a human being among human beings, in human earthly brotherhood. The Buddhist, I would say, carries through the gate of death the beauty of the world; the Christian carries the goodness of the world. They truly complement one another. The progress of Christianity consists in this: that human social relationships on Earth grow in significance for the celestial worlds. . . .

This is the very thing that we should attain through Christianity: the power to carry into the supersensible worlds what comes about in earthly evolution through our actions. We must carry into the spiritual worlds what we develop here on Earth through the thought of the risen Christ as a living being who passed through death and is alive. Therefore those human beings who would not like their social actions to be carried through death have a horror of recognizing the Risen Christ.

The world of the physical senses is really connected with the supersensible. We do not understand one unless we understand it in connection with the other. We must come once again to understand what happens on Earth by understanding the spiritual events of the great universe. We must learn not to speak abstractly of spirit and matter, but, for example, to observe how human beings once felt a connection with the divine soul and spirit of the great universe in the breathing process. Thereby we shall come to experience again the soul and spirit of the universe in the way we *can* experience it in our time. There is no other way of bringing about healing social conditions. People will cry aloud for social reform, but they will attain nothing at all. On the contrary, everything will decay more and more. The ancients might legitimately find intoxication in the breath; we moderns cannot afford to find intoxication in mere words. Words must not be a mere entrancement for us, but something that is cherished in the spirit of the old Sophia—permeating us and filling us with living wisdom.

Anthroposophy points out what is essential for social life today. It seeks to express something of this in its very name, *Anthropo-Sophia*. That too is a kind of wisdom. For the ancient Greeks, *Anthropos* went without saying. *Sophia* was wisdom for humanity. Humanity was still filled with wisdom of light. Today when one says "Sophia," people think only of science and scholarship—the ghost of Sophia. We need to draw attention to the fact that *Anthropo-Sophia* is something that proceeds from us, shines forth from us, springs forth and blossoms out of our noblest forces. We must point to this quite explicitly; we cannot leave it unsaid. Thereby, however, Anthroposophy brings renewing life into human earthly existence. Then Anthroposophy will be experienced—more spiritually, but no less concretely—as *Sophia* was in olden time. At the same time, it will bring to expression what used to live in the whole human being: namely, *Pistis*, the content of faith and a true content of knowledge—albeit, that kind of knowledge which gives human beings force and energy, such as in ancient times was contained in faith alone.

14

MICHAEL, SOPHIA, AND MARDUK

Torquay, August 11, 1924

... IN ANCIENT CHALDEA, THE FOLLOWING WAS TAUGHT: human soul
forces reach their maximum potential when human beings direct
their spiritual eye to the wonderful contrast between the life of sleep
(when their consciousness is dimmed and they are oblivious of their
environment) and the waking life (when they are clear-sighted, and
aware of the world around them). These alternating states of sleep
and waking were experienced differently thousands of years ago than
they are today. Sleep was less unconscious, and waking life was not
so fully conscious. In sleep, human beings were aware of powerful
and ever-changing images, of the flux and movement of the life of
worlds. They were in touch with the divine ground, the essence, of
the universe.

The dimming of consciousness during sleep is a consequence of
human evolution. A few thousand years ago, waking life was not so
clear and lucid as today. Objects had no clearly defined contours;
they were blurred. They radiated spiritual realities in various forms.
There was not the same abrupt transition from sleep to waking life.
The people of that epoch were still able to distinguish these two
states. The environment of their waking life was called *Apsu;* while
the life of flux and movement experienced in sleep, the realm that
blurred the clear distinction between the minerals, plants, and animals of waking life, was called *Tiamat.* Now, the teaching in the
Chaldean Mystery Schools was that when human beings, in a state
of sleep, shared the flux and movement of *Tiamat,* they were closer to

truth and reality than when they lived their conscious life among minerals, plants, and animals. *Tiamat* was nearer to the ground of the world, more closely related to the human world than *Apsu*. *Apsu* was more remote. *Tiamat* represented something that lay nearer to humanity. But in the course of time *Tiamat* underwent changes and this was brought to the notice of the neophytes in the Mystery Schools. From the life of flux and movement of *Tiamat*, demoniacal forms emerged, equine shapes with human heads, leonine forms with the heads of angels. These demoniacal forms, which became hostile to human beings, arose out of the warp and woof of *Tiamat*.

Then there appeared in the world a powerful Being, *Ea*. Anyone today who has an ear for sounds can feel how the conjunction of these two vowels (*e* and *a*) points to that powerful being who, according to these old Mystery teachings, stood at one's side to help when the demons of *Tiamat* grew strong. *Ea*, or *Ia*, later became—if one anticipates the prefix "Soph"—"Soph-Ea," *Sophia*. *Ea* means, approximately, abstract wisdom, wisdom that permeates all things. "Soph" is a particle that suggests (approximately) a state of being. Sophia, Sophea, Sopheia, the all-pervading, omnipresent Wisdom, sent to humanity her son, then known as *Marduk*, later called "Micha-el," the Micha-el who is invested with authority from the hierarchy of the angels. He is the same being as *Marduk*, the son of *Ea*, wisdom: Marduk–Micha-el.

According to the Mystery teachings, *Marduk–Micha-el* was great and powerful, and all the demoniacal beings such as horses with human heads and leonine forms with angels' heads—all these surging, mobile, demoniacal forms, conjoined as the mighty *Tiamat*, were arrayed against him. *Marduk–Micha-el* was powerful enough to command the storm wind that sweeps through the world. All that *Tiamat* embodied was seen as a living reality, and rightly so, for that is how the Chaldeans experienced it. All these demons together were envisaged as the adversary—a powerful dragon embodying all the demoniacal powers born of *Tiamat*, the night. And this dragon being, breathing fire and fury, advanced upon *Marduk*. *Marduk–Micha-el* first smote it with various weapons and then drove the whole force of his storm wind into the dragon's entrails, so that *Tiamat* burst asunder and was scattered abroad. And so *Marduk–Micha-el* was able to create out of the dragon the heavens above and the earth beneath. And thus arose the Above and the Below.

Such was the teaching of the Mysteries. The eldest son of *Ea*, wisdom, vanquished *Tiamat* and fashioned from one part of *Tiamat* the heavens above and from the other the earth below. And if, O human being, you lift your eyes to the stars, you will see one part of what *Marduk–Micha-el* formed in the heavens out of the fearful abyss of *Tiamat* for the benefit of humankind. And if you look below, where the plants grow out of the mineralized earth, where minerals begin to take form, you will find the other part that the son of *Ea*, wisdom, has recreated for the benefit of humankind.

Thus the ancient Chaldeans looked back to the formative period of the world, to the forming from the formless; they saw into the workshop of creation and perceived a living reality. These demon forms of the night, all these nocturnal monsters, the weaving, surging beings of *Tiamat*, had been transformed by *Marduk–Micha-el* into the stars above and the earth beneath. All the demons transformed by *Marduk–Micha-el* into shining stars, all that grows out of the earth, the transformed skin and tissue of *Tiamat*—*this* is the form in which people of ancient times pictured whatever came to them through the old attributes of the soul. Such information they accounted as knowledge. . . .

15

A Christmas Study:

The Mystery of the Logos

from Anthroposophical Leading Thoughts

Our study of the Michael Mystery was irradiated by thoughts of the Mystery of Golgotha. For, in effect, Michael is the power who leads humans toward the Christ along the true way of humanity's salvation. But the Michael mission is one of those that are repeated again and again in rhythmical succession in the cosmic evolution of humankind. In its beneficial influence on earthly humankind it was repeated before the Mystery of Golgotha. It was connected in that time with all the active revelations, which the Christ force—as yet external to the Earth—had to pour down to the Earth for the unfolding of humanity. After the Mystery of Golgotha, the Michael mission enters the service of what must now be achieved in earthly humanity through Christ himself. In its repetitions, the Michael mission now appears in a changed and ever progressing form. The point is that it appears in repetitions.

The Mystery of Golgotha, on the other hand, is an all-embracing world event, taking place once only in the whole course of the cosmic evolution of humankind.

It was only when humanity had reached the unfolding of the intellectual or mind soul that the ever-continued danger, which was there potentially from the beginning—the danger that humanity's existence might become severed from the existence of the divine-spiritual—made itself fully felt.

And just as the human soul loses the conscious experience in and with the divine-spiritual beings, around it emerges what we today call nature.

Human beings no longer see the essence and being of humanity in the divine-spiritual cosmos; they see the accomplished work of the divine-spiritual in this earthly realm.

To begin with, however, they saw it not in the abstract form in which it is seen today—not as physically sensible events and entities held together by those abstract ideal contents we call natural laws. To begin with, they saw it still as divine-spiritual being. They saw it as divine-spiritual being surging up and down in all that they perceived around them, in the birth and decay of living animals, in the springing and sprouting of the plant world, in the activity of water wells and rivers, in cloud and wind and weather. All these processes of being around them represented the gestures, deeds, and speech of the divine being at the foundation of "nature."

Once upon a time, humankind had seen in the constellations and movements of the stars the deeds and gestures of the divine beings of the cosmos, whose words human beings were able to read in the heavens. In like manner, the "facts of nature" became for them an expression of the Goddess of the Earth. For the divinity at work in nature was conceived as feminine.

Far on into the Middle Ages, the relics of this mode of conception were still at work in human souls, filling the intellectual or mind soul with an imaginative content.

When the sages of that time wanted to bring the processes of nature to the understanding of their pupils, they spoke of the deeds of the Goddess. Only with the gradual dawn of the spiritual soul did this living study of nature, filled as it was with inner soul, grow unintelligible to humankind.

The way humans looked in this direction in the age of the intellectual or mind soul is reminiscent of the myth of Persephone and of the mystery that underlies it.

Persephone, the daughter of Demeter, is compelled by the God of the Underworld to follow him into his kingdom. Eventually it is achieved that she spends one-half of the year only in the nether world and dwells for the remainder of the year in the upper world.

This myth of Persephone was still a great and wonderful expression of the way human beings, in an age of immemorial antiquity, had perceived and known the evolutionary process of the Earth in dreamlike clairvoyance.

In primeval times all world-creative activity had proceeded from the surroundings of the Earth. The Earth itself was only in process of becoming, and molded its existence in cosmic evolution out of the activities of the surrounding world. The divine-spiritual beings of the cosmos were the creators and molders of the Earth's existence. But when the Earth was far enough advanced to become an independent heavenly body, a divine-spiritual being descended from the great cosmos to the Earth and became the Earth divinity. The dreamlike clairvoyance of primeval humankind had seen and known this cosmic fact, and of such knowledge the myth of Persephone remained—but not only this.

For indeed, far on even into the Middle Ages the way human beings sought to know and penetrate into nature was still a relic of the same ancient knowledge. It was not yet as in these later times, when we see only according to our sense impressions, according to what appears on the surface of the Earth. They still saw according to the forces that work upward to the surface from the depths of the Earth. And they saw these "forces of the depths"—the "forces of the nether world"—in mutual interplay with the influences of the stars and elements working from the Earth's environment.

The plants in their varied forms grow forth, revealing themselves in many-colored glory. Therein are at work the forces of Sun and Moon and stars, together with the forces of the Earth's depths. The ground and foundation for this is given in the minerals, whose existence is entirely conditioned by the part of the cosmic beings that have become earthly. Through those heavenly forces that have become earthly alone, rock and stone shoot forth out of the nether world. The animal kingdom, on the other hand, has not assumed the forces of the earthly depths. It comes into being through those world forces alone that are at work from the surroundings of the Earth. It owes its growth, development, and surging life, its powers of nutrition, its possibilities of movement, to the Sun forces streaming down to the Earth. And under the influence of the Moon forces streaming down to the Earth it has the power to reproduce itself. It appears in manifold forms and species because the starry constellations are working in manifold ways from the cosmos, shaping and molding this animal life. The animals are, as it were, only placed down here on Earth from the cosmos. Only in their dim life of consciousness do they partake in the earthly realm; in their origin, development, and growth, in all that they are in order to be able to perceive and move about, they are not earthly creatures.

This mightily conceived idea of the evolution of the Earth lived once upon a time in humankind. The greatness of the conception is scarcely recognizable any longer in the relics of it that came down to the Middle Ages. To attain this knowledge one must go back, with the true vision of the seer, into very ancient times. For even the physical documents that are extant do not reveal what was really present there in the souls of humans, save to those able to penetrate to it by a spiritual path.

Now human beings are not in a position to hold themselves so aloof from the Earth as the animals do. In saying this, we are approaching the mystery of humanity as well as the mystery of the animal kingdom. These mysteries were reflected in the animal cults of the ancient peoples, and above all in that of the Egyptians. They saw the animals as beings who are only guests upon the Earth, and in whom one may perceive the nature and activity of the spiritual world immediately adjoining this earthly realm. And when they portrayed the human figure in connection with the animal in pictures, they were representing to themselves the forms of those elementary, intermediate beings who, though they are indeed on the way to humanity in cosmic evolution, purposely refrain from entering the earthly realm in order not to become human. For there are such elementary, intermediate beings—and in picturing them the Egyptians were only reproducing what they saw. Such beings, however, do not have the full human self-consciousness, which to attain we had to enter this earthly world so completely that we receive something of the earthly nature into our very nature.

Human beings had to be exposed to the fact that, though the work of the divine-spiritual beings connected with humanity is indeed present in this earthly world, *it is only their accomplished work.* And because only the accomplished work, severed from its divine origin, is present here, the Luciferic and Ahrimanic beings therefore have access to it. Thus it becomes necessary for humans to make this realm of the accomplished work of the divine, permeated as it is by Lucifer and Ahriman, the field of action for one part—the earthly part—of their life's development.

As long as humankind had not progressed to the unfolding of the intellectual or mind soul, this was possible, without human nature becoming permanently severed from its original divine-spiritual foundation. But when this point was reached, a corruption took place in humankind—a corruption of the physical, the etheric, and the astral bodies. This corruption was known to ancient science as something that was living in human nature. It was known as a thing that was necessary in order that consciousness might advance to self-consciousness in human beings. In the stream of knowledge cultivated in the centers of learning founded by Alexander the Great, an Aristotelianism lived which, rightly understood, contained this "corruption" as an essential element in its psychology. Only in a later time were these ideas no longer penetrated in their inward essence.

In the ages before the evolution of the intellectual or mind soul, humanity was still interwoven with the forces of its divine-spiritual origin, so much so that from their cosmic field of action these forces were able to balance and hold in check the Luciferic and Ahrimanic powers that reach out to humans on Earth. And from the human side enough was done by way of cooperation to maintain the balance, in the actions of ritual and of the Mysteries, wherein the *picture* was unfolded of the divine-spiritual being diving down into the realm of Lucifer and Aliriman and coming forth again triumphant. Hence in times prior to the Mystery of Golgotha we find in the religious rites of different peoples pictorial representations of that which afterward became reality in the Mystery of Golgotha.

When the intellectual or mind soul was unfolded, only through the reality could humans continue to be preserved from being severed from the divine-spiritual beings that belonged to them. Even *in* earthly life the divine had to enter inwardly, as Being, into the organization of the intellectual or mind soul that, during earthly existence, has its life from what is earthly. This took place through the divine-spiritual Logos, Christ, uniting his cosmic destiny with the Earth for the sake of humanity.

Persephone came down to Earth to save the plant kingdom from having to form itself from what belongs only to Earth. That is the descent of a divine-spiritual being into the nature of the Earth. Persephone, too, has a kind of "resurrection," but this takes place annually, in rhythmical succession.

Over against this event—which is also a cosmic event occurring on the Earth—we have for *humanity* the descent of the Logos. Persephone descends to bring *nature* into its original direction. In this case there must be rhythm at the foundation, for the events in nature take place rhythmically. The Logos descends into humanity. This occurs *once* during human evolution, for the evolution of humanity is but one part in a gigantic cosmic rhythm in which humanity was something altogether different before the stage of humanity's existence, and will be something altogether different again after this stage is passed—whereas plant life repeats itself *as such* in shorter rhythms.

From the age of the spiritual soul onward it is necessary for humanity to see the Mystery of Golgotha in this light. Already in the age of the intellectual or mind soul there would have been a danger of humanity being separated if the Mystery of Golgotha had not taken place. In the age of the spiritual soul a complete darkening of the spirit world will come about for human consciousness, if the spiritual soul cannot strengthen itself sufficiently to look back in inward vision to its divine-spiritual origin. If, however, it is able to do this, it finds the cosmic Logos, as the being who can lead it back. It fills itself with the mighty picture that reveals what took place on Golgotha.

The beginning of this understanding is the loving comprehension of the cosmic Christmas, the cosmic initiation night, whose festive remembrance is celebrated each year. For the spiritual soul, which first receives the element of intellectuality, is strengthened by allowing true love to enter into this, the coldest element of soul. And the warmth of true love is there in its highest form when it goes out to the Jesus child who appears on Earth during the cosmic initiation night. In this way humans have allowed the highest earthly spirit fact, which was at the same time a physical event, to work upon their souls; they have entered upon the path by which they receive Christ into themselves.

Nature must be recognized in such a way that in Persephone—or the being who was still seen in the early Middle Ages when they spoke of "Nature"—it reveals the divine-spiritual original and eternal force out of which it originated and continually originates as the foundation of earthly human existence.

The world of human beings must be so recognized that in Christ it reveals the original and eternal Logos who works for the unfolding of the spiritual being of humanity in the sphere of the divine-spiritual being bound up with humanity from the beginning.

To turn the human heart in love to these great cosmic facts—this is the true content of the festival of remembrance that approaches humans each year when they contemplate the cosmic initiation night of Christmas. If love such as this lives in human hearts, it permeates the cold light element of the spiritual soul with warmth. Were the spiritual soul obliged to remain without such permeation, human beings would never become filled with the spirit. They would die in the cold of the intellectual consciousness; or they would have to remain in a mental life that did not progress to the unfolding of the conscious spiritual soul. They would then come to a stop with the unfolding of the intellectual or mind soul.

But in its essential nature the spiritual soul is not cold. It seems to be so only at the beginning of its unfolding, because at that stage it can only reveal the light element in its nature, and not as yet the cosmic warmth in which it indeed has its origin.

To feel and experience Christmas in this way will enable the soul to realize *how the glory of the divine-spiritual beings, whose images are revealed in the stars, announces itself to humanity, and how the liberation of human beings from the powers that wish to alienate them from their origin takes place within the precincts of the Earth.*

Leading Thoughts issued from the Goetheanum for the Anthroposophical Society (in connection with the foregoing Christmas Study)

The activity in the evolution of the world and humanity, which comes about through the forces of Michael, repeats itself rhythmically, though in ever-changing and progressing forms, before the Mystery of Golgotha and after.

The Mystery of Golgotha is the greatest event, occurring once and for all in the evolution of humanity. Here there can be no question of a rhythmic repetition. For while the evolution of humanity also stands within a mighty cosmic rhythm, still it is *one*—one vast member in a cosmic rhythm. Before it became this one, humanity was something altogether different from humanity; afterward it will again be altogether different. Thus there are many Michael events in the evolution of humanity, but there is only one event of Golgotha.

In the quick rhythmic repetition of the seasons of the year, the divine-spiritual being that descended into the depths of Earth to permeate nature's process with the spirit accomplishes this process. It is the ensouling of nature with the *forces* of the beginning and of eternity that must remain at work, even as Christ's descent is the ensouling of humanity with the *Logos* of the beginning and of eternity, whose working for the salvation of humankind will never cease.

Sources

Prologue: Living Thinking
I. From Chapter 6, "Goethe's Way of Knowing," in *Nature's Open Secret: Introductions to Goethe's Scientific Writings*, Great Barrington, MA: Anthroposophic Press, 2000, pp. 77–78 (GA 1).
II. From *Intuitive Thinking as a Spiritual Path: A Philosophy of Freedom*, Hudson, NY: Anthroposophic Press, 1995, pp. 41, 44, 47–48, 52–53, 84 (GA 4).
III. From a Letter of August 19, 1902, in Rudolf Steiner, *Briefe I* (in *Selbstverlag der Rudolf Steiner Nachlassverwaltung*, Dornach: 1953 [GA 38]).

1. Sophia, the Holy Spirit, Mary, and Mary Magdalene
I. From "Theosophy in the Gospel of St John," lecture given November 5, 1906, Basel, in *Kosmogonie. Populärer Okkultismus. Die Theosophie an Hand des Johannes-Evangeliums* (GA 94).
II. From lecture of November 20, 1907, Basel, in *Menschheitsentwicklung und Christus-Erkenntnis* (GA 100).
III. From lecture of November 25, 1907, Basel, in *Menschheitsentwicklung und Christus-Erkenntnis* (GA 100).

2. Wisdom and Health—from *Supersensible Knowledge*, Anthroposophic Press, 1987, Lecture 9 (GA 55).

3. The Nature of the Virgin Sophia and of the Holy Spirit—from *The Gospel of St. John*, Hudson, NY: Anthroposophic Press, 1995, Lecture 12 (GA 103).

4. Isis and Madonna—lecture of April 29, 1909, Berlin, in *Wo und Wie Findet man den Geist?* (GA 57).

5. Wisdom and Love in Cosmic and Human Evolution—from *An Outline of Esoteric Science*, Hudson, NY: Anthroposophic Press, 1997, pp. 383–398 (GA 13).

6. The Being Anthroposophia—from *The Effects of Esoteric Development*, Hudson, NY: Anthropsophic Press, 1997, Prologue (no GA).

7. The Gifts of Isis—from *The Mysteries of the East and of Christianity*, Blauvelt, NY: Spiritual Science Library/Garber Communications, 1989, Lecture 3 (GA 144).

8. From the Fifth Gospel—from *The Fifth Gospel*, London: Rudolf Steiner Press, 1995, Lectures 5, 7, 9, 12 (GA 148).

9. Sophia and Achamoth—from *Christ and the Spiritual World*, London: Rudolf Steiner Press, 1983, Lecture I (GA 149).

10. The Legend of the New Isis—from *Ancient Myths and the New Isis Mystery*, Hudson, NY: Anthroposophic Press, 1994, Lecture 3 (GA 180).

11. The Search for the New Isis (I)—lecture of December 24, 1920, Dornach in *Die Brücke zwischen Weltgeistiggkeit und den Physischen des Menschen. Die Suche nach den neuen Isis, der Göttlichen Sopia* (GA 202); also in *The Search for the New Isis, the Divine Sophia*, Spring Valley, NY: Mercury Press, 1983.

12. The Search for the New Isis (2)—lecture of December 25, 1920, Dornach, in *Die Brücke zwischen Weltgeistiggkeit und den Physischen des Menschen. Die Suche nach den neuen Isis, der Göttlichen Sopia* (GA 202); also in *The Search for the New Isis, the Divine Sophia*, Spring Valley, NY: Mercury Press, 1983.

13. Sophia and Pistis—from *Weekly News for English-speaking Members of the Anthroposophical Society*, Vol. VI, No. 21, June 2, 1929. Lecture of March 26, 1922, Dornach, in *Das Sonnen Mysterium und das Mysterium von Tod und Auferstehung* (GA 211).

14. Michael, Sophia, and Marduk—from *True and False Paths in Spiritual Investigation*, London: Rudolf Steiner Press, 1985, Lecture I (GA 243).

15. A Christmas Study: The Mystery of the Logos—from *Anthroposophical Leading Thoughts*, London: Rudolf Steiner Press, 1973 (GA 26).